A John Catt Publication

D1810533

Whose History?

Essays in Perception

Edited by Caroline Ellwood

First Published 2016

by John Catt Educational Ltd,
12 Deben Mill Business Centre, Old Maltings Approach,
Melton, Woodbridge IP12 1BL
Tel: +44 (0) 1394 389850 Fax: +44 (0) 1394 386893
Email: enquiries@johncatt.com
Website: www.johncatt.com

Opinions expressed in this publication are those of the contributors
and are not necessarily those of the publishers or the editors.
We cannot accept responsibility for any errors or omissions.

ISBN: 978 1 909717 71 8

Set and designed by Theoria Design Limited
www.theoriadesign.com

Contents

Part two
Whose history do we teach?

Preface

Siva Kumari
Director General, the International Baccalaureate

Caroline Ellwood is well placed to edit *Whose History?* and I'm pleased that this book raises and addresses important questions about how history is perceived not only through aspects of historiography but by teachers deciding *how* and *what* to teach in this modern world.

This is a topic which resonates very strongly with me as today, more than ever, students and teachers should be better able to address questions of perspective with more original sources at their fingertips.

The question of 'whose history' is in, and of, itself of course intriguing. Not being a historian, I can only opine given this opportunity – firstly from the perspective of a student who studied in India, a post-colonial nation; to that of an immigrant building a professional career in the United States of America and of course, most importantly, during my time working in the professional development of teachers both in Advanced Placement and in the International Baccalaureate; to my role now as an educator who has the privilege of being in schools and talking to educators and policy makers throughout the world.

Let me share some experiences gained over the years that might illustrate to the reader just why this book is so pertinent in today's world.

It was while creating in-depth professional development for experienced teachers in the field of world literature where this issue most revealed itself: whilst discussing translated works with their students, some of the best teachers were missing the most important aspects of these works – aspects of inter-cultural understanding and an appreciation of the socio-political, and historical times in which a specific book was written. They were failing to grasp how understanding the history of that country at that time would not only add real depth to the literature, but increase the appreciation for the characters and their motivations at the very least.

Such study of multiple perspectives potentially also instils a deep curiosity about the people and the society from which the book emanated. While my experience was gained in working with teachers in the USA, the same could be said about any piece of literature, being taught by any teacher, anywhere in the world, who does not come with a good understanding of the history of the area from where the text originates. Why is this important? Because without the context, teachers were only able to read the works of literature through their lens rather than the voice of the country from which it came. It is through this experience that I realized the richness of perspectives lost in translation when teachers and students don't attend to the question of 'whose history?'

The pertinence of *Whose History?* is illustrated not only in its focus on history but because it also asks the question 'is history static?' The etymology of the word 'history', according to some sources and selectively presented here, originates from the root 'weid' meaning 'to know, to see', including the Sanskrit word 'veda' and the Greek 'historia' meaning 'finding out'.

I share this because traditionally history has been taught through a study of narratives, usually compiled in textbooks, predominately written in either a dominant language or providing dominant evidence available in a predominant language. History textbooks and curricula are often influenced by policy makers in local or national education departments or by governments who believe that their citizenry needs to learn a particular world view. These are often the realities of teaching and learning at the pre-tertiary level.

Therefore it is good that authors, as discussants, in the following pages think through whose narrative is told, whose language is being used and even through whose eye was the picture created.

I often wonder if teachers feel that now is a great time to be a teacher of history for both their sake and for that of their students. Students today are privileged in ways that those before were not, with access to original documents and recordings at the click of a mouse. Limited only by their curiosity and their ability to ask the right questions they are able to engage with first hand evidence, for instance listen to Martin Luther King's many speeches first hand rather than reading them on a page in a history textbook. They can see how his death was reported around the world by accessing the online archives of the BBC to view the news broadcast on April 4th, 1968.

They can access the whole of primary sources such as Magna Carta and watch news reels from war zones across the world. Today's access also allows students to 'see' history laterally, to understand that historical incidents do not occur in isolation nor in a vacuum. Students can compare multiple points of view at any given time regarding a particular issue. As major world events occur around the world we can access original citizen voices without the filtering by media moguls. While this may be overwhelming, it also perhaps allows the student of today to be more cognizant of 'voice' and the difficulty of meaning-making and writing history.

This can surely only bode well for the curious mind. The teachers' power it seems then is to infuse students with an energy for the study of history and to illustrate how it can be viewed from a human perspective rather than just as an accumulation of dates and a dry recounting of events. Perhaps it is even as a student views events first hand that s/he realizes the nature of perception and how it influences a particular narrative and viewpoint.

Questions of perception involve national versus international perspectives, and teachers can challenge students to think about the dominant narrative. Are all perspectives represented in the mainstream conclusions drawn about events? How much in the claims of victory of nations is ever the voice heard of those who were the losers of battles or wars? This is not to say that nations do not have the right to rally their citizenry to have pride in their victories, but more to relate that a study of history, particularly in IB schools, is well-served by a review of all points of view. And, the stunning silence of voices which are not represented should not be explained away, lazily, as the lack of an alternative viewpoint, but thought through more carefully as perhaps a lack of access to the world's heavily published languages of history or narratives that could not survive in today's accessible formats. And, to the need for more history that investigates what the missing voices might have added.

Such perception-broadening dialogues and thinking are basic to the IB mission of understanding others and their perspectives. Not only are these dialogues needed in the classroom, but also outside of them, an aspirational and pedagogical idea espoused by the IB since its inception. In today's world, access to international information is no longer always restricted by national borders. There is a growing acceptance that different cultures will interpret things differently and the idea of understanding another's point of view is part of being a global citizen. Critical thinking of this nature goes to the heart of the IB's view of international mindedness and this book opens up some of the questions that are involved in considering whose history we write, research and teach.

Contributors

Dinos Aristidou is a playwright, director and education consultant who specialises in working with educators, communities and young people, both in the UK and internationally. He is a workshop leader, examiner and curriculum consultant for the International Baccalaureate and is a part of the artistic team and a board member of the International Schools Theatre Association (ISTA). His research and interest in cultural memory, experiential and contextual learning has led to the development of site learning programmes at the SEARCH museum in Gosport and the American Museum of Natural History, New York. He has run teacher training programmes in international schools for humanities teachers on active learning strategies for the teaching of history and geography.

Richard Caston is a painter and visual arts educator. He taught for many years at the International School of Düsseldorf, Germany, where he was department head and involved in the onset of the International Baccalaureate (IB) Diploma. A long-time IB examiner and team leader, he was a regular presenter at IB and ECIS conferences and a contributor to the *International School* magazine. Richard's own work has been shown in many solo and group exhibitions, mainly in Germany and in the UK. He is a graduate of the Norwich University of the Arts and of Ravensbourne College of Art and Communication. His recent work has focused on specific exhibition themes, staged at meaningful venues, such as the 'Living Stones: Richard Caston's silent journey' exhibition at the Cathedral in Norwich, UK.

Dr Richard Caffyn is currently Principal at the International School Telemark, Norway. He has worked previously as a Principal, head of department and class teacher in international schools in Azerbaijan, Romania, Italy and Austria. He was head of research support and development for the IB at the University of Bath. His doctorate investigated the micropolitics and social dynamics of international school leadership and management, a topic about which he regularly writes and presents at conferences. His post-doctoral interests have focused on boundary management, organisational energy and expatriate subcultures in schools.

Dr Rebecca Conway is a product manager in the Assessment Projects Group at Cambridge International Examinations. She is currently responsible for managing the design and development of humanities assessments for international education reform projects. Prior to joining Cambridge, she taught history at the University of Manchester and Sheffield Hallam University. Rebecca was awarded a PhD in Modern British History in 2012.

Malcolm Davis is Director of The International School of Bremen. He has taught International Baccalaureate courses over 22 years in history, theory of knowledge, philosophy and history and culture of the Islamic world. As a middle manager in a large comprehensive school in England he introduced a history programme that attempted to address the issue of racial awareness and multiculturalism. He was head of humanities of the Vienna International School and then Head of School. He has been involved in teacher training programmes in Eastern Europe, USA and the Middle East and is co-author, with Caroline Ellwood, of *International Mindedness – A CPD Manual for Schools* (Optimus Press 2010) and a contributor to *Teaching and Learning about Islam* (John Catt, 2012).

Dr Caroline Ellwood After a career in adult education in the UK and the US where she was a Ford Foundation Fellow, Dr Ellwood moved to the international field and became head of the middle school of the Vienna International School. She was closely associated with the development of the IB Middle Years Programme, and helped pilot the history and culture of the Islamic world IB Diploma humanities option. She has a doctorate in Education from the University of London, was BP Fellow in Education at Keble College, Oxford, and has received the ECIS Award for the Promotion of International Education. She has acted as a consultant on aspects of international education and international mindedness to schools in North and South America, Africa, Australia, Europe and the Far East. She was for ten years editor of *International School* magazine and is the current editor of the *International Schools Journal* (ISJ).

Terry Haywood is Headmaster of The International School of Milan, Italy. His career in international education has included serving on the professional development accreditation and strategic planning committee of ECIS and the board of directors (Chair from 1999-2001) He was closely involved with the foundation of both the Council of International Schools and the Alliance for International Education for which he is a Trustee. His special interest lies in the promotion of international education as a learning and life experience that should be at the heart of schooling everywhere.

Dr Walther Hetzer was born on the day Marshal Badoglio announced the armistice and Italy's exit from the Second World War on the side of the Germans (8th September, 1943). He has a doctorate in history from the University of Vienna. His career included teacher of history and philosophy, various leadership roles, and Director in excellent international schools, all located in places of immense historical interest (New York, Vienna and St Gilgen in Austria, Duino-Trieste in Italy, Brussels, Abu Dhabi, Cairo). He intends to start a busy retirement, filled with family time, writing, photography, music, school design projects, mountains, and travel with his fellow educator wife Ellen to more places of historic and personal interest.

Jack Higginson is a product manager in the Humanities and Arts Group at Cambridge International Examinations. He is currently responsible for managing assessments for international customers and overseas partners. Prior to joining Cambridge, he was head of humanities and taught history in the UK and South India, and was assistant head of an Autism Resource Base. Jack holds an MA in Educational Leadership from the University of Warwick and a BA in Modern History from Hertford College, Oxford.

Dr Siva Kumari is the seventh Director General of the International Baccalaureate (IB) and is the first woman to hold the post. She joined the IB as Regional Director for Asia-Pacific and became Chief of Operating Officer of the IB, responsible for IB regions worldwide. Prior to joining the IB, Dr Kumari was the first associate provost for K-12 initiatives at Rice University in Houston, Texas, USA. She also served as associate dean and executive director of programs in the School of Continuing Studies, receiving critical acclaim for her work and winning several national and regional awards.

She has a bachelor of science degree from India, a master's degree from the University of Cincinnati, Ohio, USA, and holds a doctorate in education from the University of Houston, Texas, USA.

Roger Moorhouse is a freelance historian, specialising in modern German history. A graduate of the School of Slavonic and Eastern European Studies, University of London, he is a fluent German speaker and is the author of *Killing Hitler, Berlin at War* and most recently *The Devils' Alliance, Hitler's Pact with Stalin, 1939-1941.*

Professor Olukoya Ogen is the current Provost of Adeyemi College of Education, Ondo, Nigeria. He is also a Visiting Senior Research Fellow at CWAS, University of Birmingham, 2012-2017 as well as a Professor of History in Osun State University, Osogbo. He holds a PhD in History from the University of Lagos, and a Certificate in Trade, Growth and Poverty from the World Bank Institute, Washington DC. He was a was a Leventis Scholar at SOAS, University of London in 2008. He is currently a Co-Investigator and the Country Director of the five-year (2012-17) European Research Council Grant on 'Everyday Religious Encounter in Southwest Yorubaland'. His most recent publications include 'Variations régionales et impact localisé: analyse comparative des dynamiques du commerce transatlantique des esclaves de l'est du pays Yoruba, 1807-1850' in Guy Saupin (ed.) *Africains et Européens dans le monde atlantique (XVe-XIXe siècle).* Rennes: Presses Universitaires de Rennes, 2014, and "Nigerian Musicians' Interventions in Peacebuilding: A Socio-historical Approach' *UNESCO-IACIU Journal of African Culture and International Understanding,* No.10, Oct-Dec, 2014,

Dr Malcolm Pritchard is the Head of School at The ISF Academy, a K-12, bilingual IB school in Hong Kong. He has spent many years living in Chinese-speaking communities and counts experiential learning and language acquisition among his research interests.

Dr Rauni Räsänen is emerita professor of global education from the University of Oulu in Finland. Before her university career she worked as a primary and secondary school teacher as well as provincial advisor for language teaching. During her academic career she co-ordinated two international programmes: Intercultural Teacher Education Programme (previously Master of Education International Programme) and Education and Globalisation master's programme. Her research interests are: ethics and education, intercultural education, global education, teacher education, and higher education.

Paul Regan is currently the Founding Head of Oaktree International School Mumbai which is opening in 2016. He was also Founding Head of Oaktree International School Kolkata and the United World College in Mostar. Other positions as Head have been in Africa, the UK and the Ukraine. He graduated in Russian and has taught Modern Languages, Latin and Theory of Knowledge.

Acknowledgements

My thanks go to each of the contributors for their generous collaboration and support in the production of this collection of essays. Gratitude also to John Catt Educational Ltd for their professional help and advice. I am particularly grateful for the encouragement given to me by Publishing Director Derek Bingham who, in this and many other editorial enterprises, has been my mentor.

Introduction

Caroline Ellwood

Thousands line the streets as the cortège passes by. Two knights on horseback lead the procession; the coffin, a simple wooden box, is drawn by plumed black horses and surrounded by outriders. The crowds press forward as it passes and throw white roses. It stops before the cathedral where it is welcomed with ceremony by the Bishop to lie in state until the official burial later in the week by the Archbishop of Canterbury. Britain is burying a king.

But this is not Westminster Abbey, this is not London, this is the provincial city of Leicester where this particular king happened to be unearthed from under a car park and not only reigned 500 years ago but had a singularly violent reputation. This is Richard III.

Why have such huge crowds come out to line the streets to see a box containing a long dead, probably criminal monarch taken to be buried? Is it all part of the *Wolf Hall/Downton Abbey* historical saga TV syndrome? Are the members of the Richard III Society defending their favourite? Is this Leicester seeing the opportunities of the heritage trail? The skeletal remains were taken on a symbolic tour of Richard III memorable sites, Bosworth Field being the highlight as re-enactors in black cloaks over armour and carrying lighted torches walked behind a group of musicians playing period instruments. "Get on your knees and honour the king," was the command and replica cannon provided a 21-gun salute. How many, as they ate their 'Richard Ices', identified this corpse with Shakespeare's villainous 'bunch backed toad' who murdered his way to the throne? Or is Britain just so royalist at heart that even a 500 year-old corpse will make people wave an anachronistic Union Jack. *The Times'* leader aptly summed it up:

> Is all this knowingly absurd, or not absurd at all? Is it ancient history or very modern sentimentalism? Is it for the tourists, or done for the national soul? In every case the answer is both ...
>
> (*The Times*, March 26, 2015)

Of course love of the pageantry of history can be found in many countries and nostalgia for the trappings of monarchy still lurks in the corners of socialist nations. In 2011 Austria was the scene of the most amazing pomp and revisionist history when Otto Von Hapsburg was buried with as much ceremony as if the Empire had never been dismantled. A kilometre-long procession representing the former empire's nationalities accompanied the coffin to a funeral service in Stephansdom where the packed cathedral echoed to the *Kaiserhymne* (God preserve, God protect our Emperor, our country). Then on to the imperial crypt in company with representatives of the Houses of Hohenzollern, Saxe Coburg-Gotha, Bourbon, Leichenstein, Bernadotte, Windsor, Baden, Braganza and Montanegro.

Richard III's send-off was modest in comparison, but what the crowds who lined the streets in Vienna and Leicester were experiencing was a glimpse into the past and perhaps the first answer to the question 'whose history?' is that history can belong to anybody who wants to take an interest. Or as the Bishop of Leicester said at the burial, "Richard belongs not just to chroniclers and historians but to all of us." Indeed thousands trot through palaces and historic houses, wander around ancient monuments, visit battlefields and war cemeteries to experience a glimpse into the past. The past is indeed a 'foreign country'; it is also a fascinating place to visit. Ibn Khaldun, the great Arab philosopher, and historian noted that:

> History serves to entertain large crowded gatherings. A knowledge of history is a passport to social success, brings down the blessings of heaven on its possessor and it also explains how and why things are as they are.
>
> (Khaldun, translated by Rosenthal, 1967)

The role of history as an 'explainer' brings us to the centre of the 'whose history?' debate. The meaning of history comes from the Greek 'to know'. How historians get their knowledge in order to make their judgements has changed dramatically over time with new methods of communication and sophisticated technology.

Things were not always so complex for historians. Clio, the muse of history, celebrated the famous exploits of heroes and battles won. Herodotus, the first servant of Clio, wrote his histories, 'lest the great and wonderful deeds performed by the Greeks and Barbarians should become lost to fame'. But over the years Clio lost her status and became a servant herself. Dressed in national costume she became the handmaid of religion, colonial aspirations, political parties and economic forces. She waved flags whilst singing patriotic songs of nationalism and citizenship and worked hard for politicians. With Clotho, Lechesis and Atropos she looked into the crystal ball of the future – where she had no business to be. She would, over the centuries, search for ever more abstruse solutions to the secrets of the past. Marx claimed that as his personal midwife to the revolution of the working man she would influence the world. She did but now has the new name Cliometrics and whilst finding exciting adventures in the world of computers has lost all her mystery as freedom of information reveals her secrets. In her spare time she works as a kitchen maid for the heritage industry.

So simple young Clio, telling tales of the great and the glorious is in old age a very complex character and those who serve her have also had to change. Of course the facts of the past do not change, but for every generation our attitudes change and history is rewritten. The nature of the present influences our interpretation of the past. What could be termed 'old history' (Himmelfarb, 1987) gave a narrative of dynasties, politics and wars written from a national point of view. There was no doubt whose history was being told in *Our Island's Story* or what Britain's position was in the world. Modern historians emphasise causation, require and analyse evidence, use the methods of anthropologists, sociologists and economists and consider 'the common man' – not just kings but people. H G Wells, who never claimed to be a historian, explains that his *Outline of History* was written as a response to the disillusion of WWI and a feeling that civilisation had failed.

> Men and women tried to recall the narrow history teaching of their
> brief school days and found an uninspiring and partially forgotten
> list of national kings or presidents ... an endless wilderness of books.
> They had been taught history in nationalist blinkers, ignoring every
> country but their own.
>
> (Wells, 1920)

History, according to Wells, was 'the common adventure of all mankind, of all classes and all nations' (*ibid*). Thus he attempted to relate that adventure in vastly popular illustrated weekly instalments between 1918 and 1919, then subsequently in a two-volume publication. Here history is presented as the odyssey of man's struggle from his origins in 'unfathomable mystery' to the present 'dawn of human fellowship'. Wells' view of history is itself now a fascinating source for the knowledge, attitudes and beliefs of the time. Which poses another 'whose history?' question. Wells is telling the truth as he saw it as he wrote, but time changes perception, new evidence can be found, old evidence refuted or different events selected so we now have a different 'truth'. Eric Hobsbawm, looking backward to the First World War, saw it in relation to later events and far from seeing hope for the future saw the start of 'an age of barbarism' (Hobsbawm, 1997).

If different versions of the past can be selected then the motive behind that selection can become important. History can be used for propaganda, not just to record the past but to influence the future. As Orwell succinctly put it, 'Who controls the past controls the future, who controls the present controls the past' (Orwell, 1948).

Facts can be manipulated to give different results, knowledge is codified and generalisations made. Different historians will give a variety of versions of the causes of the First World War (see chapter 5). History is sorted into categories across time space and subject area, for example 'The Importance of European Wool Production in Medieval Times'. There is not always agreement on such divisions and modern historians are much more aware of the need for inter-disciplinarity. Teachers or often the state will choose what aspects of the world's history to include in the school curriculum to promote their own nation's point of view and develop a feeling of citizenship. Edward Said accused western historians, indeed culture of 'orientalism' (Said, 1985) and President Julius Nyerere of Tanzania (a historian himself) made a similar accusation about western historians of Africa in his opening speech to a conference he had convened to discuss African History:

> There is one thing which this conference will not have to discuss.
> That is the contention that Africa has no history. The days when
> this was seriously suggested by intelligent men and women have

now passed. Your problem at this conference is more likely to arise from the uncoordinated and sometimes undisciplined nature of the evidence and from the number and variety of books and articles published in recent years.

(Nyerere, c.1960)

Thus both the historian and the teacher are in a position of power and trust for selection involves judgement and what is considered acceptable in one period (*eg* slavery) is against the law in another. There are moral dilemmas involved in these choices where facts are used to support a theory, prove a point or reinforce the cause of a war, a political party, a religion or a controversial event. Whose and what history you teach can indeed be not just a dilemma but a danger.

Khaldun wished for history to 'explain how and why things are as they are' but it is necessary to go further and John Milton did so when he gave a necessary 'stirring' component for the lover of history:

> When there is much desire to learn there of necessity will be much arguing, much writing, many opinions; for opinion in good men is but knowledge in the making ... knowledge and understanding which God has stirred up in this city ... Let truth be in the field.

(Milton, 1644)

Explanation, discussion, a truth that shifts over time – Mr Gradgrind, 'a man of realities, a man of fact and calculations', would have been appalled. For 'facts alone are wanted in life' and the important thing was 'to never wonder' (Dickens 1854). But most history is 'wondering' ... wondering about the available facts and so producing opinions.

Who produces those opinions? Who writes the history ? Who controls the curriculum and how should it be taught? What message will go into a text book? How does history impinge on aspects of culture such as art and drama? How important is our own history or that of our institutions? Is history a moveable 'truth'?

It is a consideration of questions like these that will form the basis of this book:

Part One – Whose history? Of historians and history
Part Two – Whose history do we teach?

References

Dickens, C (1995) *Hard Times*. London: Penguin Classics. (Original work published 1848)

Himmelfarb, G (1987) The New and the Old History. Cambridge, Mass.: Harvard University Press.

Hobsbawm, E (1997) *On History*. London: Wiedenfeld & Nicolson.

Khaldun, I (1967) The Maquiddimah, translated by Franz Rosenthal, abridged and edited by Dawood N, J. London: Routledge and Kegan Paul.

Milton, J (2014) Areopagitica and Other Writings. London: Penguin Classics. (Original work published 1644).

Nyerere M. J 'Speech to the Conference on African History' in Roberts, R and James, S (1998) History for Theory of Knowledge Teacher's Guide.

Orwell, G (1980) 1984. London: Penguin Classics. (Original work published 1948).

Said, E (1985) Orientalism. London: Penguin Books.

Wells, H. G (1920) *The Outline of History*. London: Cassel and Company.

Part one

Whose history?
Of historians and history

Chapter 1

Whose history? Whose language?

Malcolm Pritchard

以古為鑒，可知興替...(With history as a mirror, one can know the rise and fall of dynasties...)

Emperor Taizong, Tang Dynasty (597-649)

History is our never-ending search for meaning through contending words, languages, cultures, and interpretations. It is not the 'dead hand' of the past, but a potent living weapon in the present struggle for identity and meaning that transcends clans, communities, and countries. The interpretation of history and defining key events of the past are also powerful forces in shaping the future actions, attitudes and aspirations of individuals and nations. Like territorial conflict, we struggle to retain possession of the past whilst staking out a claim to own the future.

The key medium in which and through which we engage in the fight to own history is language, in both the spoken and written word. Our words, in any language, are the frontline troops doing battle between the past, present, and future. An oft-quoted and somewhat tongue-in-cheek saying, translated from Yiddish and associated with the sociolinguist Max Weinreich, suggests that:

> A language is a dialect with an army and navy...
>
> (א ‏ראַרפּש א זיא טימ דיאלעטקאַ ואַ ימראַ ואַ םלֿפאַט *a shprach eez a deealekt mit an armee un flot*).

(Boyle, 2014; Friedman, 2003)

The more influential a language becomes, the more it develops the accoutrements of power. At the pinnacle of influence, a distinctive culture emerges from a critical demographic mass of speakers, and armed with a language and a culture, a country is born (Hobsbawm, 1990). One might paraphrase Weinreich by saying: a country is a culture with an army and navy. Nations, cultures, and languages are associated with the projection of power, the assignment of authentic identity, and the potential for conflict driven by self-preservation and assertion of a discrete cultural identity, with its own version of the past. Being ethnolinguistically 'right' is perhaps one form of might.

On the authorship of history, Churchill, Machiavelli, even William Wallace, have been credited with the saying, 'History is written by the victors.' Its truth strikes us as self-evident. Max Lerner makes the more interesting and provocative statement:

> The so-called lessons of history are for the most part the rationalizations of the victors. History is written by the survivors.

(Lerner, 1989 [1943])

This principle is well understood globally: those left behind have indeed adopted this sentiment, word for word, in languages such as Chinese (历史是由胜利者书写的). It points to the seemingly self-evident truth that when nations, cultures, and languages come into contact, the victors who emerge from the inevitable competition and conflict are afforded the privilege of writing the definitive historical record.

What may be overlooked in this truism is that the language in which the victor chooses to record history is also significant, not just the content. In fact, the language(s) of the victorious at a socio-political level reflect the dynamic state of the ongoing struggles between competing cultures and civilizations and their respective languages. Hidden within those languages and their grammars are artifacts that reflect deeper inter-linguistic and inter-cultural conflicts, adaptation to new circumstances, and evidence of evolutionary socio-linguistic change. Across the globe in the early decades of the 21st century, the languages, indeed the very words used to record histories, are the product of socio-cultural interactions and conflicts, from the individual through to the international, from the personal to the political, the mercantile to the military.

The relationship between a nation, its language(s), its culture, and its history is complex and has become increasingly so in a globalizing world where we can no longer assume that there is a one-to-one correlation between these elements.

This chapter is concerned with nations, their histories, and the role of language in shaping perceptions of past events, current trends, and, perhaps, predicting future developments. It is not about anyone's history, *per se*, but seeks to explore the interplay between history, languages, and nations through some leading questions: for example, what is the nature of history? What is the nature of language and thought? And what role might these play in shaping our view of history?

The following discussion explores history through the lens of language, examining the nature of language and its relationship to thought, the linguistic building blocks of history, and the extent to which language itself might influence the way in which human experience is captured, recorded, and remembered. A brief review of the Sapir-Whorf Hypothesis, focusing on the vexed question of linguistic determinism, provides a frame of reference for this discussion.

What is history?

Human knowledge is, to a great extent, informed by experience and the study of past events. Is human knowledge, however, derived from the straightforward presentation of clear, well-defined, and incontrovertible fact through the medium of value-neutral language? Or is it the result of carefully curated, experientially and culturally informed meaning making? At an ontological level, we might even ask if history exists independently of human thought?

In answering the question, 'What is history?', the influential British historian and philosopher, E H Carr, replied that it is a continuous process of interaction between the historian and his facts, an unending dialogue between the present and the past. He added that, 'Interpretation is the lifeblood of history' (Carr, 1987 [1961]). Thus, in Carr's view, history is an act of interpretation, or meaning making, and all history might be construed as the history of thought. Rather than a process of placing a set of agreed facts in correct sequence to create an accurate historical record, the historian's interaction with 'historical fact' might be construed in a more adventurous and dynamic fashion:

> The facts are really not at all like fish on the fishmonger's slab. They are like fish swimming about in a vast and sometimes inaccessible ocean; and what the historian catches will depend partly on chance, but mainly on what part of the ocean he chooses to fish in ... the historian will get the kind of facts he wants.
>
> (Carr, 1987 [1961])

While history appears to be about the past, it is also inextricably and intimately intertwined with the present (Carr, 1987 [1961]). The historian's choice of language and lexicon reveal much about the purpose, context and culture, and underlying philosophy of the author. Extending Carr's metaphor a little further, what the historian chooses to call the fish caught is also of importance.

There is no neutral refuge in this process. Seemingly indisputable facts are still open to interpretation and re-interpretation and, according to Churchill, personal opinion:

> For my part ... leave the past to history, especially as I propose to write that history myself.
>
> (Churchill, 2012 [1947])

Another expression of this view comes from the author of *A People's History of the United States*, Howard Zinn (1970), who observed: 'The historian cannot choose to be neutral; he writes on a moving train.'

Whether we are seeking to understand history from the ancients (Bede, 731 [2015]), the radicals (Zinn, 1980), the classicists (Gibbon, 1782 [2012]), or the modernists inspired by Hobsbawm (1990) or Carr, among others, there is much more than dates, places, and people to consider. Whether fishing or commuting, there is the clear presence of *movement* and *intent* in the process of recording history. History does not appear as the sterile product of static observation, fixed in time and space; it emerges dynamically and interactively from engaged human participants on a journey from somewhere to somewhere else, who perhaps exercise some degree of volition. The words of historians are themselves laden with many meanings, explicit and implicit, intended and, perhaps, unintended.

While the deeper questions of import to historians of all hues, the tensions between causation and chance, lie beyond the scope of this discussion, the cultural and linguistic contexts surrounding any act of interaction with historical data for the purposes of making present meaning from the past cast a shadow that should not be ignored or underestimated.

The limits of language and the shaping of history

The nature of language and its impact on thought, and by extension, history, is a rich field for discussion among academics: philosophers, linguists, educationalists, and historians. An early authority in this field, von Humboldt asserts that the difference between languages is not found in sounds and signs, but in the ways in which languages represent the world (Formigari, 1999). Wittgenstein's famous solipsism states, '*The limits of my language* mean the limits of my world (2010 [1922]: italics in the original).' Our world ends where our words fail. What our language cannot express, our history cannot record.

On the connection between what happens and what we think as a result, Halliday assigns a more universal and non-deterministic role to language, stating that '...language is the essential condition of knowing, the process by which experience becomes knowledge' (Halliday, 1993; emhasis in the original). The scope and nature of a language might therefore play some role in shaping how we come to understand and interpret our experience of the world. Through the medium of language, individuals and communities construct artifacts that encode and record meaning – knowledge – out of their experiences of the world. This construction of meaning is essentially a socially mediated process, albeit one that is shaped by the environment in which the social interaction is conducted (Piaget, 2002 [1923]; Vygotsky, 1986 [1934]; Wells, 1999).

Thoughts are constructed in response to human experiences within a physical, social, and cultural context. Through social interaction, the semiotic tool of language is used to make meaning, which in turn creates cultural structures in the form of shared patterns of understanding, behaviors, and attitudes (Wells, 1999). Language is the primary mechanism for human social interaction and through which humans create semiotic artifacts derived from experience (Halliday, 1993; Vygotsky, 1986 [1934]).

As humans are born biologically and socially 'unfinished' and therefore dependent, this creates the need for a lengthy phase of reliance on caretakers for basic physical needs (Arendt, 1977). This dependency might also be construed as a biological mechanism developed from a clear and specific adaptation necessary for cultural organisms. Human immaturity at birth provides the mechanism by which cultural knowledge is shared by the parenting generation through the medium of language and internalized in the infant. Infants in this phase of development are exposed to recurrent and culturally structured patterns of activities that shape adult attitudes and behaviours.

According to Vygotsky, infant inner speech develops through a long cumulative series of functional and structural changes in cognition driven by social interaction in which the structure of speech mastered becomes the basic structure of thinking (Vygotsky, 1986 [1934]). Language is a fundamental survival skill that is both produced by and contributes towards socialization. The diverse ways of comprehending and communicating human experience through language are necessary for the survival of the species (Lakoff, 1987). Infants begin noticing, ordering, representing, and remembering experiences and phenomena. In this phase, the central role for language is the categorization of experience. There is an external logic that shapes categorization and representation, as this is the main way in which infant humans make sense of their experience (Lakoff, 1987).

The notion of representation, the naming of things encountered and experienced, is an important aspect of language development that bears further discussion. Arendt (1977) asserts that the urge to speak is the quest for personal meaning, not objective fact. The need to make meaning is to make sense of whatever has occurred. This may or not be motivated by a desire to create knowledge. It is, however, connected with the quest to construct understanding in an unfamiliar world:

> The sheer naming of things, the creation of words, is the human way
> of appropriating and as it were, disalientating the world into which,
> after all, each of us is born as a newcomer and a stranger.
>
> (Arendt, 1977)

We derive our categorization systems during childhood through social interaction, which suggests that categories are shaped by culture and environment and are largely the product of experience and imagination. Categories take on an existence beyond the things they contain and as such to change the concept of any category is to change the way in which we understand the world.

When in everyday use, most categorization is largely automatic and unconscious. We only notice it when we encounter something that is problematic because it does not fit the existing systems of naming. Different cultures organize and categorize domains of knowledge, according to custom and experience (Lakoff, 1987). Where these objects in the experienced world are different, unique to setting, they will undoubtedly influence the language used to create and describe the categories in the local language.

This leaves open the strong probability that a phenomenon or culturally privileged object, artifact, or relationship in one language may be completely invisible or irrelevant to another. The evolution of environmentally and experientially differentiated languages is in part the history of humanity. Linguistic diversity is a form cognitive pluralism, which facilitates the evolution of differently shaped and contrived semiotic tools to record, combine, represent, and remember experience in distinctive, context dependent, ways (Lakoff, 1987). This linguistic evolution is manifested in the myriad forms of grammatical structures, which unconsciously reflect distinctive features of thought itself, not just objects of thought.

Returning to the theme of language and history, if our understanding of the past is constructed through the medium of linguistic artifacts, then we must accept the possibility that specific manifestations of semiotic encoding, indeed the encoding system itself, might exert some influence over what can be reasonably inferred or understood from the artifact. The extent to which the grammar and lexicon of a language might inform or even constrain the construction of meaning lies at the centre of what became known as the Sapir-Whorf Hypothesis in the mid 20th century. This hypothesis contends that environment shapes language, and by extension thoughts, in particular ways, while disregarding or de-emphasizing others (Feist & Gentner, 2007; Sapir, 2000 [1921]).

Languages, especially members of quite different language families, differ in important ways from one another. One view is that the grammatical structure and lexicon of a language influence or determine how its speakers perceive the world, and in a largely systematic way (Swoyer, 2003). This idea of linguistic *determinism* proved to be highly influential in the 20th century and even found expression in the fictional 'Newspeak' of George Orwell's *Nineteen Eighty-Four*, in which Orwell explores the notion that the removal of problematic words might prevent 'thought-crime' (Orwell, 2014 [1949]).

While there is a near universality of belief that each language is unique in its ability to express certain ideas and differs from every other language, strong opposition to the Sapir-Whorf Hypothesis emerged in the late 20th century. Building on Chomsky's notion of a universal grammar, this school of thought contends that there is no evidence to suggest that languages differ in the way they shape cognition, that language does not shape the way in which we experience the world (Chomsky, 1986; Schuh, 2011; Scovel, 1991).

Chomsky's theory of language rests on the idea that language is in fact independent of cognition with its own separate modular system (Lakoff, 1987). Languages provide a cognitive toolkit of representational resources that augment the capacity for encoding experiences and reasoning; they facilitate and enhance, but do not ultimately replace or prevent the construction of understanding (Feist & Gentner, 2007). Thus, the experienced world may exert influence on language at a lexical level, but in a way that is not materially different to any other language, and this influence does not prevent or promote cognition. The labels change, but our thoughts remain largely unaffected.

For example, there are terms that reflect peculiar, if not unique sets of circumstances and cultural referents, and these words may defy translation into other languages, often due to the lack of a comparable cultural or environmental context (Scovel, 1991). In such cases, words may be borrowed from another language to serve a particular purpose. Many linguists, therefore, accept that languages adapt and evolve, but also assert that the strongest extra-linguistic influence is manifested in lexical, rather than phonological or syntactical differences (Scovel, 1991). Whorf's evidence in attempting to show that all ethnolinguistic communities have a unique way of seeing the world, erred in asserting that speech and language structures are largely invariant or immutable, which was subsequently demonstrated to be false (Dorian, 1991).

A more recent and robust expression of opposition to Whorfian linguistic determinism, championed by McWhorter, asserts that while the idea that language shapes thought and changes the way we see the world is 'mesmerizing', it is largely a 'hoax' (McWhorter, 2014). Citing the largely inconclusive evidence in support of linguistic determinism generated through clinical experiments that explore color boundaries in Russian and English, McWhorter believes that the world looks much the same in all languages (Hoge, 2014; McWhorter, 2014). The functions of language, such as categorization, reflect universal linguistic phenomena (McWhorter, 2014).

The many critics of Sapir-Whorf support the notion of the largely universal nature of the non-lexical elements of language, such as syntax and semantics. The near universal phenomenon of mutual lexical borrowing between languages, such as the huge number of loan words in English and many other languages, demonstrates an innate human capacity to innovate linguistically when a native term does not serve to communicate an idea. The question of whether this practice of lexical innovation could be construed as an influence on cognition, however, remains a hotly debated proposition.

One of the problems with the theories of those opposed to Whorfian linguistic determinism is that relatively little is known about the particular connections between a particular language and mental life (Lucy, 1996). Categorization systems have been studied in many languages in a comparative fashion, but the symbols and mechanics of cognition, the 'language of the mind', has been more impervious to scrutiny. Where deeper understanding of these connections has been sought through studies of cognition, problems emerge when working with a single language, privileging one language and cultural perspective in comparative studies (Lucy, 1996).

Naming systems, such as words for colors, have offered the most distinctive and clinically observable differentiating features of specific languages and have therefore been the focus of many experiments that aim to explore the lexical boundaries of naming systems (John-Steiner, 1991). It has been more difficult to move from differentiating linguistic categorization into non-linguistic thinking processes (Lakoff, 1987). Evidence of the interdependence of language and thought remains the target for contemporary supporters of Whorf (John-Steiner, 1991).

Challenges to the universalist views of Chomsky and, more recently McWhorter, have emerged on the basis of empirical evidence that points to certain spatial and categorization predispositions imposed on speakers and writers of certain languages (Boroditsky, 2009, 2011). For example, the many ways in which languages order, compare, and group the consequences of human experience have been of particular interest to linguists. The spatial orientation of speakers is also believed to be shaped significantly by the language used (Boroditsky, 2009).

In comparison to other languages, Chinese offers some stark contrasts. Its orientation to history is the opposite of English: forward or front is the past, behind or back is the future; last month is on top, next month is below (Boroditsky, 2001). The Chinese face their past, not their future:

前事不忘後事之師 (*qian shi bu wang, hou shi zhi shi : don't forget the past, it guides the future…*

(Chinese proverb)

The Chinese term 'context' (上下文) refers to that which comes before (above) and after (below), reflecting the orientation of traditional written script – from top to bottom.

A further example is offered by languages with counting systems that are less complex than others, interpreted as a consequence of cultures that place less emphasis on quantification (Boroditsky, 2001). The languages of the indigenous peoples of northern Australia, such as the Warlpiri, have few terms for quantities (none, one, two, many, infinite), reflecting a culture that traditionally does not emphasize keeping count (Dixon, 2010). The Warlpiri have a rich vocabulary describing kinship, etiquette, and personal interaction, suggesting that this phenomenon is the result of cultural emphasis rather than linguistic impoverishment (Dixon, 2010).

In the many dialects of Chinese, the importance of familial ties in Chinese culture means that it is virtually impossible to avoid specifying the exact nature of a relationship between blood relatives. Chinese language doesn't permit deliberate obfuscation through the use of vague terms like 'sister' or 'uncle'. The richness of the Chinese lexicon describing familial relationships reflects an emphasis on the exact nature of blood ties that is not emphasized to the same extent in other languages (Fen, 2007). The 212 kinship terms in common use in modern Chinese create a sensitivity to familial relationships because of the social necessity of precision when identifying and addressing another member of the family; this rich lexicon of kinship terms forces the speaker to maintain a constant awareness of familial ties (Qian & Piao, 2007).

While the color blue and what it might be called in Russian offers evidence of some terminological imprecision in English, there are some challenges to the universalist assumption of a single conceptual system (Lucy, 1996; Winawer *et al*, 2007). Lakoff describes this in a somewhat novel fashion, suggesting that conceptual systems are butchers, with reality serving as the carcass; carving the carcass is just a matter of naming and habit, the chunks are either smaller or larger, but the beast is still the same (Lakoff, 1987). Citing von Humboldt and echoing Whorf, Slobin asserts that there resides in every language a unique characteristic world-view that shapes cognition in some way:

> Whatever else language may do in human thought and action, it surely directs us to attend – while speaking – to the dimensions of experience that are enshrined in grammatical categories.

> (Slobin, 1996)

Rejecting the purported linguistic neutrality of the universalists, Slobin asserts that unique personal experience leads to the construction of a discrete, individual understanding of the world, the articulation of which is informed by the shape and structure of the interlocutor's speech:

> The language or languages that we learn in childhood are not neutral coding systems of an objective reality. Rather, each one is a subjective orientation to the world of human experience, and this orientation affects the ways in which we think while we are speaking.

> (1996)

Our mental analogue of the world is an internal reconstruction of our external experiences and the categories we inherit from those around us, or create ourselves. This model reflects a highly individual and subjective combination of experiential realism and imaginative speculation. The gestalt properties of thought cannot be further deconstructed in a reliable manner (Lakoff, 1987). Our experience of the world shapes our thinking through language as we prepare to verbalize our experiences through speech (Hoge, 2014).

State of the linguasphere
The foregoing discussion brings us to an important question regarding the importance of languages to humanity. A language stands as a unique artifact created or evolved by a group of people to communicate with each other directly and where preserved or recorded in some way, with speakers across time. It contains the accumulated experiences and wisdom of those who have used the language and speaks to those who will use the language in the future. As the carrier for all human experience, constructing, recording and communicating the totality of human knowledge in culturally and cognitively unique ways, language deserves our respect and attention; the management and preservation of specific languages perhaps deserves closer scrutiny.

In the same way that biological diversity is considered a global ecological asset, the sum total of the world's languages, the 'linguasphere', reflects the relative state of linguistic diversity and vitality. At the time of writing, there are 7,102 recognized languages still in use globally. Papua New Guinea has the highest number of languages in the world: a population of just over 4,000,000 speaking 839 languages (Paul, Simons, & Fennig, 2015); this is followed by Indonesia, Nigeria, and India, each with 707, 526, and 454 languages respectively. Eight languages are currently spoken by around half of the world's population (Paul *et al*, 2015).

This apparent vitality conceals some alarming trends for those who believe that linguistic diversity, a marker of cultural diversity, is healthy for humanity (De Schutter, 2008). The percentage of world languages with declining populations of first language speakers is 35%: in 2015, there were 1531 endangered languages (22%) and 916 dying languages (13%) (Paul *et al*, 2015). Since 1950, 367 human languages have become extinct, an average of six per year, but well short of the oft-cited number of one every 14 days. Other authorities place the proportion of world languages 'at risk' as high as 46%, although Krauss' estimate of 90% is now considered to be overly pessimistic (Wiecha, 2013). The Ethnos Project, dedicated to preserving indigenous languages, also asserts that the oft-cited statistic of a language extinction event occurring fortnightly is exaggerated, but the actual loss of culture and language (one every four months) is still seen as alarming (Oppenneer, 2014; Thurman, 2015).

States with large numbers of languages spoken by small minority populations, such as Papua New Guinea, Indonesia, and Australia have experienced an acceleration in the decline of minority languages, often because younger speakers perceive a social or economic advantage in neglecting an ancient language in favor of a more prestigious and financially rewarding language (Mufwene, 2003). In such places, linguistic pluralism is a war of words, with socio-political power and prestige as the main prize.

The phenomenon of linguistic extinction points to the existence of an extra-linguistic mechanism that leads to a tension or struggle between languages. The relative vitality of a language at any given time is a dynamic state. The forces that empower a language – cultural, economic, political, technological, and social – are the same forces that impoverish it. Languages evolve; they also rise and decline.

Post-Nationalism and the ethnolinguistic identity

As social and cultural beings, we are born and grow up sharing a common language and history with others. If there are enough of us, our social, cultural, and economic critical mass may allow us to form a larger grouping – a 'nation'. The contemporary definition of a 'nation' typically invokes the idea of a large group of people born with a distinctive and shared cultural and linguistic connection occupying a geographically or politically defined territory.

Defining the concept of the nation is somewhat problematic, partly because the concept itself is a relatively recent development, and partly because the excessive number of exceptions defeats attempts at definitive description (Hobsbawm, 1990). Sri Lanka and its interlaced communities of Tamil and Sinhalese speakers provide an apposite example of this difficulty. The overlapping ethnic and political boundaries found in Africa are similarly confusing and complex.

Nations are difficult to define cartographically, linguistically, ethnically, and politically. Superficial similarities of ethnicity may conceal deep-seated differences of history. Nations have thus been defined in ethnolinguistic terms, but in fact national identity does not reside solely in a language: the 'post-national' state is not necessarily coterminous with a discrete nation with a single language (Boroujerdi, 1998; Branchadell, 2012; De Schutter, 2008). Nations are often conflated with the more politicized notion of the 'state', which pertains to self-governance and sovereignty. States are defined in politico-military terms. There are of course many nation states, but there are also many stateless nations (UNHRC, 2010).

There has been a fundamental shift in the underlying principle of modern nation-states, first codified in the Treaty of Westphalia, which assumed that a nation would be demarcated by a border within which would be found a single language, culture, religion and government. Known as the *linguistic territoriality principle* (De Schutter, 2008), this Westphalian correlation of the state with a single ethnolinguistic nationality is no longer the standard model of statehood in a linguistically heterogeneous global community.

The imposition of linguistic unification implicit in this traditional model is, to some, both socially undesirable and politically unachievable, particularly in countries such as India or Papua New Guinea (De Schutter, 2008). Moreover, the relevance of monolingualism as the defining criterion for defining a nation is dwindling. To resort to an ethnolinguistic definition of national identity is to misunderstand the impact of multicultural and multilingual challenges to the citizen of the modern state. Just as ideology is more than a constellation of ideas, similarly, language is more than a constellation of discourses, or an 'army of words' striving to be heard as a single voice in the struggle for national purity (Boroujerdi, 1998).

Language can authenticate the identity of a distinct cultural grouping, or anonymize a number of cultural groupings sharing a common 'borrowed' language (De Schutter, 2008; Woolard, 2005; Xue & Zuo, 2013).

An authenticating language offers individuals membership of a self-defining group that reflects the community's values and its cultural identity. It serves as the carrier and core of culture; it is the 'crystallization' of a single culture, the distinctive marker of a discrete group of people (De Schutter, 2008; Xue & Zuo, 2013). An authenticating language and the identity of the individual are inextricably intertwined and as such, some assert that it has no existence apart from its culture (Sapir, 2000 [1921]). As such, linguistic purity and conformity are manifestations of homogeneism, where even small differences are seen as dangerous and centrifugal and are to be eliminated (De Schutter, 2008; Woolard, 2005). Attempts to enforce linguistic purity through the imposition of rules or restrictions on the use of foreign loanwords by community authorities are examples of this phenomenon.

A language may also offer its speakers freedom from any form of identity or labeling through its ubiquity; it is the linguistic equivalent of the 'view from nowhere' (Branchadell, 2012; Woolard, 2005). Neutral, unaligned, unaffiliated, unencumbered with political, social, or cultural impediments, such a language might facilitate communication not possible through media more closely aligned with interested parties. This perspective sees language primarily as a tool of communication, as a conduit for conveying information, but without authenticating membership of a distinctive group (Branchadell, 2012).

Accordingly, some states are home to more than one language; some languages are spoken in more than one state. Both circumstances create the potential for intra- and inter-national tensions: the former creates tensions over national identity; the latter creates tensions over ownership. Both phenomena create the potential for a plurality of historical narratives. Take English for example: who owns it? Attributed variously to Oscar Wilde, George Bernard Shaw and Winston Churchill, the quip that Great Britain and the United States are two nations separated by a common language humorously illustrates the issues of ownership in English speaking world (O'Conner & Kellerman, 2009). The same words may have different meanings, and different words carry identical meanings.

Several countries around the world serve as examples of linguistic pluralism within a single political entity, reflecting conflicting cultural or national affiliations, often arising from political or military accommodations of territorial aspirations. In Europe, violation of the unified nation-state-language equation is not unusual: Austria, Belarus, Belgium, Bosnia & Herzegovina, Cyprus, Finland, Ireland, Luxembourg, The Netherlands, and Switzerland have all identified more than one 'official language' for their respective nation states (Paul *et al*, 2015), with varying degrees of success in maintaining a degree of peaceful co-existence between the official languages of state.

The tensions between the languages are fracture lines in national unity and community identification, suggesting that multiple narratives regarding history, the present and future are operational in these countries. Historical examples that stand out are the multiple ethnolinguistic blocs that were eventually amalgamated into the Republic of India, or the German-speaking Sudetenland in the former Czechoslovakia. Some of these fracture lines are interpersonal, with different segments of the community speaking different languages (multilingualism) and some are intrapersonal, with individuals speaking multiple languages, either willingly or reluctantly.

An example of contemporary diglossic tension is found in the Canadian province of Quebec, where the Francophone majority has asserted a cultural identity at odds with the wider Anglophone Canadian polity (Dunn & West, 2011). During the Quiet Revolution of the 1960s, Quebec made French the common language of public life through which Quebecers of all origins would communicate among themselves (Dunn & West, 2011). The success of the 'revolution' might be measured in the 79% of Quebecois who reported French as their mother tongue in 2006, with an even higher figure, 81.8%, reporting French as the language most used at home (Branchadell, 2012). Carving out a Francophone 'nation' within a state, however, has effectively created two narratives, two histories, *Two Solitudes* (MacLennan, 2008).

Catalonia offers an interesting case study to compare and contrast with the previous example. Castilian Spanish is spoken by 55% of the population in Catalonia, but Catalan is the dominant language among those claiming a Catalonian identity, who number just under 40% of the total population in the region (Branchadell, 2012). The strong cultural identification between the minority Catalonians and their language, however, has proven to be a barrier to the promotion of Catalan beyond the native speaking community. The shift in policy to de-ethnicize Catalan was intended to increase its status and usage by non-Catalan speakers, a move which also threatens the power of Catalan as a culturally distinctive and unifying feature of Catalonian culture (Branchadell, 2012). In order to gain popularity, Catalan risks losing its distinctive identity.

One language: multiple states

In contrast to intra-national linguistic tensions discussed in the foregoing paragraphs, some linguistically homogeneous groups may cross national boundaries. The spread of Russian across many former members of the Soviet Bloc has created some linguistic tensions. In modern day Ukraine, for example, a politically significant proportion of the population in the east of the country speak the language of a neighbouring country, Russia, thus giving rise to a cultural conflict that has quickly escalated into a military and territorial battle, with casualties on both sides. The declared native language of Ukraine is spoken by just 67.5% of the population, with Russian second at 29.6%. When surveyed on languages spoken or used (rather than 'mother tongue'), the proportion of speakers of Ukrainian and Russian was roughly equal (Branchadell, 2012). The language map marks the political fault lines of the current conflict in Ukraine, but the penetration of Russian into the remaining areas of the country point to a troubled future of cultural and linguistic plurality.

China: many nations, many languages, divergent histories

The most populous country in the world with the longest unbroken written history, the People's Republic of China (PRC) is a single political entity with 56 nationalities, eight major language groups, 313 dialects, 22 provinces, and four self-governing municipalities. It is a polyglot, multicultural collection of clans and nationalities that stand in marked contrast to the Westphalian model of the single nation-state-language model. The Chinese national language, also the most spoken first language in the world, is known as 'Mandarin', Putonghua (普通話), Guoyu (國語), or Huayu (華語). It is the most spoken first language in the world, but its apparent prevalence masks a complex dynamic between the national language and some powerful regional dialects.

Chinese, in its written form, is distinguished from all other languages by its unique pictographic-logographic script. While spoken Chinese comprises myriad and mutually unintelligible spoken dialects, because the Chinese script conveys meaning through symbols and not sounds, this permits written communication between Chinese-literate groups that do not share a common spoken dialect (Paul *et al*, 2015). Chinese characters sit at the heart of the unbroken, millennia-long history of the Chinese people. The script simplification reform movement in the 1950s in the PRC has introduced a second written form for the most common 25% of Chinese characters. These two scripts now straddle a political divide that separates Chinese communities across the globe, from Shanghai to San Francisco, depending on whether the simplified or traditional characters are used.

The war of words in the Chinese-speaking world does not cease with the written form of the language. The relative status of the dialects continues to generate heated debate on-line, particularly over the notions of dialect prestige and historical provenance (Salibra, 2010; Xu, 2014). Northern dialects, particularly Mandarin, are deemed by southern Chinese speakers to be suspect due to the supposed foreign, especially Manchurian, influences on the language (Chen, 2010). The choice of the official language for the newly founded Republic of China following the Xinghai revolution of 1911 continues to generate heated debate online, with speculation that there was a close vote between Cantonese and Mandarin (Roswell, 2013). Mandarin (or Putonghua) has been the national spoken language of both 'Chinas' and is an official language of Singapore.

The current status and future of Cantonese is a complex and highly political and cultural question that extends well beyond the boundaries of the People's Republic of China. The cultural prestige of Cantonese is asserted by southern Chinese bloggers citing the purported historical authenticity and longevity of Cantonese over Mandarin (Chen, 2010). This is but one manifestation of the ethnolinguistic divide between northern and southern China. Cantonese remains the dominant language in the Hong Kong Special Administrative Region (SAR), at least in spoken form (Snow, 2010). It was, until relatively recently, the Chinese dialect most likely to be heard outside of China, predominating in 'Chinatowns' around the world, but particularly in North America, parts of South East Asia, and Australia (Semple, 2009). The official role of Cantonese in the Hong Kong SAR after the conclusion of the 'Basic Law' treaty in July 2047 remains unclear, but there are highly politicized and starkly polarized debates online about this question (Salibra, 2010). The apparent educational ambiguity surrounding the status of Cantonese in Hong Kong poses questions for its future vitality and influence beyond the social sphere in a future where Putonghua is increasingly prominent (Lee & Leung, 2012). In Chinese communities in other parts of the world, historically dominated by Cantonese, the struggle between Cantonese and Putonghua is clearly evident, with Putonghua winning through sheer numbers (Semple, 2009).

Similar debates are taking place over the status and perceived decline of Shanghainese, one branch of the second largest dialect group in China, the Wu group of languages. One reason for the apparent decline of Shanghai dialect is the influx of migrants from other dialect speaking areas who see no economic advantage in learning Shanghai dialect (Huang, 2013; Xu, 2014).

Many contributions to the online debate within the Chinese-speaking world on the struggle between the dialects assert the prestige and historical authenticity of Cantonese or Shanghainese. There is the claim that both dialects can prove a longer history, or that ancient poetry when read in either dialect rhymes, something that is claimed not to be the case in Mandarin (Huang, 2013; Lee & Leung, 2012; Salibra, 2010; Xu, 2014). Uniquely for the Chinese, however, there is the issue of modern written Chinese, which corresponds closely with the national language, but not with some of the major spoken dialects. Cantonese is in fact a group of spoken dialects, rather than a written language. There is no standard way of writing Cantonese, although many informal or quasi-official variants of standard Chinese characters have been created to cater to this need. These are unintelligible to any non-Cantonese reader.

The 'histories' of China, reflected in the myriad journals, commentaries, publications, weblogs, and other formats, offer sharply divergent views of the past, the present, and the future of 'Greater China'. The script, grammar, and vocabulary all communicate a great deal about the writer, culturally, socially, and politically, before the content has even been considered. Chinese offers an interesting case study of form versus substance, where the form of the script itself conveys meaning independently of its semantic content. The use of traditional characters locates the writer geographically, educationally, and to an extent politically. The use of certain grammatical particles and structures similarly locates the writer within 'Greater China'. The gap between spoken Chinese dialects and modern written Chinese, in either traditional or simplified characters, creates its own norming dynamic that will continue to influence the evolution of Chinese in the 21st century.

The potential for Chinese to extend its influence beyond its boundaries into non-ethnically Chinese communities will depend somewhat on its political influence, and its capacity to confer economic advantage or cultural prestige.

Transnationality and global English

No exploration of the relationship between history and language would be complete without some reference to the English language and its place in the global struggle between words and cultures. In a process that has spanned centuries and gathered increasing cultural and political momentum and geographical coverage, English, or 'Globish' has emerged from the rise and fall of empire, industrial and technological dominance, and the global conflicts of the 20th century, as the global *lingua franca* at the start of the 21st century (EurActiv, 2013; McPeek, 2012; Popan, 2011). For example, there is increasing evidence of a preference for English in international transactions, in the commercial, scientific, political, and even cultural sphere (*The Economist*, 2001; Xue & Zuo, 2013). The histories studied in many schools, particularly 'internationally-minded' schools, are largely written in English. In Europe, English has steadily reinforced its status as Europe's new *lingua franca*, with 94% of upper secondary students learning English as a foreign language, with overall figures increasing from 73% to 83% in just one year; just over 51% of EU citizens speak English as either their first or other language (Maracz, 2012).

This trend is also reflected beyond Europe, with English increasingly taking on the role of the new 'Latin', a global *lingua franca* (Abdullah & Chaudhary, 2012; Silverberg, 2015). English is also increasingly exerting a major influence on the lexical and grammatical development of other languages, both within Europe and beyond (Maxwell, 2006). Under the influence of contact with English, the Chinese language has modernized and evolved during the 20th century, acquiring new grammatical structures and lexical items derived directly from English (Pritchard, 2014).

The internet has opened up a new front in the war of languages and the potential for English to 'pollinate' other languages online can only increase (Maxwell, 2006). Web-based language is estimated to be more than 50% English. It might be claimed that the history of computers and computer languages, even those developed for use in non-English speaking contexts, would not be possible without reference to English, although the extent of lexical influence is limited to the 100 or so English-based command terms needed for most programming languages (Programmers Stack Exchange, 2011).

Due to economic and political influence of English there is an emerging perception of its linguistic and even cultural hegemony arising from what is perceived as an unidirectional flow of influence from English to other languages and cultures (Xue & Zuo, 2013). This view asserts that the burgeoning cultural dominance of English is the new 'colonialism' and that English has become a weapon in a cultural war that threatens the social discourse of other countries (Xue & Zuo, 2013).

The flow of linguistic influence, however, is not unidirectional. The penchant of speakers of English to borrow from other languages reflects at one level a pragmatic practice of linguistic innovation and flexibility. However, much more than this, the practice is also an efficient way of borrowing not just a word, but a cultural perspective, a world view, even a history, with the simple adoption of a foreign term. For example, the extent to which a language freely accommodates loanwords from other languages and naturalizes or conventionalizes those words with little resistance may be significant. English is linguistically 'docile'; it is highly malleable and open to accommodate foreign borrowings without fear of culturally defensive reactions from its global community of speakers.

English speakers, in fact, are prone to using foreign words, even when existing English terms may perform an identical linguistic function. For example, English speakers tend to use the German loanword *schadenfreude* when the English term *epicaricacy* exists with roughly the same meaning, at least in the dictionary. Is this practice pointing at something deeper than the need for a new word to describe something new? In the dying days of the Soviet Union, *glasnost* (openness) and *perestroika* (restructuring), were certainly not imported because such words did not exist in English at the time. The words were imported to convey a much deeper and comprehensive meaning attaching to the political, cultural and even historical context that created these terms in their native context in the first place. These nuances of meaning were simply not part of the native English terms. They are possibly intended to capture an aspect of *zeitgeist*. In fact, the Russian loanwords cited have not maintained the currency of the age in which they were borrowed and have now assumed a place in history, but for a time, they conveyed quite precisely a particular meaning and worldview.

Current loanwords from Arabic may serve a similar purpose in English, importing both a specific definition and its surrounding cultural context: *jihad* (holy war), *jihadi* (holy warrior), *fatwah* (judgement), *burqa* (veil), *imam* (priest), *caliph* (successor or ruler), *caliphate* (ruler's jurisdiction), join much older words that have already taken deep root in English, such as algebra, alcohol, hazard, kismet, candy, jar, and zero. Orange, the perennial poet's puzzle for its lack of an English rhyme, was also borrowed from Arabic.

English itself is both a product of enthnolinguistic conflict and a major combatant in the contemporary cultural battle over linguistic influence. It is a rich amalgam of influences and borrowings, some voluntary, others imposed. Broadly speaking, the influence of Norse, Norman French, German, and Latin on English reflects the unique history of the English speaking peoples, both at war and in times of peace. The history of the English language clearly demonstrates the capacity for conflict and invasion, either military or cultural, to shape a language. Linguists generally agree that a large percentage of English is essentially borrowed from the languages of invading powers, mostly French and Latin, suggesting a strong, if somewhat imposed, predisposition towards accommodation and adaption, lexically and grammatically in English. It is of course a purely linguistic irony that the term used in English to describe its current common language status, *lingua franca* (language of the Franks), is itself a loanword (as is 'loanword' – *lehnwort* from German).

Conclusion: Whose History?

We are left in the end with two relatively straightforward questions. Whose history, and whose language? While it is easy to construct this as a conflict between competing cultures and tongues, given the foregoing discussion on the nature of human experience, thought, language, and history, the answer to these questions of language and history is 'ours'. The interplay between language and history is complex and nuanced. A language and the history it tells are human cultural artifacts capturing a unique set of experiences at a certain point in time, neither of which will ever come again.

From the evidence examined here, there appears to be no unique, one-to-one relationship between a language and a culture, between a language and the history it tells. A single culture may embrace more than one language and a language may act as the carrier for more than one culture. Where one language is inextricably intertwined with a homogeneous culture or nationality, it serves as a form of human boundary to demarcate the territory occupied by its speakers. When cultural identity and nationality are no longer identified through a language spoken by a group of people, for example English in some countries, the role of the language moves into a different dimension of ethno-social function. Language shapes culture, but culture also shapes the development of language: both are ultimately permeable and malleable (Boroujerdi, 1998).

Our survival skill, practiced from birth, is to observe, to absorb, to mimic, to label and categorize our experiences, which shapes how we remember these things later in life. Our linguistic and experiential frame of reference compels us to observe certain things, while perhaps ignoring others. The pattern of social interaction that builds slowly towards the completion of enculturation similarly privileges certain attitudes, actions, and aspirations, while neglecting others. Through our experiential frame of reference, we may or may not become aware of our biases and may therefore choose to make adjustments or proceed regardless. From this we construct our distinctive, subjective histories in microcosm.

The imaginative interplay between language and thinking, experience and meaning, results in the production of a seemingly infinite range of artifacts, spanning the entirety of human endeavor. If language operates under a common set of specifications, there perhaps should be a greater evidence of homogeneity in linguistic artifacts across the history of humanity; this is not in evidence. While the purposes of language may be largely equivalent across different cultures, and this equivalency of function may create the perception that all languages are equal, the highly individual and experiential nature of the construction of meaning and the product of that construction, reflect the unique circumstances of each member of the human race. It is this uniqueness and the making of individual meaning that must be considered carefully before dismissing linguistic determinism.

What does emerge from this brief exploration of the ownership of language and history is that each language is a unique human construct that shapes the historical narrative in ways inextricably bound to the language and the cultural context in which the narrative is created. Languages contend for territorial dominance, grow and mature like living organisms. Languages transcend their original ethnic identity and migrate to other cultural 'life support systems', where they serve the needs of other cultural groups. Languages become trapped in cultural or demographic dead-ends and fade into extinction. Each language coins a phrase that captures an experience like no other; each history tells a story like no other. Our languages, like our histories, are precious and irreplaceable living artifacts that reflect the chaos, contention, and complexity of human experience.

References

Abdullah, S. S., & Chaudhary, M. L. (2012). *English as a Global Lingua Franca*. Paper presented at the International Conference on Education, Applied Sciences and Management, Dubai, UAE. psrcentre.org/proceeding.php?catid=68&type=1&mode=detail

Arendt, H. (1977). *The Life of the Mind*. New York: Harcourt, Brace, Jovanovich.

Bede. (731 [2015]). *Historia Ecclesiastica Gentis Anglorum* Vol. About Education Classic Literature. Retrieved from classiclit.about.com/library/bl-etexts/bede/bl-bede-preface.htm

Boroditsky, L. (2001). Does Language Shape Thought? Mandarin and English Speakers' Conceptions of Time. *Cognitive Psychology, 43*(1), 1-22.

Boroditsky, L. (2009). How Does Our Language Shape the Way We Think? *Edge: Conversations*. Retrieved 5 April, 2015, from edge.org/conversation/how-does-our-language-shape-the-way-we-think

Boroditsky, L. (2011). How Language Shapes Thought: The languages we speak affect our perceptions of the world. *Scientific American, 304*(2), 62-65.

Boroujerdi, M. (1998). Contesting Nationalist Constructions of Iranian Identity. *Critique: Journal for Critical Studies of the Middle East, 7.12*(Spring 1998), 43-55.

Boyle, J. (2014). What is the difference between a dialect and a language? [Weblog]. Retrieved from www.quora.com/What-is-the-difference-between-a-dialect-and-a-language

Branchadell, A. (2012). One Nation, One (Common) Language? Language and Nationalism in 21st Centry Catalonia. Retrieved from Recode Working Paper Series website: www.recode.info/wp-content/uploads/2013/02/Branchadell-Albert-2012-RECODE.pdf

Carr, E. H. (1987 [1961]). *What is History?* (2nd ed.). New York, NY: Penguin.

Chen, M. (2010). Cantonese is Authentic Chinese, Mandarin is actually the language of foreign enslavement (广东话才是正宗的汉语，"普通话"其实是被胡人奴化的语言). Blog Retrieved from malcolmchen.blog.epochtimes.com/article/show?articleid=25657

Chomsky, N. (1986). *Knowledge of Language: Its Nature*, Origin, and Use. Westport, CT: Praeger.

Churchill, W. S. (2012 [1947]). Parliamentary Speeches. In A. Jay (Ed.), Oxford Dictionary of Political Quotations. Oxford, UK: Oxford University Press.

De Schutter, H. (2008). The Linguistic Territoriality Principle - A Critique. *Journal of Applied Philosophy, 25*(2), 105-120.

Dixon, R. M. W. (2010). *The Languages of Australia*. Cambridge, UK: Cambridge University Press.

Dorian, N. C. (1991). Linguacentrism and Language History. In R. Cooper & B. Spolsky (Eds.), *The Influence of Language on Culture and Thought: essays in honor of Joshua A. Fishman's sixty-fifth birthday* (pp. 85-100). New York, NY: Mouton de Gruyter.

Dunn, W., & West, L. (2011). The Quiet Revolution. *Canada: A Country by Consent*. Retrieved 25 April, 2015, from www.canadahistoryproject.ca/1960s/index.html

EurActiv. (2013, 30 September). Eurostat: English Reinforces its status as Europe's 'lingua franca'. Retrieved 16 August, 2014, from www.euractiv.com/culture/english-reinforces-supremacy-eur-news-530728

Feist, M. I., & Gentner, D. (2007). Spatial Language Influences Memory for Spatial Scenes. *Memory & Cognition, 35*(2), 283-296.

Fen, X. (2007). English and Chinese Culture Differences from Linguistic Viewpoint. *Canadian Social Science, 3*(5), 99-101.

Formigari, L. (1999). Idealism and idealistic trends in linguistics and the philosophy of language. In P. Schmitter (Ed.), *Sprachtheorien der Neuzeit* (pp. 230-253). Tübingen: Gunter Narr Verlag.

Friedman, V. A. (2003). Language in Macedonia as an Identity Construction Site. In B. D. Joseph, J. DeStefano, N. G. Jacobs, & I. Lehiste (Eds.), *When Languages Collide: Perspectives on Language Conflict, Language Competition, and Language Coexistence* (pp. 257-295). Columbus, OH: The Ohio State University Press.

Gibbon, E. (1782 [2012]). *History of the Decline and Fall of the Roman Empire* D. Widger (Ed.) Retrieved from www.gutenberg.org/files/25717/25717-h/25717-h.htm

Halliday, M. A. K. (1993). Towards a language-based theory of learning. *Linguistics and Education, 5,* 93-116.

Hobsbawm, E. J. (1990). *Nations and Nationalism Since 1780: Programme, Myth, Reality.* Cambridge, UK: Cambridge University Press.

Hoge, K. (2014). Review: The Language Hoax: Why the World Looks the Same in Any Language, by John H. McWhorter. *Times Higher Education.* Retrieved from Times Higher Education website: www.timeshighereducation.co.uk/books/the-language-hoax-why-the-world-looks-the-same-in-any-language-by-john-h-mcwhorter/2014926.article

Huang, S. Y. (2013). Loss of dialect a crisis for ancient language. *Shanghai Daily.* Retrieved from China.org.cn website: www.china.org.cn/opinion/2013-08/09/content_29669554.htm

John-Steiner, V. (1991). Cognitive Pluralism: A Whorfian Analysis. In R. Cooper & B. Spolsky (Eds.), *The Influence of Language on Culture and Thought: essays in honor of Joshua A. Fishman's sixty-fifth birthday* (pp. 61-74). New York, NY: Mouton de Gruyter.

Lakoff, G. (1987). *Women, Fire, and Dangerous Things: What Categories Reveal about the Mind.* Chicago, Il: The University of Chicago Press.

Lee, K. S., & Leung, W. M. (2012). The Status of Cantonese in the Education Policy of Hong Kong. *Multilingual Education, 2*(2), 1-22.

Lerner, M. (1989 [1943]). Epilogue *It is Later Than You Think: The Need For a Militant Democracy* (pp. 253-258). New Brunswick, NJ: Transaction Publishers.

Lucy, J. (1996). The Scope of Linguistic Relativity: An Analysis and Review of Empirical Research. In J. J. Gumperz & S. C. Levinson (Eds.), *Rethinking Linguistic Relativity* (pp. 37-69). Cambridge, UK: Cambridge University Press.

MacLennan, H. (2008). *Two Solitudes.* Toronto: New Canadian Library.

Maracz, L. (2012). Multilingualism in Europe: Policy and Practice. *European Studies, 29*(2012), 21-35.

Maxwell, K. (2006). From metrosexual to metrosessuale: the global influence of English in the creation of neologisms. *MED Magazine.* March, 2006. Retrieved 15 August, 2014, from www.macmillandictionaries.com/MED-Magazine/March2006/36-New-Word-Neologisms.htm

McPeek, T. (2012, 20 February). The Future of The English Language as a Global Lingua Franca. Retrieved 15 August, 2014, from floridalinguistics.com/?p=641

McWhorter, J. H. (2014). *The Language Hoax: Why the World Looks the Same in Any Language*. New York, NY: Oxford University Press.

Mufwene, S. (2003). Language Endangerment: What Have Pride and Prestige Got to Do with It?. In B. D. Joseph, J. DeStefano, N. G. Jacobs, & I. Lehiste (Eds.), *When Languages Collide: Perspectives on Language Conflict, Language Competition, and Language Coexistence* (pp. 324-347). Columbus, OH: The Ohio State University.

O'Conner, P. T., & Kellerman, S. (2009, 24 May). 'Origin of the Specious'. *The New York Times*.

Oppenneer, M. (2014). Status of the Ethnosphere: New Statistics about Language Loss Across the World [Web Blog]. Retrieved from www.ethnosproject.org/status-of-the-ethnosphere/

Orwell, G. (2014 [1949]). Nineteen Eighty-Four. *George Orwell Novels: The books, essays and letters of George Orwell*. Retrieved 23 August, 2014, from georgeorwellnovels.com/books/nineteen-eighty-four/

Paul, L. M., Simons, G. F., & Fennig, C. D. (Eds.). (2015). *Ethnologue: Languages of the World* (18th ed. Vol. 2015). Dallas, TX: SIL International.

Piaget, J. (2002 [1923]). *The Language and Thought of the Child* (M. Gabain & R. Gabain, Trans.). London: Routledge.

Popan, C. (2011). English as a Lingua Franca or the New Global Latin: Sociolinguistic Considerations from the Conference Interpreter's Standpoint. *Cognitie, Creier, Comportament, 15*(2).

Pritchard, M. (2014). Languages in Competition and Conflict: mechanisms of linguistic evolution. *The International Schools Journal, 34* (1), 33-44. Woodbridge, UK. John Catt Educational.

Programmers Stack Exchange. (2011, 21 August 2011). Non-English-based programming languages. Blog Retrieved from programmers.stackexchange.com/questions/35501/non-english-based-programming-languages?lq=1

Qian, Y. F., & Piao, S. (2007). *Chinese Kinship Semantic Structure and Annotation Scheme*. Paper presented at the Corpus Linguistics Conference, Birmingham, UK.

Roswell, M. (2013). Did Cantonese almost replace Mandarin as the standard spoken version of Chinese? Why did Mandarin win out? Web Blog Retrieved from www.quora.com/Did-Cantonese-almost-replace-Mandarin-as-the-standard-spoken-version-of-Chinese-Why-did-Mandarin-win-out

Salibra, L. (2010). 7 Reasons Cantonese is Dying & Mandarin is King [Blog]. Retrieved from www.larrysalibra.com/2010/02/25/7-reasons-cantonese-is-dying-mandarin-is-king/

Sapir, E. (2000 [1921]). *Language: An Introduction to the Study of Speech*. New York: Bartleby.

Schuh, R. (2011, 21 September). Reply to Lera Boroditsky "How Languages Shapes Thought" (Scientific American, February 2011). Retrieved 22 August, 2014, from www.linguistics.ucla.edu/people/schuh/lx001/Discussion/d01_response_to Boroditsky.pdf

Scovel, T. (1991). Why Languages Do not Shape Cognition: Psycho- and Neurolinguistic Evidence. *Japanese Association of Language Teachers Journal, 13*(1), 43-56.

Semple, K. (2009, 21 October). In Chinatown, Sound of the Future is Mandarin. *The New York Times*, p. A1.

Silverberg, E. (2015). 'Englishisation' - Is it working? *Japan Today*. Retrieved from: www. japantoday.com/category/lifestyle/view/englishisation-is-it-working

Slobin, D. (1996). From "Thought and Language" to "Thinking for Speaking". In J. J. Gumperz & S. C. Levinson (Eds.), *Rethinking Linguistic Relativity* (pp. 70-96). Cambridge, UK: Cambridge University Press.

Snow, D. (2010). Hong Kong and Modern Diglossia. *International Journal of the Sociology of Language, 2010*(206), 155-179. doi: 10.1515/IJSL.2010.052

Swoyer, C. (2003). The Linguistic Relativity Hypothesis. Retrieved 15 August, 2014, from plato.stanford.edu/entries/relativism/supplement2.html

The Economist. (2001, 20 December). The Triumph of English: A world empire by other means. *The Economist*. Retrieved from www.economist.com/node/883997

Thurman, J. (2015). A Loss for Words: Can a Dying Language be Saved?. *The New Yorker, 2015*.

UNHRC. (2010). Declaration on the Rights of Persons Belonging to National or Ethnic, Religious and Linguistic Minorities. New York: UN Human Rights Commission.

Vygotsky, L. S. (1986 [1934]). *Thought and Language* (A. Kozulin, Trans.). Cambridge, MA: MIT Press.

Wells, G. (1999). *Dialogic Inquiry: Towards a Sociocultural Practice and Theory of Education*. Cambridge: Cambridge University Press.

Wiecha, K. (2013). New Estimates on the Rate of Global Language Loss. Retrieved from rosettaproject.org/blog/02013/mar/28/new-estimates-on-rate-of-language-loss/

Winawer, J., Witthoft, N., Frank, M., Wu, L., Wade, A., & Boroditsky, L. (2007). Russian blues reveal effects of language on color discrimination. *Proc Natl Acad Sci U S A*, 104(19), 7780-7785. doi: 10.1073/pnas.0701644104

Wittgenstein, L. (2010 [1922]). *Tractatus Logico-Philisophicus* (C. K. Ogden, Trans.): Project Gutenberg.

Woolard, K. A. (2005). Language and Identity Choice in Catalonia: The Interplay of Contrasting Ideologies of Linguistic Authority. Retrieved from: www.ihc.ucsb.edu/ research/identity_articles/WoolardNov5.pdf

Xu, J. Q. (2014). Shanghai Dialect Locked in Tug of War with Mandarin. *China Daily USA*. Retrieved from chinadailyusa.com website: usa.chinadaily.com.cn/ epaper/2014-02/28/content_17313346.htm

Xue, J., & Zuo, W. J. (2013). English Dominance and Its Influence on International Communication. *Theory and Practice in Language Studies, 3*(12), 2262-2266.

Zinn, H. (1970). What is Radical History? *History is a Weapon*. Retrieved from: www. historyisaweapon.com/defcon1/zinnwhatisradicalhistory.html

Zinn, H. (1980). *A People's History of the United States* Retrieved from www. historyisaweapon.com/zinnapeopleshistory.html

Chapter 2

Whose history? Whose nation?

Caroline Ellwood

Across the world and the generations people have maintained their identity by the preservation of a collective memory. History was used to record great events, reinforce religious belief, create good citizens, maintain the power of the state and ensure a loyalty to the nation. Isaiah recommends that you should 'Consider the rock you were hewn from and the quarry from which you were cut' (*Isaiah*, 51.1) But where is the quarry? Who owns it now? And who did the cutting?

Any history, even a chronological list of facts, is subject to the motivations of the selector and nowhere is that motivation more explicit than in the way history has been used through the centuries to provide and inculcate specific messages of citizenship, behaviour, morality and heritage. Facts are chosen by the historian. 'Millions have crossed the Rubicon, but only Caesar's journey is notable' (Carr). The way that history is taught, what is remembered, what is selected and emphasised and what is ignored can make or destroy values and create or ruin the identity of a nation.

President Mitterrand, defending the permanent place of history in the French Baccalaureate, maintained that 'A people which loses its memory loses its identity' (Mitterrand, 1984). But how trustworthy is that memory and who decides which memory is correct and what kind of an identity is being preserved? History is 'remembered' and 'forgotten' in different ways by different people. The history of West and Equatorial Africa is likely to be remembered rather differently by President Mitterrand (and French Baccalaureate students) and an African. Chinua Achebe vividly illustrates this difference of perspective in his analysis of Conrad's story *Heart of Darkness*. The French man the gunboats, but Achebe was 'one of those strange beings jumping up and down on the bank, making horrid faces' (Achebe, 1990).

What can be termed a collective memory is found in heroic sagas like *Beowulf* or the *Kalevala*, in folk heroes like Robin Hood, saving the nation, icons like Jeanne d'Arc and traditions like the burning of Guy Fawkes. The celebration of some noble act or sacrifice on behalf of the tribe or nation becomes a ritual act of remembrance. This is often recorded in poetry or drama where the original story becomes changed and adapted over time like the English Mummers Plays, the Spanish *Moros y Cristianos* and Shi'ah celebrations of Ashura.

Henry Kissinger in his book, *World Order* (2014), emphasises the importance of The Peace of Westphalia (1648):

> a turning point in the history of nations because the elements it set in place were as uncomplicated as they were sweeping. The state,

not the empire, dynasty or religious confession, was affirmed as the building block of European order. The concept of state sovereignty was established.

(Kissinger, 2014)

By the late 18th century in Europe the reinforcement of a sense of a country's identity was being promoted by the way national history was interpreted and written. However the initial impetus of the French Revolution was to cut across boundaries and promote the brotherhood of man, an enthusiasm that prompted Wordsworth, travelling in France, to write how 'a benignant spirit was abroad which might not be withstood' (*The Prelude* Book 1X).

France announced in a decree in 1792 that it would 'accord fraternity and assistance to all peoples … who shall wish to recover their liberty'. (Thompson 1948). With this kind of neighbourly encouragement for insurrection, coupled with the flight of a frightened aristocracy, the poetic rapture did not last long. For all the acclamation of the international brotherhood of the Revolution it was, once the wars began, essentially a French affair. Napoleon's Empire was an expanded France, not a united Europe. Nor were the settlements of the Congress of Vienna based on ideas of European unity but reinforced the integrity of national identity and a balance of power of the powerful.

This was a balance of European national groups and did not of course include the nations of great swathes of the rest of the world which the European powers felt free to absorb into their own 'stories' wherever possible. The various nations that in turn have claimed the Falkland Islands provide a fascinating and ultimately deadly history of ownership and nationalism. Europe may have evolved into a balance of national powers; the rest of the world was open to the claims of whoever got there first, and could by war keep possession or grab as the prize of victory. As a book like *The Patriotic Historical Reader* puts it at the end of a series of descriptions of how 'races of savage men of the lowest type' have been civilised by Britain, 'The British Empire is a great one, indeed the greatest the world has ever seen' (1890 Collins).

The history that children learned was the story of their own nation. England's story began with the seeds of greatness sown by Julius Caesar and his civilising influence, followed by her conversion to Christianity, the founding of parliament, and then proceeding by way of a series of great events and inspiring leaders to become the most important power in the world: a power whose expansion and success was uniquely favoured by God.

H E Marshall's *Our Island Story* concluded with the comment, 'In reviewing the latter portion of our history we find many reasons for gratitude to the Almighty Dispenser of events'. *Our Island Story*, revised in 1909, with its exciting tales of heroism (Drake, Wolfe, Nelson, Clive *etc*) brought the story up to date and reinforced the status of the national heroic and patriotic stereotype with the inferiority of other races. It did however graciously note that 'the Indians have taken kindly to cricket' (*Ibid*).

The selection of facts and events to reinforce a nation's identity is not peculiar to Britain. Selected events and the tales of heroes have provided the story of the emergence of a nation from the exploits of the Greeks right through to the emergence of modern China. Patriotism provides the basis for success and success depended upon a military spirit that would create an enthusiasm for combat and therefore a willingness to join the fight and die for one's country. Throughout the 19th century each of the European leading nations – Britain, France, Russia, Austria and the newly united Italy and Germany – all used history to reinforce not just an idea of identity but also of militarism as they jockeyed for positions of influence. War was not just a necessary event; it was noble and to die for your country was a privilege.

Each country embroiders into the cloth of its history moments of significance that become illustrations of success or greatness. Millen points out how such dates, enshrined in meaning for a particular nation, can be totally unknown by others. Few except historians know the significance of 1864 for the Danes (Schleswig Holstein); 1871 for the Italians (Unification); 1431 for Romania (birth of Vlad III); and what does 1617 signify for Sweden? (Millen 2015).

Each of these examples reinforces identity just as the way many school text books reflect a specific interpretation of the past. For many centuries the role of the historical narrative as presented to young people was to serve the nation state. The proposed curriculum for British schools in 1904 shows clearly the expected result from the topics:

> Course 3. Emigration to the Colonies (to bring out the need for
> and value of emigration and the dash, energy and pluck
> necessary to carry it out).

> Course 4. Modern government and why men go to prison.

> Course 5. The Question of Imperial defence.
> (Goldsmith College, 1904).

To 'pluckily' defend your country and to serve in the army, work as a colonial administrator or indeed as a missionary was to show patriotism for the mother country and spread its values to the native population. This patriotic and militaristic fervour across Europe would culminate in thousands of recruits, each assured of their own country's greatness and eager to show their love of and loyalty to a monarch and a nation, being slaughtered in World War One. *'Dulce et dacorum est'*... each country gave its own version of events to prove that their cause was righteous (see also chapter five).

In the late 19th century the newly united German nation created a centralised education system that also controlled teacher training and the text books that were used. Bismarck was well aware of the power of education in bringing together the disparate parts of the new nation. As the lawyer says to the irate Captain Trotta when he complains that the school text book is not telling the truth about his role in the Battle of Solferino: 'All historic events are rewritten for school use ... they can find out the truth later on.' (*The Radetsky March*, Roth 1932)

Written in 1932, Roth's novel illustrates the way militarism dominated 19th century life in both Austria and Germany. With all the horrors of WW1 revealed as the ultimate result of the great powers competing for supremacy, it is no accident that the background reality of the time the novel was written is Hitler moving to power through another reinforcement of militarism. Because he was a Jew, Roth's books were burned in the Nazi book burning ceremonies of 1933. Hitler's determination to use not just history to serve the militaristic needs of the state, but the whole curriculum, is found expressed in his aims for education that:

> All subjects, German Language, History, Geography, Chemistry and Mathematics must concentrate on military subjects, the glorification of German heroes and leaders and the strengths of a regenerated Germany.
>
> (Angriff 27th October, 1939)

History would, however, have a special place in this aim and provide

> An ardent love of country and a passionate spirit of national patriotism ... out of the abundance of great names in German history the greatest will have to be selected and presented to our young generation in such a way as to become solid pillars of strength to support the national spirit ... so that pupils on leaving school will not be a pacifist but a whole hearted German .... and take as its crowning task the understanding of racial purity.
>
> (*Mein Kampf*, 1939)

It is a statement that, apart from the chilling last sentence, would still meet with the approval of both patriotic leaders and citizens of a number of countries today. Indeed, leaders from every age have realised the value of selecting a version of history that gives support to their claims, making sure that it was reinforced by suitable propaganda. The winner's version is the truth or, as the African proverb says, '*Gnatola ma no kpon sia, eyenabe adelan to kpo mi sena*' (Until the lion has his own storyteller, the hunter will always have the best part of the story).

If the European leaders and rulers saw history's role as reinforcing the aims of the state, Karl Marx was busy promoting a different stance. Taking the point of view of the lion, he saw the purpose of history not from the top down but from the bottom up. Maintaining that 'the history of all previous societies has been the history of class struggle' Marx proposed a political solution that would promote the working class. He saw a struggle, rooted in the proletariat, based on economics with the necessary aim of revolution if it was to be achieved. Such a revolutionary movement would cross national boundaries. Economic forces, he maintained, determine, shape and define all political, social, cultural, intellectual and technological aspects of civilisation:

> The history of all hitherto existing society is the history of class struggles... All previous historical movements were movements of

minorities, or in the interest of minorities. The proletarian movement is the self-conscious, independent movement of the immense majority, in the interest of the immense majority.

(The Communist Manifesto, 1848)

Marx maintained that to understand history you needed to study more than political history, and what have become known as Marxist Historians attempt to make sense 'not of this or that part of history but of the whole of history'. (Himmelfarb 1987)

> To understand history you need to study both economics and psychology and sociology... In studying such transformations it is always necessary to distinguish between the material transformation of the economic conditions of production, which can be determined with the precision of natural science, and the legal, political, religious, artistic or philosophic – in short, ideological forms in which men become conscious of this conflict and fight it out.
>
> (The Communist Manifesto, 1848)

This all-encompassing view of the role of history as a catalyst, coupled with the impact of the industrial revolution, slowly brought about a change from the study of past politics, leaders and wars. The interpretation of history as sometimes on a bumpy ride but always moving toward a better destination no longer fitted a world with a conscience about inequality and poverty. Society was no longer seen in terms of a stable feudal system, as the popular hymn *All things bright and beautiful* expressed it:

> The rich man in his castle, the poor man at his gate
> God made the high and lowly and ordered their estate.
>
> (Cecil Alexander, 1895)

Society was in fact dynamic and changing and, come the revolution, men will eventually throw off their chains.

In Britain, a social conscience was reflected not just in attitudes to history but also in literature. A notable change occurred in the subjects and themes of the novel as illustrated by Disraeli (*Sybil*, or *The Two Nations*), Gaskell (*North and South*), Dickens (*Hard Times*) and Eliot (*Felix Holt, The Radical*). As ideas of socialism developed and trade unions gained more power a 'socialist' history emerged. Charles Booth published *Life and Labour of the People in London* (1887); J and B Hammond produced *The Village Labourer* (1911) and *The Town Labourer* (1917). Detailed accounts of the foundation of trade unions and early socialist movements were recorded with the purpose of spreading socialist ideas and demands for suffrage and changes in the law.

Considerations of the purpose of history were not peculiar to Marx and socialist or communist writers. The rapid changes in technology and demography that created appalling social conditions for the poor encouraged historians like Carlisle in Britain, Ranke in Germany and Michelet in France to question the aims of historiography and extend the writing of history into new directions.

Widening the field in subject matter, skills and purpose, patriotic drum and trumpet history was no longer a sufficient explanation of a complex interconnected world or indeed the identity of a state. More importantly there was now conflict about what that explanation might be. Marx had wanted the 'workers of the world to unite'; the reality was a reinforcement of national identity that in 1914 encouraged such patriotism that millions were prepared to die to protect it.

However the war that started as one of the most patriotic in history, involving millions of volunteers, produced a disillusion that included all sides of the conflict. What had it all been for? Historians produced different explanations and politicians proposed opposing solutions to the post war emergence of a series of dictators. National interpretations of events proved misleading. Historians could now disagree, dates became less firm, the study of sources was moved to the surface – not just the background work of the scholar before writing the text.

History was now not just a story but a theory of what had happened in the past and the purpose became to prove that theory beyond doubt. Two world wars and the decline of empire meant that the focus of history moved beyond the narrowly national to a European, then a world view. European scholars who had assumed an educational high ground that gave them the right to document and judge the history of 'the silent, sullen peoples' (Kipling, 1899) had to readjust to the fact that 'non Europeans could think' (Dabashi, 2015}.

The history of colonial independence and its results is now more than a century old and crosses continents, religions, traditions and languages. No longer is that history written by the ex-colonialists themselves. Post colonial historians now give critical scrutiny to the actions of early colonists and their patriotic actions are reassessed as attitudes changed. Such opinions as that expressed in *Prester John* by the popular novelist John Buchan reveal a world that is now totally alien.

> I knew the meaning of the white man's duty. He has to take all the risks ... that is the difference between white and black, the gift of responsibility, the power of being in a little way a king, and so long as we know and practice it we will rule not only in Africa alone, but wherever there are dark men who live only for their bellies.
>
> (Buchan 1910)

As colonial power faded and countries gained independence, the old nationalism which had assumed the right to transfer values, religion and of course commerce to the colony receded. However the urge to bestow democracy as a legacy did not. Just as the message of the European school text books of the past had been the glory of empire and support for the nation, the message after WW2 was anti-fascist, anti-communist and democratic. Not everyone has agreed with this view:

> The persisting blindness of superiority continues to hold the belief that all the vast regions of the globe should develop and mature to the level of contemporary Western systems, the best in theory,

45

the most attractive in practice, that all those other worlds are but temporarily prevented by wicked leaders or by severe crises or by their own barbarity and incomprehension from pursuing Western pluralistic democracy and adopting the Western way of life. Countries are judged on the merit of their progress in that direction. But in fact such a conception is a fruit of Western incomprehension of the essence of other worlds, a result of mistakenly measuring them all with a Western yardstick.

(Solzhenitsyn, Harvard commencement speech 1995)

This Western bias is also criticised by historians of the Islamic world. *The Crusades Through Arab Eyes* (Maalouf, 1984) brought a quite different perspective to the European version of events with the result that students now study both sides of the story. Said's comments on how the history of the orient had been hijacked by western historians is now no longer true (Said 1978). Islam has its own historians and indeed always did have.

However the fact that the West presumed to not just log the past but control the future by all kinds of interventions meant that there is a common history. The intricate interconnected if meddlesome past, together with economic developments, have made links that cannot be ignored. As Frankopan points out in his book *The Silk Roads: A New History of the World* perspectives have changed. The history of the Middle East and the nations along the Silk Road has been warped by the West's assumption of superiority and thus not just a conqueror's right but a moral right to organise, name and delineate national boundaries.

The recent violent history of the Middle East has shown that Western interventions in pursuit of democratisation have not worked well and through terrorism the benefactor has turned round to bite the giver. '... what we are witnessing ... are the signs of the world's centre of gravity shifting... back to where it lay for millennia' (Frankopan 2001).

Islamic religious fervour is its history and its motor just as Christianity and commerce founded the British Empire. The basis of the Islamic State of Iraq and Syria (ISIS) is to return to the ideals and sharia law of the Caliphate of the Prophet; in fact a historical recreation of a sixth century empire to be established by force, a new nation founded to recreate the past. Here, history and religion combine just as they had done in mediaeval Europe and the combination provides an incentive and a cause both powerful and luring to people who feel alienated in a world of rapid change. Far from being 'a foreign country', the past is a comforting haven of security and stability.

In fact, in spite of the increased interest in world history and the debunking of any kind of patriotic approach which characterised much of the teaching and writing of history in the years after WW2, the role of history in nation-building never went away. For new young nations it is part of consolidating the state. For nations asserting a particular choice of government it has to reinforce that choice. North Korean history consists of learning of the past glories of the state, the record of 'Great Kim Il Sung' and castigating the USA (*Daily Mail* report 2012). Text books in countries as far apart as

China, the USA and Russia all make historical analysis dependant on an ideology that supports the state (Ferro 2003).

Counter to this have been attempts by the Council of Europe to eliminate propaganda and prejudice from history teaching. From the 1950s there have been periodic meetings bringing together teachers, academics and authors to consider ways to offset bias and prejudice in history teaching and text books (Council for Cultural Co-operation, 1986). Post WW2 changes of pedagogy in the West have gone a great way to free history from extreme nationalism and jingoism through consideration of sources, analysis of propaganda, recognition of bias and the encouragement of discussion rather than rote learning. Showing the flag and playing the national anthem at the Olympic Games and football matches should, it is suggested, be sufficient reinforcement of nationality. Indeed the focus has moved from 'our nation' to 'our world' with the development of regional studies and global studies. It is ironic therefore that the new century has seen a revival of history as the servant of the state.

When in 2013 the then Secretary for Education, Michael Gove, proposed a new curriculum for England with the history component made up of a chronological journey through what made Britain great, there was an uproar from teachers and historians. How could it be, after all the efforts to free history from *Our Island Story* and the great reforming debates of the 1970s to expand the history syllabus and bring in European and world history, that there could be a return to a 'pub quiz history curriculum' (Evans, 2013).

Having accepted that Britain's history, now and indeed always, has involved more than just the natives of England, Wales, Scotland and Ireland we would go back to a patriotic narrative of high points and heroes in the emergence of a 'Great' Britain. The politicians were proposing a state school history based on chronology and selected facts. Primary school children would start with the origins of Britain and the medieval period. After the age of 11, pupils would study modern history.

> All of the developments over the past half-century – in economic, social, cultural, and other kinds of history – that have made history so exciting as a discipline are pushed to the sidelines in favour of a political narrative that might have been lifted straight from a text book written in the 1930s.
>
> (Evans 2013)

How did this happen? What made an experienced politician like Gove propose a history syllabus that in basic terms said 'Whose History? Our History'. Why did this syllabus, presented in the belief that it would give pupils 'a sense of national identity', create such a furore of opposition from historians, teachers and The Historical Association, speaking on behalf of its 6000 members?

The answer can be found in the coming together of a number of different issues that had been simmering in British society and politics for more than half a century. It involves political and social problems arising from immigration, fears of terrorism, policies in the Middle East and Afghanistan and a mixing of the aims of teaching history with those of creating good citizens. It is also an illustration of Benedetto Croce's theory that history focusses on the problems of its own times just as much as on those of the past. 'All history is contemporary history' (Croce 1921).

So history is given the role of offsetting the dilution of Britishness caused by successive waves of immigration, protecting 'core British values' and, as a hopeful result, the combating of Islamic extremism. Britain, unlike America, did not have a policy of unification through a common allegiance to the nation. As the Russian Jewish immigrant Quixano proclaims in Zangwill's play:

> America is God's crucible, the great melting pot where all races are
> melting and reforming ... Frenchmen, Irishmen and Englishmen,
> Jews and Russians, into the crucible with you. God is making America.
> (Zangwill 1908)

Britain from the 1960s onwards tried to embrace diversity with a policy encouraging multiculturalism whilst at the same time attempting to create a socially cohesive society based on 'Britishness'. As the numbers of immigrants from south Asia, the Caribbean and Africa steadily rose, the attempt to balance the competing claims of diversity and solidarity brought an increased concern. In 1968 there was a growing fear that core values of democracy were being lost so that 'in this country in 15 or 20 years time, the black man will have the whip hand'. This was from a letter quoted by Enoch Powell in what became known as 'the rivers of blood speech'. Powell urged parliament not just to stop immigration, but to provide the process for 're-emigration'. Otherwise, he warned, 'Like the Roman I seem to see the river Tiber foaming with much blood' (Powell 1968).

Far from immigration coming to a stop or people returning to their original countries, numbers have steadily increased, bringing passionate debate, social unrest, riots and considerable legislation for 'equality'. Different world events, such as the wars in Afghanistan and Iraq, and changes in the composition of the European Community, brought waves of different nationalities that compounded the problems of integration and increased pressure on jobs, housing, and schools. By the census of 2011 there were 7.5 million foreign-born residents in Britain; 37% of Londoners were born outside the UK; and 2.7 million of these were Muslims (Census returns, 2012). The policies developed to accommodate this influx included integration, community cohesion, emphasis on equality and the active promotion of 'Britishness'. To this can be added a growing fear of Islamic fundamentalism infiltrating schools and resulting in terrorist acts.

It is against this background that Gove's attempts to create a history syllabus that promoted 'core British values' should be seen. The response was a robust opposition to the teaching of 'a glorious British past' and 'prescriptive content'. Instead there was a demand for 'an international perspective' and 'a high quality history education that equips pupils to think critically, weigh evidence, sift arguments and develop perspective and judgement'. Gove's response was indeed a 'weighing of the evidence' put before him and a modification of the curriculum. Much of the content was removed, optional projects included and world and local history broadened the programme (*The Times*, 23rd June, 2013).

The British case study illustrates the dilemma faced by politicians, historians and teachers of many nations. For Britain is of course not the only country facing the issue of mass immigration and terrorism, combined with rapid change and economic fragility. Social cohesion aims to promote a common goal of what it means to be part of a particular nation, to share its goals and language, have a sense of belonging, work for the good of that group. A common knowledge of the origins of that nation are a part of the aim, but it can be dangerous when history is selected specifically to serve that goal. It can become even more explosive when fear of the incomer, the immigrant, provokes the building of physical barriers to keep out the 'other' (Palestine, Hungary, Calais).

The very act of selection assumes that things will not only be included, but some will be left out. When that exclusion covers up aspects of a nation's history that are morally dubious or against a modern interpretation of human rights, then the question of censorship arises. History abounds with examples of behaviours and policies that were accepted at the time, but are now considered not just reprehensible but cruel and inhumane – slavery, and the subjugation of women being but two.

European countries that trampled over borders and the rights of indigenous populations can find many reasons why this was ultimately for the good of the country concerned. Arguments over what can be considered 'a just war' tend to be based on treaties and border settlements initiated by powerful empires: Palestine/Israel; claims to the Falklands; Serbia/Bosnia; Russia/Ukraine... the list could go on. The question of genocide is barely considered other than in relation to 'the Holocaust', which itself has become mixed with the nationalism of Israel and its claims to land. The massacre of the Armenian nation by the Ottomans, Stalin's eradication of the Kulaks, the appalling killings in Rwanda, are all examples where 'selection' becomes an important part of a nation's view of itself.

The history of Japan presents an example that illustrates a number of these points. This is a nation that has caused enormous suffering by cruel treatment of prisoners in WW2, the Nanking Massacre and the killing of ethnic Koreans, yet they themselves have suffered by the dropping of the atomic bombs on Hiroshima and Nagasaki.

From 1903, with a brief interval when the Americans were in charge after WW2, the teaching of Japanese history has always been prescriptive and standardised. Based on respect and obedience to the Emperor/ Father whose power originates in a number of myths, history provides an ideology to serve the divine mandate that creates the Japanese nation. Ferro illustrates this in his study of Japanese text books pointing out that they represent both a code and an ideology. Government issued, they affirm kokutai – the foundation of the nation, its past and character. The function of education is not to reveal what actually happened...

> Its aim is to encourage patriotism, to identify the people with the Emperor... Our children must be taught the continuity of Japanese

history, the glorious achievements of the emperors and the actions of their loyal subjects and learn what a privilege it is to be Japanese.

(Ferro 1984)

A report in *The Times* (8th May, 2015) headed 'History is rewritten for Japanese pupils' explains that teachers must choose their textbooks from a list approved by the Ministry of Education. 'None of these mention the Nanking Massacre where as many as 300,000 Chinese were killed' (*The Times*, 8th May, 2015). Criticism of Japan's attitude to its history also surfaced when the 70th anniversary of the defeat of Japan by the allied campaign in the Pacific in WW2 was marked. The victors still look for Japan to face what *The Times* called 'its historical guilt' and show 'atonement' (8th May, 2015).

Saying sorry for past historical misdeeds is a comparatively modern idea and fraught with problems, from the 'guilt clause' of 1918, to responsibility for the slave trade, to Germany and the Holocaust (see chapter six). How far must nations go on apologising for past misdeeds? According to Ferro, Japanese historians are themselves divided on whether their history should be re-evaluated and *kokutai* dismantled (Ferro 1984).

In a world of wars, conflicting ideologies and shifting populations, how far is it legitimate for a country to protect its identity by selecting the best interpretation of its national story? Japan's idea of *kokutai* upholds a common culture. So do the government-approved text books of France where, tradition has it, that French students across the country all turn over the same page at the same time. Surely, once the Westphalian system of state sovereignty became the norm, then each country felt it had the right to its own interpretation of the past. These selected and often sanitised histories were of influence when contact was limited. As the printing press got going, telephone, telegraph, and the advanced media of today made communication not just rapid but easily available, then records of events proliferated and it has become more difficult to conceal facts. Once evidence is available for interpretation, then history can never be just an official story.

It also must be noted that, as so often in history, what works one way in one area is countered by events in another. Growth of the importance of single states was paralleled by movements for federalism and unity. The attempts to unite workers across the world in socialism, the bringing together of European countries in union, the growth of global markets and the interdependence of monetary concerns, all cut across national boundaries. Similarly the foundation of the United Nations and the Declaration of Human Rights are attempts to see issues in global terms.

Whilst history will still be presented by many countries as a narrative to support the state and its culture, so that 'whose history' studied is 'our history' a number of developments are working to bring a more discursive approach.

This is aptly illustrated by an exploration of how the discipline has changed and developed. Acton in 1896 asserted, with reference to his editing of the *Cambridge Modern History*, 'It is a unique opportunity of recording, in the way most useful to the greatest number, the fullness of the knowledge which the nineteenth century is about.' By 1967, the view had changed dramatically to '...since all historical judgements involve persons and points of view, one is as good as another, there is no 'objective' historical truth.' (Elton 1967).

This attitude has been reinforced through the proliferation of history as a popular subject of analysis and comment on the media. A growing market for non-fiction and fiction on the subject of history has brought an understanding that there is often not just one story but a number of interpretations. Television has linked history to archaeology, architecture, cookery, dance, music *et al* and history is seen as exciting and an adventure in not just understanding but interpretation of events.

Thus, except in the most totalitarian states, even though history may still be seen as factually-based, nevertheless the skills expected of the historian are now part of the pedagogy. Cognitive capability in critical thinking, problem-solving and analysis, coupled with the ability to discuss and defend a point of view, have become part of the curriculum not just in history but in most subjects. It is recognised that simply to regurgitate a series of facts does not just make a poor historian: it produces an ill-educated citizen. Added to which the availability of search engines gives any individual the opportunity to do their own historical research.

Judgements based on understanding and evidence do not necessarily imply a lack of patriotism. One nation's history does not necessarily imply denigration of others. Even as we walk along the path of our own country's story we can see the importance of the borders we share and the mountain peaks of other neighbour nations around us. If the history student is encouraged to see history as not presenting 'the truth' but a selection of possible interpretations of the facts then, as Ibn Khaldun suggests, ' we can avoid idle gossip and uncritical acceptance of historical data'. The student can also have a voice and an opinion considering both the local and the global and can gain a greater understanding of the interconnected world in which we live.

Whose history is studied in our ever more multicultural societies is still quite likely to be slanted towards a national story. Humans need to belong to a tribe and be part of an identifiable group. A nation at war will still demand unquestioning support. Selections from the past will be used to support the decisions of the present. What is important is to have the opportunity to see beyond one's own experience and culture, one's own nation's motivations and interpretation of the historical 'truth' to an appreciation of other perspectives ... and to have the freedom to question and judge accordingly.

Bibliography

Achebe, C., *The Song of Ourselves*, New Statesman, February 9th 1990.

Againt Bias and Prejudice, Council for Cultural Co-operation. Strasbourg 1986.

Alaxander, C., *"All things bright and beautiful"*, Complete Anglican Hymns Old and New, Kevin Mayhew Ltd, 2000.

Buchan, J., (2010) *Prester John*, originally published 1910, Wordsworth Classics.

Croce, B., (1921) *Theory and history of Historiography*, translation by Douglas Ainslie, Editor: George G. Harrap.

Dabashi, H., (2015) *Can Non- Europeans Think?* Zed Books.

Elton, G. H., (1967) *The Practice of History*, Collins Fontana.

Evans R., *New Statesman*, March 15th 2013

Ferro, M., (1984), *The Use and Abuse of History*, Routledge Classics.

Frankopan, P., *The Silk Roads: A New History of the World*, Bloomsbury 2005.

Gleig G. E., (1853). *A school history*, acessed WWW 15.7.15, Goldsmith College Prospectus 1804.

Kipling, R., (1899) *The White Man's Burden*, first published *New York Sun*.

Hitler, A., *Mein Kampf* (1939). Translated by James Murphy, Hurst and Blackett.

Ibn Khaldun., (19670), *The Muquaddimah*. Translated by Franz Rosenthal, Routledge and Kegan Paul 1967.

Kissinger, H., (2014), *World Order*. Allen Lane 2014.

Maalouf, A., (1984) *The Crusades through Arab Eyes*.' London.

Marshall, H. E., (1905) *Our Island Story*. T. C. & E. C. Jack.

Marx, K., *The Communist Manifesto*, 1848, Project Gutenberg.

Millen, R., *The Times*, 11.5 15. *Dates that Matter* (1617 – Coronation of Gustavus Adolphus).

The Patriotic Historical Reader, 1890, Collins.

Powell, E., Transcript of speech to West Midland Conservatives, Birmingham, April 20th 1968. Census 2011 – Official returns accessed 16.4. 2015.

Solzhenitsyn, *Harvard commencement speech* 1995.

Thompson, J. M., (1948) *French Revolution Documents*, Basil Blackwell.

Wordsworth, W., *The Prelude* Book 1X, 1950, J. M. Dent.

Zangwill, I., (2011) *The Melting pot*, 1908, Forgotten Books.

Chapter 3

Whose history? My history

History as a Personal Memory

Walther Hetzer

I started writing this in Cairo in early December 2014, on a clear and sunny day. Everyday the news reports new Middle Eastern calamities from countries whose borders were drawn up after 'The Great War', borders for which almost whimsical artificiality is made visible everyday by the chorus of tribes, terrorist groups and nationalists dreaming of new demarcations and identities. Even the medieval idea of an 'Islamic Kalifat' has re-emerged in a terrifying and poisonous form. Week after week, the news seems to become more ominous, more threatening. Geoffrey Barraclough's claim that all history is contemporary history, that we always move from our understanding of today's world and look back to see when today's issues first become visible is still valid, but it has become difficult to select 'today's issues' in a seemingly chaotic situation.

I continue writing this during a winter break in Vienna. The bookstores show innumerable World War One recollections, images, diaries, and poetry anthologies. Christopher Clark's masterly *The Sleepwalkers* lies next to a pile of books dedicated to immediate 'causes' of the war. I wonder whether the present musing on how Europe slipped into that war will be matched in 2018 by equal attention to how the 'peacemakers' arranged its end? What will the Middle East be like in three years, what the world?

Vienna, the former imperial capital, is one of my present 'homes'; it shapes my image of World War One, just as my life in Italy and Belgium contributed greatly to it. Vienna in many ways still represents our ideas of *fin de siècle* culture, powerfully expressed in Schorske's *Fin De Siecle Vienna*. Right now I am reading Eric R Kandel's *The Age of Insight*, a superb attempt to understand the unconscious in art, mind and brain, starting in the Vienna of 1900. This is where my father as a young boy in 1916 saw the funeral cortege of Emperor Franz Joseph proceed through the *Mariahilferstrasse* towards St Stephen's Cathedral in the very centre. The final destination was the Hapsburg crypt, the *Kapuzinergruft*, Joseph Roth's evocation of a vanished world. My father must have stood there with my grandmother Hermine. She died when I was very young and I now remember her less well than my more stylish grandmother Elizabeth (whose father was a cavalry major in the Austro-Hungarian army – he is said to have bred wolves and might have even fought a duel, according to family lore).

All this is a century in the past, much too far away for personal reminiscing but nevertheless evoking continuous reference points of a very personal nature. Many of my father's Austrian generation in the interwar period had turned their backs on modernist, cosmopolitan, intellectual, Jewish

Vienna. In a strange reversal of chronology, 1914 with its rich cultural, artistic and intellectual echoes still reverberating seems closer to me than 1938 and its incomprehensible tragedies.

In a side street of the *Mariahilferstrasse* is the *Kriegsarchiv*, the Imperial War Archive. As a PhD candidate in history, I researched my thesis there, smelled the unique archival scent, opened countless boxes of Hapsburg sources, files, ledgers, documents, letters, imperial edicts, and photographs. I tried to analyze how the demands of various nationalities within the dual monarchy presented difficulties for the penultimate Austro-Hungarian minister of war, Franz von Schoenaich (1906–11). His attempts to reform the common army and provide sufficient financial appropriations to maintain it as an effective force were only partially successful. More than in inventories, strategic considerations and proposed budget allocations, I became increasingly interested in the cast of characters shaping the unfolding Austrian drama, complicating the life of von Schoenaich: in the Chief of Staff Conrad von Hoetzendorf, with his incessant appeals for a 'preventive war' already strongly argued during the Bosnian Annexation Crisis of 1908; in the heir to the Hapsburg throne, Crown Prince Franz Ferdinand, with his reform ideas for the monarchy and his attempts to influence military developments as well as foreign policy. Reading the *Neue Freie Presse* and the *Reichspost*, my archival primary sources were complemented by very 'Viennese' stories, such as the ongoing rumours about the stern Chief of Staff and his pursuit of the wife of a rich industrialist. I filed photographs of Franz Ferdinand, an enthusiastic hunter posing with hundreds of dead animals piled up in front of him. I read *Die Fackel*, Karl Krauss' biting criticism of the last years of the dying monarchy. It is easy to stray during research.

Part of our 'understanding' history and of building some empathy with events as grand as a World War is that certain images push themselves into our mind, to remain there even if we do not always endow them with explicit meaning. The Vienna Arsenal, where I often went with my history students, contains countless military uniforms from all reaches of the vanished monarchy. The rooms have the look of a costume collection for an operetta: helmets topped with feathers or spikes, epaulettes, even a piece of leopard skin, surrounded by all manner of flags and banners. The mosaic of nationalities and ethnicities show Austria Hungary as a *Vielvoelkerstaat*, origin of nostalgic myths and less nostalgic realities.

What sticks in my mind long after, however, from the thousands of exhibits in the Arsenal, is not the colourful and operatic fluff but rather an enormous piece of steel, more than a foot thick, pierced like butter by the shell of the largest of the German guns; the vast painting by the expressionist Albin EggerLienz, of soldiers crawling through the mud, chtonian creatures always ready for a dance of death; and of all the fanciful uniforms, the jacket of Franz Ferdinand from Sarajevo – cut open after he was shot – faint rusty blood stains still visible.

Personal images act as aids for grasping an event as enormous as a war. For six happy years in the 1980s, I was teaching at the United World College of the Adriatic in Duino, the Italian and Slovene village close to Trieste, Austria's 1914 port in the Mediterranean. As I sit here in the

Vienna of December 2014, I know from the weather report that fresh snow has fallen today in the Italian Dolomites, covering the fortifications carved out a century ago for mountain warfare. Today this is a climber's paradise, where I often went with my students. In the war it was the site of an unprecedented struggle between the Austrians and Italians, vying for possession of the high ground and clear sight lines. Some of today's *vie ferrate*, secured climbing paths up vertical mountain faces, were started in 1915 on the limestone faces of the Marmolata, the Tofana, the Tre Cime. One climbs past endless galleries, corridors and tunnels, carved inside the mountains, with windows opening to the world below.

In today's world, we climb with lightweight equipment, secured by rope and harness. We pass clusters of barbed wire rusting for almost 100 years, see a few of the crude original wooden steps and ladders, broken crates left in a niche, a piece of cable used to haul provisions and ammunition up to the highest observation post. None of us can imagine how soldiers managed to survive a brutal winter there. I do remember once meeting a friend of my Austrian grandfather who manned one of these observation posts high up in the rock-face. What he remembered in his old age was that warm food hauled up to his eagle's post always arrived cold.

Trenches (always difficult to dig in the hard limestone) and fortifications of both World Wars are everywhere around Duino, mixed with the natural *dolinas* so typical of the Karst. My students at the time diligently traced some of them, both for the history classes as well as for creating accurate maps for orienteering competitions. Mount Ermada, key point of some of the *Isonzo* battles, is close by, dominating the Karst. The Austrians transformed it into a major bulwark against Italian assaults. There is a photograph of the building, now housing most of the classrooms of the UWC of the Adriatic. In Austrian hands in 1917, Duino was shelled heavily prior to the last Italian offensive. In the image, a huge shell hole shows in the roof of the building, right above where we held our class that was to explore the causes of war many years later.

Before the war, in 1912 Rainer Maria Rilke, one of the greatest poets, was a visitor at Duino Castle, a guest of Princess Marie von Thurn und Taxis. There he started writing his *Duino Elegies*. The Great War affected Rilke deeply and the *Elegies* remained unfinished and unpublished until 1923. The *Sentiero Rilke*, a wonderful footpath along the coastal cliffs, offers views of the Carso and the Bay of Trieste in the distance, the white speck of Miramare Castle clearly visible at the entrance to the bay. It was built for Emperor Franz Joseph's brother, Archduke Maximilian, who was shot in Querétaro as Emperor of Mexico. Miramare hosted Franz Ferdinand for two months in the spring of 1914, before he went off to Sarajevo in July for his fateful encounter with the three 19-year-old youths, now alternately called terrorists or freedom fighters. Gavril Princip and his companions seem curiously similar in their mixture of gullibility, idealism, naivete and lack of prospects to some of the youths drawn to radical causes today.

Not far from Duino are two other sites and images with diametrically opposed effect on me: Redipuglia and San Martino del Carso. The guidebooks state with uncanny precision that Italy's largest war *sacrarium* in Redipuglia contains the corpses of 39,857 identified Italian soldiers and 69,330 unidentified. In a nearby cemetery, around 14,000 Austro-Hungarian soldiers are buried. Inaugurated in September 1938 with Mussolini in attendance, its 22 gigantic stone steps are pure fascist architecture. The immense porphyry sarcophagus of the Duke of Aosta (75 tons), commander of the 3rd Army, flanked by the tombs of four of his generals, holds indisputable pride of place. The roll call of '*Presente*' is carved with endless repetition in the rising steps. "Presente, presente, presente." In the commemorative park is an inscription: '*Dulce et decorum est pro patria mori.*' I resisted the temptation to tell my students how deeply repulsive this gigantic heap of stones is to me.

Historical echoes resonate easily in this border country. On top of the hill there is a column, brought there from the nearby military and commercial Roman center of Aquilea, meant to commemorate the victims of all wars. It is more touching than the gigantesque glorification below. At the nearby mouth of the Timavo river, already prominent in Virgil's poems, a bronze sculpture of the *Lupi di Toscana*, the Tuscan Wolves of military fame during Italy's wars of independence, looks out over an original section of the Roman Road, the Via Timavo of AD 200. It also points up to the slopes of Mount Ermada. A couple of hundred meters up from there is a small and unheralded grotto containing the remains of an altar of Mitra, the Persian cult popular with the Roman legions of the time.

Layers and layers of history, layers and layers of wars, borders and demarcations exist. With the collapse of the Austro-Hungarian monarchy, the borders around Duino were set in the Paris treaties, with Italy receiving parts of Friuli/Venezia Giulia. From then on, Trieste with its Piazza Unita D'Italia was considered sacred nationalist territory by the Italian right. Istria, still ancestral home of Italian fishermen settling there since Venetian times, and much of the Dalmatian coast below it went to Croatia. My history students traced the post World War One maps, already aware that equally complicated tasks lay ahead, namely sorting out the arrangements in the region after 1945.

Establishing borders after the Second World War was extremely difficult in some areas and took longer than the arrangements made after 1918. Only in 1975 was the Treaty of Osimo signed by Yugoslavia and Italy, dividing what had been the 'Free Territory of Trieste'. After 1954, Italy had provisionally administered Zone A and Yugoslavia had administered Zone B. In class, instead of following the trenches and battle lines of the First World War, we traced the ethnic complications created by these zones, replete with new nationalistic and linguistic divisions still lingering today in Duino and the region.

The president of the UWC of the Adriatic, the former Italian parliamentarian Corrado Belci, provided a strong personal connection. As a local politician he had been politically involved in the establishment of the Treaty of Osimo. At the time, sentiments of Italian right-wing nationalists resenting the recognition of the border resulted in death threats against him. Even late in the 1980s, when the Duino students organized a charity march to the Piazza Unita D'Italia in Trieste, it was made clear to us that our student speaker, a Slovene speaking girl from Istria, should think carefully about uttering even one word in Slovene on that square. This could cause serious repercussions for her and the college. The school was ready to support her and left the decision to her. Flavia only spoke Italian.

Moving on to one more small digression in time, I think of lunch in the summer of 1991 with Slovene colleagues from Ljubljana and Maribor in the Istrian town of Piran. Fishermen were on this coast long before the Romans, Venice added beautiful buildings when it ruled the Adriatic, and Austria had its time here. We met at the end of a school year, as the end of Yugoslavia seemed near and Slovenia was about to declare its independence. None of us around the table knew what was going to happen. We did expect some crisis of words and a lot of political maneuvering, but could not imagine that yet another 'Balkan War' was going to break out so soon. During the December break that followed, I went back to Duino and with a friend drove up from there to a small fogbound Croatian town in a van full of school supplies. The Serbs had just bombed the city of Vucovar; 3000 refugees had found refuge in the local school. Driving back from there across the Italian border, established with such difficulty years before and geographically so close, we exchanged the world of refugees for the affluent world of vacationers packing up their skis for the winter holiday.

History is personal history, full of images, memories, and emotions. We do not always know why some impressions resonate deeply with us. Maybe more than all those that I have mentioned above, I think of a plaque in the small village of San Martino del Carso. My students and I had walked there from a nearby mountain plateau, after visiting one of the sites of the first massive poison gas attacks on the Italian front. San Martino del Carso is a placid and attractive place, set in the grey limestone hills covered by red leafed scrub in the fall. It became the title of a poem by Giuseppe Ungaretti, displayed on an old wall at the entrance of the village. Both poem and plaque are more personal and vivid in my memory than most images of the Great War.

Di queste case - Non è rimasto - Che qualche - Brandello di muro
Di tanti - Che mi corrispondevano - Non è rimasto - Neppure tanto
Ma nel cuore - Nessuna croce manca
E' il mio cuore - Il paese più straziato

Of these houses
nothing
but fragments of memory

Of all who
would talk with me not
one remains

But in my heart
no one's cross is missing

My heart is
the most tormented country of all

Valloncello Dell'albergo Isolato, 27 August 1916 - *Translated from the Italian by David McDuff and Jon Silkin; from The Penguin Book of First World War Poetry, edited by Jon Silkin.*

Chapter 4

Whose history? Whose sources?

Colonial border manipulations and the poverty of archival records in Ikaleland, south-eastern Yorubaland, Nigeria

Olukoya Ogen

Introduction

This chapter, through a critical assessment of local historical genres and a successful engagement with ethnography as well as an exploration of musical genres and linguistic patterns, examines the potential and historiographical rewards of other sources in bringing about a counter historical ideology that runs contrary to the existing official Western-influenced and hegemonic accounts on the history of the Ikale speaking people of southeastern Yorubaland.

Significantly, it exposes some of the banal views on the Ikale that are still being bandied about even in the 21st century due to the excessive reliance on official colonial accounts and analyses the 'injustice' done to the Ikale nation by British colonial overlords through the systematic and well co-ordinated dismemberment of Ikale common territorial and cultural landscape. The chapter unequivocally affirms that clearly misguided are those modern African historians who would *a priori* construct the pre-colonial history of Africa with facts that are strictly derived from European chronicles and accounts without paying due attention to the wealth of historical information contained in African oral traditions and ethnography.

Ikaleland, broadly defined in its geographical, dialectal and cultural scope, is bounded in the north by Odigbo and Idanre local governments areas, and in the south by Ilaje and Ese-Odo local governments areas. All are within Ondo State, southwest Nigeria. In the east, Ikaleland is bounded by Ovia south west local government of Edo State, and to the west, by Ogun Waterside local government area of Ogun State, southwest Nigeria. Thus, the Ikale people share common borders with seven major Nigerian groups, the Edo, the Idanre, the Ondo, the Ijebu, the Ilaje, the Apoi and the Izon. Ikale's total surface area has been estimated at about 176,584 hectares.[1] Its geographical location makes it a frontier zone par excellence and a major theatre of cultural intermingling.

Some popular colonial-derived views on the Ikale-speaking people

For long Ikaleland has been at the receiving end of great historical distortions and fundamentally flawed stereotyping. Interestingly, for more than a decade now, a major intellectual focus of the present author has been the debunking of the myths, insinuations and age-long historical prejudices currently masquerading as Ikale history.[2] In fact, as recently as 2010, one of the leading Yoruba historians in Canada, Olatunji Ojo, opined that 'In the 17th century the Arogbo were Ijo, they became Ikale and Yoruba in the 18th and 19th centuries.'[3] He concludes that 'Evident in these narratives is the Yorubanisation of a previously non-Yoruba group.'

Indeed, Ojo was in his best elements when re-echoing the prejudiced and stereotyped views of European missionaries, British officials, colonial anthropologists and their local lackeys on Ikale socio-economic and political superstructure. For Ojo and these commentators, even up to the 19th century, the Ikale had no king to unite them; they lived in hamlets in a primitive state; and were socially lower than other Yoruba.[4] The Ikale were also painted as a people who had 'no market where they buy and sell provisions' because they were 'averse to trade'.[5] They were also described as 'half-naked, greasy bodied, dirty and covetous people'.[6]

For these 'Hegelian' tirades, James Beale Africanus Horton's 1868 response to the degrading and humiliating remarks about Africans and more specifically the people of Abeokuta by colonial anthropologists seems very apt. To be sure, Horton was magnanimous enough to the extent that he simply attributed these false and unfair remarks to ignorance.[7] Interestingly, in spite of the efforts of fine minds like Horton and the monumental efforts of the Ibadan School of History from the 1960s to the '80s to correct these racist views about Africans, the big question remains: what could be responsible for the re-echoing of these banal views even in the 21st century and sometimes by African historians themselves? What is presently being hawked about appears to be an admixture of anti-Ikale sentiments derived from jaundiced colonial accounts and age-old misconceptions.

We are fortunate to have other sources to reconstruct the political economy of the Ikale speaking people, especially the accounts of some European officials as well as scholars who lived among the Ikale or conducted field studies in Ikaleland. One of these is Paul Richards of University College, London.[8] Richards stayed long enough in Ikaleland and understood perfectly the resilience and social dynamics of Ikale agricultural practices. According to him:

> The Ikale in the 19th century had not shown themselves to be especially peripheral and backward. They had participated as strongly as any other group in the mercantile networks of the Nigerian littoral … their main interest in supplying this regional system with food rather than in participating in the overseas trade directly, reflected strong comparative advantage, since there were few other areas so well placed to make good the food deficits of the creek and delta trading communities. That Ikale specialisation in food production was not just second best is shown by the fact that they vigorously expanded their supply to delta towns such as Sapele and Warri, and eventually as far as Lagos.[9]

Paul Richards is of the opinion that settlements on the mainland Ikale region 'have a long history of involvement in trade, and the majority of the larger periodic markets in the Okitipupa region are to be found in this boundary zone'.[10] He went further:

> The creek and Lagoon waterway system on the southern margin of Ikale country has been a major inter-regional trade route for many centuries, linking places as far apart as Whydah and trading centres in the Niger Delta.[11]

It is indubitable that the ancient pre-colonial socio-political and economic organisation of the Ikale people was a sharp contrast to the picture painted by the missionaries and early colonial anthropologists who described the Ikale people as a 'lowly and barbarous people',[12] indolent, lacking in self-confidence and bereft of any sense of organization.[13] It is highly ironical, but in a way interesting that Mr Mathews, the District Officer, eventually owned up and admitted that:

> The old system of administration in the Ikale country shows a thorough organisation existed for the Oloja and his council of Ijamo chiefs down to the young boys of about five years of age who were formed into Otu or companies, and Native Administration would be simplified enormously today if the same organisation was still in existence.[14]

No wonder, the Acting Resident, Ondo Province, applauded Ikale's pre-colonial system of administration and strongly recommended a reversal to the Otu system and the Ijama institution which the British officials had earlier derided and denigrated.[15]

Limitations of time preclude an elaborate examination of all the issues raised above. However, the salient points have been made. It is, therefore, apposite at this juncture to briefly zero in on the colonial manipulations of Ikale borders and its larger implications for the Ikale nation.

Colonial border manipulations along the Ikale-Ondo-Ijebu-Edo borderlands

It is also important to interrogate briefly the historical dynamics of colonial border demarcations in Ikaleland, especially along the Ikale-Ondo, Ikale-Ijebu and Ikale-Edo borderlands. I argue that colonial border manipulations were basically targeted at control over economic resources, increased tax revenues for favoured groups as well as effective and an efficient administration. The resultant effect was the institutionalised territorial dismemberment of the Ikale territorial landscape and cultural enclave. Cultural affinity and the factor of geographical contiguity were ignored by the British colonial officials in order to rationalise the downsizing of the Ikale country.

More significantly, I will be highlighting some instances of official dishonesty on the part of the British colonial administrators and judicial officers who were saddled with the task of border delineation and the settlement of border disputes. Indeed, salient historical facts were distorted and judicial officers deliberately ignored veritable evidence not in the primary interests of the British colonial administrators.

The scenario in pre-colonial Ikaleland was particularly compelling. Confronted with a vast territory made up of 14 kingdoms with each kingdom inundated with several settlements in a heavily-forested area of Yorubaland, the British officials had to devise expedient means of administering Ikaleland. One of the major strategies employed was the systematic dismemberment of Ikaleland for ease of administration.

The eastern-most end, comprising the Ikale kingdoms of Akotogbo, Ajagba and Ijuoshun, was cut off and renamed Bini Confederation Area or Ado-Ikale.[16] The western-most end and parts of Osooro kingdom, comprising several towns and villages like Ayila, Aiyede, Ibu, Arijan, Ajegunle, Okebi, and so on, were excised and placed under Ijebu Province. It is interesting to note that the Ikale people placed under this province were renamed Ijebu-Ikale.[17] In the north, several Ikale settlements like Lafe, Oja Baale, Lowo, Agbabu, Onishere, Epewe, Umobi, and so on, were removed from the Okitipupa Division and merged with Ondo Division.[18]

Recourse to history came in handy in an attempt to rationalise and justify these artificial divisions. Unfortunately, it was a one-sided history; history from the point of view of the Benin, Ijebu and Ondo traditional authorities as well as their local collaborators, all acting in concert with the British colonial officials. Meanwhile, for the people of Ajagba, Akotogbo and Ijuoshun, the official claim was that they had little or no cultural, historical and linguistic connection with the Ikale.

The Abodi and other Ikale monarchs later pointed out that the people of the Bini Confederation are *bonafide* Ikale people who had been attending meetings at Ikoya from time immemorial until about 1916 when, as a result of the long distance from the other Ikale towns, they were given their own court at Akotogbo. However, the Assistant District Officer, Okitipupa Division, C I Garvin, the author of the *Ikale Intelligence Report*, recorded that this claim was a fabrication.[19] As usual, Mr Garvin started off his defence of the *status quo* by luxuriating in subjective history. He opined without any convincing evidence that the history of Akotogbo, Ajagba and Ijuoshun proclaimed them to be independent Edo units and that the language spoken as well as the indigenous organisation of these kingdoms are fundamentally different from that of the other Ikale kingdoms.[20] The point being emphasised here is that the British officials found the distortion of the historical account of the Ikale people expedient in order to justify the continued excision of this area from Ikaleland.

Moreover, an attempt was made in 1937 by the District Officer, Okitipupa Division, to merge the Ikale kingdom of Iyansan with the Bini Confederation. Again, the weapon employed was a misrepresentation and distortion of the authentic history of the people of Iyansan. In a letter dated 29th May, 1937, to the Resident, Ondo Province, the District Officer claimed that:

While visiting Iyansan on 24th May, 1937, the Oloja and chiefs surprised me by saying that they feel their connection with Ikale to be something of a mockery and that they would much prefer to join with the Bini Confederation. They said that they spoke the same language, had the same interest and were geographically intimately connected with the Binis. They added that they were Ikales only in name ... it is hardly necessary to dilate upon the many and obvious difficulties of administering Iyansan as part of Ikale, nor upon the corresponding advantages of inclusion in the Bini Confederation.[21]

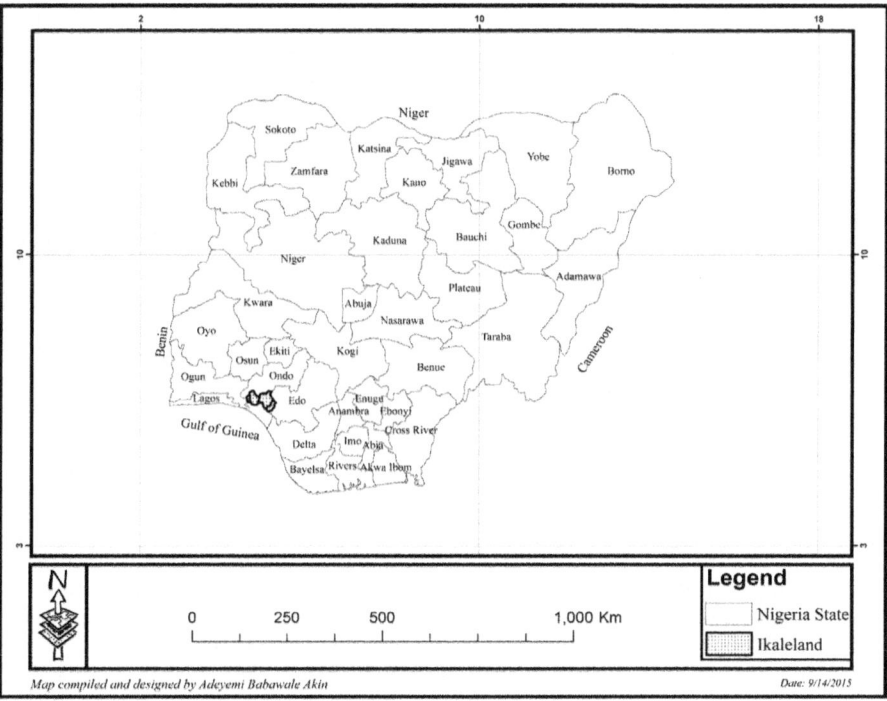

Fig 1: Map of Nigeria showing Ikaleland.

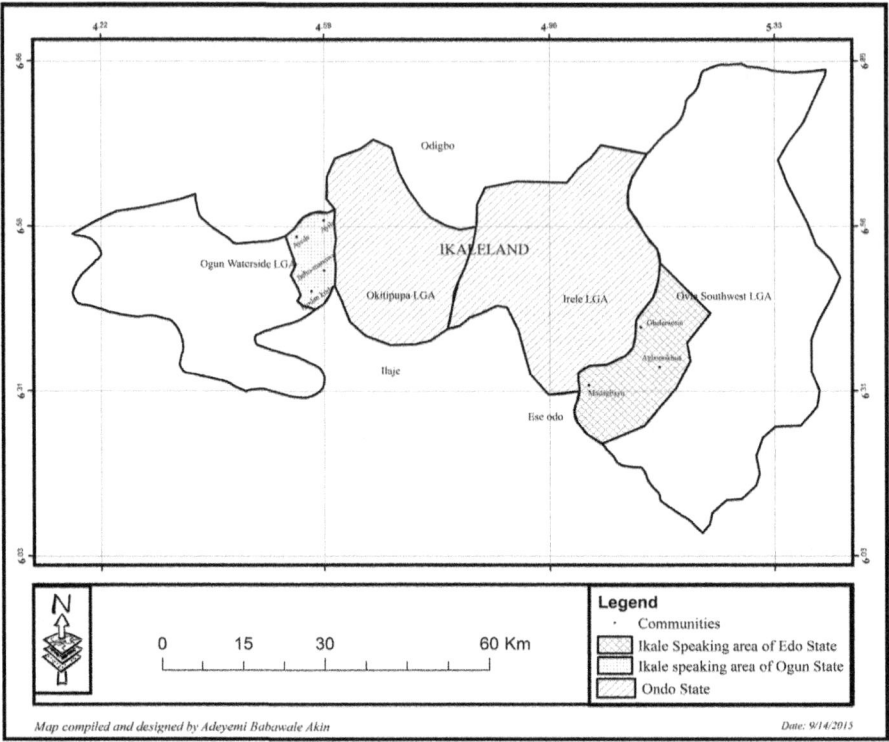

Fig 2: Map showing geographical extent of Ikale speaking people of Southeastern Yorubaland.

Surprisingly, the Resident replied that the Ikale Council was unanimous in opposing the move to merge Iyansan with the Bini Confederation. He went further to argue that contrary to the claim being made by the District Officer, 'Iyansan people have never suggested that they are not Ikale.'[22]

But apart from the case of the so-called 'Ado-Ikale', even more compelling was the use to which history was put to justify the excision of several Ikale settlements, a few of which include Lafe, Oja Baale, Onishere, Epewe and Umobi in the north of Aye kingdom and their merger with the Ondo Division. It should be borne in mind that A R W Sayle, the District Officer of Ondo Division, had in an earlier judgement on 19th June, 1922 placed these Ikale settlements within Ikale's administrative and cultural enclave in the north of Aye kingdom.[23] Again, Mr Matthews wrote in 1932 that:

> Much information has been obtained regarding the history of the Ikale people and there is evidence to show that the Ikales have occupied land north of the present boundary (*ie* north of Aye district) from older times.[24]

However, Justice A P Pennington saw things differently and ruled in 1923 that the Ikale 'are descendants of slaves who escaped from Benin to the

Yoruba country'[25] and, as such, the Ikale cannot lay claim to a distinctively Yoruba territory. As a matter of fact, the Osemawe of Ondo relied on the Benin theory of origin and the ruling of Justice Pennington to put up a ludicrous claim to the entire Ikale country including the kingdoms lying within the Bini Confederation.[26]

Nevertheless, the real reason why these Ikale settlements were placed under Ondo Division was to come to light in April 1928, when His Honour Major F H Ruxton held meetings with the traditional chiefs at Okitipupa and Ondo. It was at this meeting that he confessed that the then colonial boundary had nothing to do with ethnic origin or the ownership of land but with the jurisdiction of the two commissioners of the Provincial Court.[27] Indeed, on 17th February, 1937, H G Aveling, the Resident of Ondo Province, at a meeting with the Abodi pointed out the lopsidedness and unsatisfactory nature of the political boundary between the Ondo and the Ikale. He, however, insisted that the boundary must not be tampered with for ease of administration.[28]

To further buttress the point that the facts of Ikale history were either ignored or glossed over by the British colonial officials in order to rationalise the downsizing of the Ikale country for efficient administration, the case of the Ijebu-Ikale is also worth citing. As noted earlier, the large expanse of land lying between the Gbaragada and Ofara rivers, where the Ikale people had settled for several centuries, was cut off and merged with Ijebu Province. The British authorities turned a deaf ear to the vociferous protests of the people of Aiyede, Ayila, Lowo, Arijan, Igodan-Kuda, Ajegunle, Okebi, and so on – who were part and parcel of the Osooro kingdom – to be placed within the same administrative unit with their kith and kin. The principled opposition and agitations by the Abodi and other Ikale monarchs against this development were also ignored.[29] It is interesting to note that on 15th June, 1922, A R W Sayle, District Officer of Ondo Division, admitted that:

> The claim of the Ikales to that portion of land between the
> Gbaragada and Ofara Rivers at present under Ijebu-Ode ... with
> reference to these claims, that of the Ikales would appear to be fully
> justified – the people in the land in dispute are Ikales and look upon
> the Abodi of Ikoya as their paramount chief.[30]

Again, the recommendations by Captain Mackenzie and Mr White in 1922, and that of Mr Matthews in 1932, that the Ikale people are the rightful owner of the parcel of land in dispute were turned down by the Lieutenant Governor, Mr Buchanan-Smith.[31] The Governor added that if the Ikale people inhabiting the disputed land were desirous of joining their brethren in the Ikale heartland, they were free to do so but that the existing boundary would not be altered.[32] Furthermore, between 10th and 11th April, 1913, F L Tabor, the District Commissioner, Ondo and G S Hughes, District Commissioner, Epe met at Ayila and reported:

> The Ayila people are Ikales as also are the people of Arijan and Aiyede
> and there is no doubt that formerly the Ikales farmed the land up to the
> Ofara river. The effect of making the Gbaragada River the boundary

is that the Ikales are now cut in two and the power of the Abodi, the king of the Ikales is considerably diminished. In our opinion, the Ofara River should be the boundary between Epe and Ikale but we hesitate to suggest any alteration at present, as the result would be an addition of a piece of country to the Ondo district far removed from headquarters and increasing the unwieldy size of the district.[33]

It is indubitable from the preceding analysis that the 'Ijebu-Ikale' are Ikale people and the land which they occupy is part and parcel of the Ikale landscape. Curiously enough the Ijebu's claim, which was supported by the British authorities, was that the Ikale are from Benin and the disputed land was owned by the Onipe of Ibu and since the Awujale of Ijebuland is the consenting authority to the Onipe throne, it follows that the Awujale is the owner of the land between the Gbaragada and Ofara Rivers.[34] Ironically, the Onipe of Ibu admitted in several correspondence that the Onipe has a biological connection with the Ikale people and that the majority of the people of Ibu are Ikale.[35] In fact, Alademomi Kenyo reports that:

> Ubu which once figured among the oldest clan districts comprising Ikale, has long been cut from the country and administratively included in Ijebu province. The Oba and his people have consequently been deprived of the privilege of doing things in common with their original people in Ikale.[36]

Under the full glare and active support of the British colonial administrators, the Awujale, by relying on the Benin theory of origin and his historical claims to these Ikale settlements, started conferring chieftaincy titles on a number of Ikale traditional authorities and even threatened that the Abata of Aiyede would have to surrender his appointment as President of the Arijan Native Court if he (the Abata) ventured to return to the Osooro kingdom.[37]

The several instances cited above are pointers to the fact that the British colonial officials deliberately distorted the origin and history of Ikaleland in order to justify these border manipulations. Indeed, available evidence suggests that they actively encouraged several historical distortions, all in a bid to drastically reduce what these officials termed 'the already unwieldy size'[38] of the Ikale country.

Conclusion

Over the years, the totality of my ethnographic experiences in several parts of Yorubaland, the Benin and Delta regions, the Bakassi Peninsula and the 'Yoruba' inhabited districts of Sierra Leone, has taught me that no archive or library, no matter how well-stocked, could match an in depth ethnographic survey of ones' study area. These writers cocooned themselves in the archives and relied almost exclusively on the biased and half-baked accounts of missionaries and British officials who merely passed through the coastal fringes of the Ikale country.

There is no proof that any of them stayed for more than one night in any of the few Ikale villages and towns that they passed through. Yet, they felt they knew enough about the socio-political and economic dynamics of Ikaleland to make their sweeping but fundamentally flawed pronouncements. The colonial historiographical trinity of 'know the archive, know the past, write the story' has been revealed as sham in theory and practice for a good many thinkers and history practitioners for some time now.[39]

By relying on the multidisciplinary tools of historical linguistics, especially empirical comparative dialectology and lexico statistics, ethnography, social anthropology, totemism, Ifa corpus, the Ikedu tradition, praise names and so on, my research has firmly established the fact that the Ikale are heirs to an ancient and cultured civilization. Given its post-modern theoretical leanings, the thesis also establishes an empirical basis for Yoruba identity studies. The work opines that Ikale pre-colonial history cannot be the history of the activities of invaders but that of the indigenous Ikale people, far beyond what British, Benin and Ife-Oyo imperialism could have made.

Colonial border gerrymandering in Ikaleland resulted in the institutionalised territorial dismemberment of the Ikale territorial landscape and the multiple partitioning of a hitherto single Ikale cultural enclave. Salient historical facts, cultural affinity and the factor of geographical contiguity were ignored by the British colonial officials in order to rationalise the downsizing of the Ikale country, ostensibly for ease of administration and the optimal utilisation of economic resources.

From a comparative standpoint this chapter is of the view that the afore-mentioned colonial border interventions aggravated intergroup conflicts in this strategic borderland region and the long term effects continue to adversely affect harmonious intergroup relations among the affected groups. This scenario is also played out among several other Nigerian groups.[40]

The prevailing brief critique of aspects of Ikale's colonial historiography and the rendition of its border problematic reveal the fact that Africa is still faced with the challenge of how to reconstruct an autonomous historical science of its peoples and showcase an indigenous historiography that is devoid of the trauma of colonial historiography and Western historiographic dependence. The Ikale's case reveals that, by failing to take into consideration the facts embodied in Ikale oral sources, in order to crosscheck the reliability of European based sources, the colonial cum official inferences on the Ikale people are defective and inevitably the current jaundiced version of Ikale history is also fundamentally flawed.

Thus, if it goes unchallenged, we will be doing dreadful damage to the validity and credibility of oral sources and the interdisciplinary genre of historical methodology.

Indeed, the bastardisation of Ikale history has moulded contemporary attitudes between the Ikale and other Yoruba subgroups and this perhaps explains why the Ikale are generally regarded and treated as 'peripheral Yoruba' by other groups. The bottom line is that official histories and colonial constructions of ethnic identities, stories of migrations and borderland histories have important implications for historical reconstructions and cultural expressions.

Notes and References

* The archival sources for this study were drawn primarily from parts of the archival research conducted for the 'Knowing Each Other: Everyday religious encounters, social identities and tolerance in southwest Nigeria' Research Project (Grant agreement no. 283466), funded by the European Research Council (ERC).' I thank the Principal Investigator, Insa Nolte, for granting the permission to use parts of the archival data obtained for the research project.

(Endnotes)

1   Olukoya Ogen, "The Ikale of South-Eastern Yorubaland, 1500-1900: A Study in Ethnic Identity and Traditional Economy." Ph.D., thesis, University of Lagos, 2006. See also Olukoya Ogen, "Geography and Economy in Southwestern Nigeria: A Critique of Colonial Anthropology on the Pre-colonial Economic Geography of Ikaleland" Ife Journal of History, Vol. 4, No.2., 2007, 59 &en8) and Abiodun Ijose, A Brief History of Osooro and How Ilutitun was Founded, (Lagos, 1990).

2   Some of these works include; Olukoya Ogen, "Exploring the Potential of Praise Poems for Historical Reconstruction among the Idepe-Ikale in Southeastern Yorubaland" History in Africa: Journal of Method Vol. 39, August 2012, pp.77-96.
Olukoya Ogen, "The Slave Trade and its Abolition in the Ikale-Yoruba Country, 1650-1890" Lagos Historical Review. Vol. 9, 2009, pp.68-82.
Olukoya Ogen, "Identity Formation among the Ikale-Yoruba: The Poverty of Colonial Records as Sources for the Reconstruction of Pre-colonial African History." Leventis Seminar, Centre of African Studies, University of London, United Kingdom, 11 December 2009.
Olukoya Ogen, "Geography and Economy in Southwestern Nigeria: A Critique of Colonial Anthropology on the Pre-colonial Economic Geography of Ikaleland" Ife Journal of History, Vol. 4, No.2, 2007, pp.203-224.
Olukoya Ogen, "The Akoko-Ikale: A Revision of Colonial Historiography on the Construction of Ethnic Identity in Southeastern Yorubaland" History in Africa: Journal of Method, Vol. 34, 2007, pp. 255-271.

3   Olatunji Ojo., "Slavery and the Slave Trade in Ikale, Yorubaland': A Rejoinder." Lagos Historical Review, 10, 2010, 129.

4   Ibid., 122 and 139 n17 -18.

5   G3A2, 1880, 125: [D. Olubi], "Journals extracted, half-year to December 1879"

6   CA/058, 161: S. Johnson, "Journal Extracts for half-year to June 1880"

7   James Africanus Beale Horton, West African Countries and Peoples, British and Native: And a Vindication of the African Race. (Cambridge: Cambridge University Press, 2011, first published in 1868), 20-43; Daniel J. Paracka, The Athens of West Africa: A History of International Education at Fourah Bay College, Freetown, Sierra Leone. (New York: Routledge, 2003), 42-43.

8   Paul Richards, Indigenous Agricultural Revolution. (London: Hutchinson, 1985); "Landscapes of Dissent – Ikale and Ilaje Country, 1870-1950" in J.F. Ade-Ajayi and J.D.Y. Peel (eds.) Peoples and Empires in African History. (London: Longman, 1992).

9   Richards, Landscape of Dissent, 169

10   Ibid, 163

11   Richards, Indigenous Agricultural Revolution, iii

12   NAI. The Annual Report for Southern Nigeria, 1907.

13   NAI. Ikale Intelligence Report, 2.

14   NAI. Ikale Assessment Report, 186.

15   NAI. "Covering Report on an Intelligence Report on the Ikale District of the Okitipupa Division of Ondo Province", F.B. Carr, 1934, 13-15.

16   NAI. Ikale Intelligence Report, p.4; NAI. An Intelligence Report on the Bini Confederation Area, pp. 1-2 and NAI. Ikale Assessment Report, p. 64. See also Ade Obayemi, "The Yoruba and Edo-Speaking Peoples and their Neighbours Before 1600" in J.F. Ade Ajayi and Michael Crowder (eds.) History of West Africa, Vol.1. (London: Longman, 1976, 224).

17   NAI. Ondo Prof. 1/1, File No. 502, Vol. III, "Ondo-Ijebu Boundary: Question as to Proper Demarcation of". See also NAI. CSO 26/4 30030: "Ikale-Ijebu Boundary" in Ikale Assessment Report, pp. 231-237.

18   NAI. CSO 26/4 30030 "Ondo-Ikale Boundary" in Ikale Assessment Report, pp. 224-227.

19   NAI. Ikale Intelligence Report, p.4.

20   Ibid., p.229.

21   Ibid., p.224.

22   NAI. Ondo Prof. 1/1, OP. 243 "Letter From the District Officer, Okitipupa Division to the Resident, Ondo Province" Ref. No. O. W. 117/201 of 29th May, 1937.

23   Ibid, also see the Resident's minutes on the District Officer's letter in long hand.

24   NAI. "Ondo-Ikale Boundary" pp. 224-230.

25   Ibid., p.229.

26   Ibid., p.224.

27   Ibid and oral interview with HRH Oba J. Turoti, the Larogbo of Akotogbo, 25 July 2004.

28   Ibid. p. 227.

29   Ibid., p.230.

30   For a history of these agitations and the role played by the colonial officials in frustrating these moves, see for instance NAI. Ondo Prof. MLG (W) 8/7 "Abata of Aiyede" J. Wann, 8 June, 1932, p. 2, NAI. Ondo Prof. 502/Vol. III "Ondo-Ijebu Boundary, pp. 506, 552 and 526-527 and NAI. Ondo Prof. OP 113/32 Okiti Division "Report on the Proposed Formation of Ikale Native Administration" 29 November 1932, p.2.

31   NAI. "Ikale-Ijebu Boundary" pp. 234-235.

32   NAI. Ondo Prof. 1/1, File No. 502, Vol. III "Ondo-Ijebu Boundary, Question as to Proper Demarcation of" p. 526.

33   Ibid.

34   NAI. "Ikale-Ijebu Boundary" pp. 234-235.

35   Ibid., p. 235, NAI, Ondo Prof. 1/1, File No. 502 Vol. III "Ondo-Ijebu Boundary, Question as to Proper Demarcation of" p. 552 and oral interview with HRH Oba H.A. Enigbokan, the Onipe of Ibu, Onipe's Palace, Ibu, 19 July 2004.

36   Alademomi Kenyo, A. Founder of the Yoruba Nation. (Lagos, 1959) 44.

37   NAI. Ondo Prof. 1/1, File No. 502, Vol. III "Ondo-Ijebu Boundary, Question as to Proper Demarcation of" p. 499. NAI. Ondo Prof. MLG (W) 8/7 "Abata of Aiyede" J. Wann, 8 June, 1932, p. 2.

38   NAI. "Ikale Ijebu Boundary" pp. 232-233.

39   For details of the historiographically interesting Marwick-Munslow debate, see Arthur Marwick, The New Nature of History: Knowledge, Evidence, Language (Palgrave, 2001) pp. xvi, 334. 'A Review' by Alun Munslow. Available online at History in Focus: What is History? www.history.ac.uk/ihr/Focus/Whatishistory/munslow5.html (Accessed 15 August 2015)

40   Omolade Adejuyigbe, Boundary Problems in Western Nigeria: A Geographical Analysis. (Ife: University of Ife Press, 1975). See also R.T. Akinyele "Historiography of Nigeria's External and Internal Boundaries." In R.T. Akinyele (ed.) Academic Disciplines and Border Studies. (Lagos: University of Lagos Press, 2007).

Chapter 5

Whose history? Whose evidence? Whose guilt?

Case study: World War One

Caroline Ellwood

And when I look at a history book and think of the imaginative effort it has taken to squeeze this oozing world between two boards and typeset, I am astonished. Perhaps the event has an unassailable truth, God saw it. God knows. But I am not God. And so when someone tells me what they heard or saw, I believe them, and I believe their friend who also heard or saw, but not in the same way, and I can put these accounts together and I will not have a seamless wonder but a sandwich laced with mustard of my own.

Jeanette Winterson,
Oranges Are Not The Only Fruit
(1991, London, Vintage).

Marking the anniversaries of special events – births and deaths of the famous, important historical incidents, even the publication of certain books or artistic performances – is very much a part of a celebrity-conscious society. A blessing to teachers looking for added interest, to organizers of festivals and broadcasting, it can also become a tedious ritual: the 150th anniversary of *Alice in Wonderland* in 2015; C P E Bach's 300th anniversary in 2014; 2016 will be another 'Shakespeare Year'.

However, few people could not have noticed (particularly those living in Europe), that 2014 was the centenary of the start of World War One and there is no doubt that such a catastrophic and cataclysmic event is deserving of not just commemoration but also reassessment. The fact that it affected the lives not just of Europeans but had global repercussions; the influence that the events of the war and its final outcome had on future history; the impact that the tragedy of the deaths of over eight million (and 20 million wounded) had on society; the impact on the arts, and particularly literature, mean that it is featured in almost every school curriculum.

If history teaching is to encourage the skills of assessment of evidence, relationship of cause and effect, and understanding that historians can come to different conclusions using the same facts and as a result be able to discuss this with confidence, then World War One presents just the challenge necessary.

Christopher Clark makes the point that:

...the outbreak of war in 1914 is not an Agatha Christie drama at the end of which we will discover the culprit standing over a corpse in the conservatory with a smoking pistol. There is no smoking gun in this story, there is one in the hands of every major character. Viewed in this light, the outbreak of war was a tragedy not a crime.

(Clark, 2002).

Perhaps part of the 'tragedy' of the story, especially in the long term, is that Germany was the one labelled as having perpetrated the crime – found guilty and then had to pay a severe price for its guilt. Was Germany to blame for the start of World War One? Contemporary historians would say yes, indeed there was a clamour not just to blame but to punish. "We shall squeeze the German lemon until the pips squeak" is the famous quote attributed to Sir Eric Campbell-Geddes in 1918. However, recent publications give a more varied response.

   A useful start is the general perception after 100 years (teachers could get students to do a survey). There would be little doubt of the response in Britain. As the centenary commemorations got going, a government minister warned:

> It would be a tragedy if this just became an anti-German Festival. Equally it would be a tragedy if we forgot what happened, why we fought, if we forgot we won.
>
> (Eric Pickles, quoted in *The Times*, 10th June, 2013).

Certainly the commemorative events across Europe and beyond became an occasion for a reassessment.

> What does the First World War mean to you? Is it endless rows of poppy strewn graves stretching across Flanders fields. Or ... *Oh What a Lovely War* or Blackadder desperately trying not to go over the top... More than any other conflict popular perceptions of the Great War have been shaped by cultural interpretations. Perhaps most importantly the war poets... As a nation Britain understands the Second World War as a struggle with clear moral dimensions; our understanding of the First World War is a little muddier. Why did we fight?
>
> (Glancy, 2013)

Why did anybody fight? Ben MacIntyre (2013) agrees that 'The first World War is "morally muddier than the second"', pointing out that the war was 'suffused with notions of duty and deference ... Edwardian imperialism and honour'. Added to and encouraged by this was a general enthusiasm across all countries for war. The war was greeted by excited crowds in all the capitals of Europe, but it was by no means clear for what the various nations were cheering.

   Each country considered the war a war of defence, a call to arms to save the nation; a conviction that to die for one's country was not just a duty but an honour and a sacrifice worth making was common to all belligerents. Each country poured out propaganda to support this idea of defence against an implacable and evil enemy and the need for patriotism. A British sermon aptly sums up this attitude:

They went down the dark valley with a song because they had kept their souls. It is all too great for words, too beautiful to regret, this thing the lads have done. For surely life has no other value than this – to put it to beautiful use – ... when bullet or shrapnel found them or bayonet thrust became the sharp eye of eternity to enfranchise them into a new life – they pleased God.

(Allen, 1915)

In *All Quiet on the Western Front*, Remarque describes the enthusiasm with which most of his class joined the army in 1914: 'They were besides themselves with joy.' (Remarque, 1929).

Enthusiasm for the war was a mixture of nationalism and religion. That the war 'pleased God' was a common sentiment and a necessary justification for the conflict. Each of the four heads of state of the major combatants – The Tsar, Kaiser Wilhelm, Emperor Franz Joseph, King George V – was not just ruler of a nation but an anointed religious head of a church, and in each country the war was described in religious terms. Whilst the interpretation of Christianity was in fact somewhat different, all assumed that God was on their side.

God must stand on Germany's side because we fight for truth, culture and civilisation, human progress and true Christianity. The belt buckle worn by German soldiers had stamped on it *Gott mit uns*.

(Knightly, 2015)

An Austrian Padre directed his troops:

Let us acknowledge clearly and unequivocally that Jesus' commandment 'love thine enemies' applies only to individuals, not between nations. In the struggle of the nations there is no room for loving one's enemies. Here the individual soldier need have no scruples. In the heat of the battle... Jesus' command of love is suspended, in combat killing is no sin but a service to the fatherland, a Christian duty – indeed a service to God.

(*ibid*)

The Bishop of London, Arthur Winnington Ingram, echoed the same sentiment:

Everyone that loves freedom and honour are banded in a great crusade to kill Germans, to kill them not for the sake of killing but to save the world, to kill the good as well as the bad, to kill the young as well as the old, to kill those who have shown kindness as well as those who crucified the Canadian sergeant, who supervised the Armenian massacres, who sank the *Lusitania* and who turned the machine guns on civilians in Aerschott and Louvain – and to kill them lest the civilisation of the world itself be killed.

(Hardie, 2015)

So whose God was listening? The Good Soldier Swejk summed it up in his wise and idiotic, cynical and perceptive way:

Preparations for the slaughter of mankind have always been made
in the name of God or some supposed higher being which men have
devised and created in their own imagination ... the great shambles of
the world war did not take place without the blessing of priests.

(Hasek, 1921)

He then goes on to tell a story about how a German drum head mass was
bombed and the chaplain was declared a martyr. Then, 'Our aeroplanes
prepared the same kind of glory for chaplains on the other side.' (*ibid*)

In the atmosphere of 'glory and sacrifice', as countries vied for colonial
power, armed themselves for a future war, used propaganda to exploit
their nationalism and manoeuvred through a series of crises, was the war
inevitable and was it all the fault of Germany? Post-war there had seemed
to be no doubt as the victors decided on the future of Europe: Germany was
to blame and indeed this was strongly supported by the German historian
Fischer who, writing in the 1960s and '70s, argued that Germany had been
planning for the war since 1912 (Fischer, 1973).

However as the 2014 centenary came nearer a number of historians took
the opportunity to reassess the evidence as to Britain's involvement in the
war and its causes. Their conclusions, which varied considerably, provide
another example of the importance of whose history we accept. Professor
Gary Sheffield puts forward the importance of maintaining the 'balance of
power' but also considers the 'moral dimension':

> Britain went to war for Belgium and the balance of power. Outrage at
> Germany's violation of the treaty by which it had guaranteed Belgian
> integrity helped to bring a united nation into the war. WW1 was not an
> aberration in British history but simply another round in a long struggle
> to prevent one continental state from dominating the rest. There is also
> a moral dimension. A German-dominated Europe would have been a
> very dark place. German troops murdered 6500 Belgian and French
> civilians and torched the city of Louvain ... Democracy and liberalism
> would have been extinguished in most of continental Europe.
>
> (Sheffield, 2014)

Professor Niall Ferguson, far from considering the war as a moral
imperative, considers that the war was avoidable:

> Britain's entry into the war was the biggest error in modern history.
> The nation could have coped well with a German victory in Europe,
> and it would have been in Britain's interests to stay out in 1914. Even
> if Germany had defeated France and Russia, it would have been
> a pretty massive challenge on its hands to try and run the newly
> dominated German Europe and would have remained significantly
> weaker than the British Empire in naval and financial terms. Britain's
> involvement turned a continental war into a world war.
>
> (Ferguson, 2014)

Professor Chris Clark reiterates the idea (found in many school text books)
(Traynor, 1992; Culpin & Henig, 1990) that the war was the inevitable

result of a series of interlocking alliances. Once these alliances came into play then, like 'sleepwalkers', Europe moved inevitably into war.

> The key decision makers – kings, emperors, foreign ministers, ambassadors, military commander and a host of lesser officials – walked towards danger in watchful, calculated steps. The outbreak of war was the culmination of chains of decisions made by political actors with conscious objectives, who were capable of a degree of self-reflection, acknowledge a range of options and formed the best judgement they could on the basis of the information they had at the time. Nationalism, alliances and finance were all part of the story – and shaped the decisions that in combination made war break out.
>
> (Clark, 2012)

Author Max Hastings viewed the war as a catastrophic blunder:

> Many Europeans anticipated with varying degrees of enthusiasm that the two rival alliances would sooner or later come to blows. Far from being regarded as unthinkable, continental war was viewed as highly plausible, and a by no means intolerable, outcome of international tensions. Europe had 20 million regular soldiers and reservists, and each nation developed plans for every contingency in which they might be deployed. The conflict was really the result of an interlocking series of miscalculations by all the principal actors. Europe did not sleepwalk into war, it blundered into it.
>
> (Hastings, 2013)

Allan Mallinson blames fate ... the war was predestined to happen in a world sleepwalking into conflict.

> Fate – the power or principle that predetermines events ... seems to have been the bringer of that war. How but for some malign force could the assassination of an Austrian archduke in a place few outside the Balkans could find on a map, send the Royal Navy to its battle stations and the British army to France? Fate made statesmen and officials purblind, unable to see the consequences of arms races, treaties and threats, so they sleep walked into war.
>
> (Mallinson, 2014)

The trigger that started the war was on the gun in the hand that shot the Archduke of Austria in June 1914. What happened after that is the result of a coming together of the histories of a number of separate states but, as Mallinson sees it, fatefully interlinked countries. If we follow the story as Clark and Hastings recount it, then the war is less inevitable than the result of the specific actions of certain countries. How the facts of history are interpreted depends on the researcher. 'Blundering' and 'sleepwalking' seems a rather inadequate explanation of such a catastrophe as WW1.

What is necessary in order to have an informed opinion is a close look at the events from the point of view of each of the involved countries in turn. A start for this is *The Lost History of 1914: How the Great War Was*

Not Inevitable by Jack Beatty. He looks in detail at the events leading up to the war from the point of view of each of the main protagonist countries. Taking no overarching view he describes

> the military overturning civil government in Germany, revolution stalking autocracy in Russia, political fanaticism threatening parliamentary democracy in England, incipient nationalism among its eleven peoples haunting the Austro Hungarian Empire, imperialism in Morocco straining the honour of France and poisoning relations with Germany.

(Beatty, 2012)

However it is in the dauntingly complex history of the Balkans that the final clues must be found.

The Balkan problem is interlinked to the decline of the Ottoman Empire and the resultant instability in the region as predators lurked ready to descend on any weakness and nationalism burgeoned in populations released from the heavy hand of authority. Indeed, the history of the Balkans in the 19th century and through to today is an ideal illustration of the dilemma posed by whose history we choose to tell. The problems of the region are a bewildering convolution of the importance of ethnicity, religion, language and boundaries as defining a nation.

They are also the key to the start of WW1, with Austria-Hungary's relations with an ambitious Serbia possibly the major short-term cause of the war. In the weeks after the assassination of the Crown Prince, events moved in an almost leisurely pavan towards crisis as Serbia was forced to respond to unacceptable demands from Austria-Hungary. The commitments of alliances slotted into action and Germany took the opportunity to invade Belgium.

All the recent histories presenting an analysis of why WW1 took place reveal a complex of motivation, intention, bellicosity, greed and accident. However, writers nearer the event produced histories to rationalise the role of their own nation. Compiled in the aftermath of an extraordinarily bloody war, each country produced official records that were abundant but rarely unbiased. Poetry, war diaries, letters all added to the constant lists of dead and wounded to give each country a specific view of the bravery and sacrifice of 'their boys' and their life in the trenches and the various battle zones.

Just as God was on 'their' side, so their nation was in the right. One hundred years later, to read much of this evidence is to weep for the similarity of experience and futility of the enterprise as each side slaughtered the other over years of attrition. Seigfried Sassoon in *Memoirs of an Infantry Officer,* Ernst Junger's *In Stagerwittem* and Henri Barbusse in *Le Feu* all recount suffering in similar ways and echo the same emotions.

> ... these are not soldiers, these are men. They are not adventurers or warriors, designed for human butchery – as butchers of cattle. They are the ploughmen or workers that one recognises even in their uniforms. They are uprooted civilians. They are ready, waiting for

the signal of death and murder, but when you examine their faces
between the vertical ranks of bayonets, they are nothing but men.

(Barbusse, 1916)

Most of these 'men' were not professional soldiers. WW1 armies were
made up not just of recruits, but of conscripts and this was a global war
which involved whole populations. The Battle of Waterloo equalled any
of the battles of WW1 in brutality and loss of life (50,000 in one day) but
it was fought by professional armies, not whole populations. It was this
total involvement together with the long drawn out inability of one side
to overcome the other across a no-man's land that stretched hundreds of
miles and the proliferation of hostilities across the globe that made the end
of the war not just a question of making peace but of blame and also of
punishment. Not a 'Congress' of nations to restore the balance of power
and draw up a series of treaties, as in Vienna in 1815, but a gathering of the
winners which would name Germany as the villain and proceed to punish
its guilt.

When the representatives of Germany arrived at the railway carriage
parked at Compiegne to surrender they expected to be part of an 'armistice';
an agreed cease fire as had been suggested in the preliminary talks by
President Woodrow Wilson in his address to the Senate in January 1917:

It must be a peace without victory ... Victory would mean peace
forced upon the loser, a victor's terms imposed upon the vanquished.
It would be accepted in humiliation, under duress, at an intolerable
sacrifice, and would leave a sting, a resentment, a bitter memory ...
Only a peace between equals can last.

(Traynor, 1992)

In addition, Wilson set out '14 Points' listing ways in which Europe could
achieve his aim of 'a peace between equals'. To understand why he failed
(and in its turn the League of Nations), it is necessary to look at how each
of the participating countries had survived the war and what each hoped to
get out of a peace. Certainly all populations were exhausted, economically
distressed and desiring an end to hostilities.

Every country had social problems and there was civil war in Russia,
Ireland, Germany, the Balkans and Turkey. The war had provided
opportunity for border disputes to flare up between Russia and Finland
and Poland. As the crown heads of Germany and Austria disappeared into
the night and the Tsar, already stripped of any power, was assassinated
together with his whole family, it was in a period of acute social turmoil that
the victors met at Versailles to hammer out a new Europe.

Once again it is important to look not just at the story from the point of
view of one of the participants, but realise the complexity of motivations,
the shifting loyalties and the national imperatives that brought about the
different responses and actions at Versailles.

'Peace without victory' was certainly not the aim of the 'victors' who were
very clear about who had started the war and who had won. That Germany
was solely responsible for the outbreak of World War I was officially reported

77

to the Paris Peace Conference by a 'Commission on the Responsibility of the Authors of the War', which was chaired by American Secretary of State Robert Lansing. Lansing refused to allow any Germans to take part in his deliberations, and firmly supported France in the idea that Germany must pay. Thus the vitally important 'guilt clause' was included in the Versailles peace treaty:

> Article 231. The Allied and Associated Governments affirm and Germany accepts the responsibility of Germany and her allies for causing all the loss and damage to which the Allied and Associated Governments and their nationals have been subjected as a consequence of the war imposed upon them by the aggression of Germany and her allies.

The German representatives had no choice but to sign the treaty in the very Hall of Mirrors where they had triumphed over France in the war of 1871. France had her revenge as the treaty did not just declare Germany's responsibility, but returned Alsace Lorraine, stripped her of her colonies, reduced her army and as a final humiliation presented a reparations bill of 226 billion RM (£22 billion). Whilst this was later reduced to 132 billion RM, it was not just this crippling debt that had to be found; Germany was subjected to a total stripping of her industrial and agricultural assets. France was to receive '500 stallions, 30,000 fillies and mares, 2,000 bulls, 90,000 milch cows, 1000 rams, 100,000 sheep, 10,000 goats. Belgium was to receive a similar list of livestock' (Treaty of Versailles, Annex 4, 6).

Was the Versailles settlement an act of revenge that would poison the future of Europe and lead to the dictatorship of Hitler, or was it reasonable in the circumstances? It is difficult for historians not to justify their opinions by a knowledge of later events; however, there were critics at the time who foresaw dire results arising from the punitive tenor of the treaty.

> The future of Europe was not their concern; its means and livelihood was not their anxiety. Their preoccupations, good and bad alike related to frontier and nationalities, to the balance of power, to imperial aggrandisement, to the future enfeeblement of a strong and dangerous enemy, to revenge and to the shifting by the victors of their unbearable financial burdens on to the shoulders of the defeated.
>
> (Keynes, 1919).

Most people were not so far sighted, seeing no further than a war-torn society in turmoil. "The whole of Europe is filled with the spirit of revolution," said Lloyd George in 1919, "the whole existing order in its political, social and economic aspects is questioned by the mass of the population from one end of Europe to the other." The stability provided by monarchical systems dissolved, it seemed, overnight and each of the major combatants had internal social problems.

Russia erupted into revolution, as did Germany, Austria and Hungary. France and Britain both feared the spread of Bolshevik ideas on the one side and the extreme right on the other. Britain faced civil war in Ireland and the outbreak of riots in Egypt (1919) and revolts in Iraq and Palestine (1920). The Balkans, cradle of WWI hostilities, continued to simmer with ethnic religious and nationalist strife. It was as though whoever was guilty of opening Pandora's box, be it Germany or not, had released a potential for violence that would never stop and would change the world. "The hate and the evil is greater than ever," D H Lawrence said on Armistice night (Ferguson, 1998).

More hopeful was the message of President Wilson. His 14 points to settle Europe after the war were based not on labelling a guilty Germany but reconciliation and included the idea of 'a general association of nations ... of great and small states alike'. Here was the seed of an idea which with the formation of The League of Nations created the possibility of a balance of national power that included all states, large and small, providing a forum to promote peace. This was a vision of a world order, where peace would be maintained through open diplomacy, democracy would be enshrined as a principle and there would be agreed and shared rules – 'a community of power'.

Hindsight clearly shows the hopelessness of this aim as even the U S questioned its feasibility. Roosevelt likened it to Aesop's truce between the wolves and the sheep where as a guarantee of good faith the sheep sent away the watchdogs and were quickly eaten by the wolves (Kissinger, 2014). Indeed the American Senate repudiated the entire settlement. Nor did it promote reconciliation, since Germany was not included until 1926.

Nevertheless, although Wilson died a disillusioned and sick man and the League of Nations turned out to be a failure as a maintainer of international order or peace, it did provide the impetus for another and later attempt at world government through the formation of the United Nations.

As for outcomes it is easy from the high mountain view of today to look backwards and see a clear road leading from the labelling of Germany as guilty for the First World War to reparations, the rise of Hitler and guilt for the Second World War. However as the discussions of the causes of the WWI have shown, there are few straight lines in history and many ways of interpreting the facts. Certainly by retrospective analysis the consequences were WWII and the Cold War.

Searching the evidence is the role of the historian, however interpretation of that evidence will differ; nationality, culture and religion will influence perceptions of whose history is discussed and assessed. The 'muddy' origins of WWI will continue to present a challenge but perhaps in the end it is the poet that can give the greater insight and the final word:

> ...I mean the truth untold,
> the pity of war, the pity war distilled...
> I am the enemy you killed, my friend.
>
> (Wilfred Owen, *Strange Meeting*, 1918)

Bibliography

Barbusse, H. (2003) *Under Fire*. Penguin Modern Classics.

Beatty, J : (2012 'The Lost History of 1914 : How the great War was not Inevitable', Bloomsbury.

Bond, B : (1984) 'War and Society in Europe, 1870 -1970', 1984, Fontana.

Clark C : (2012) 'The Sleepwalkers, How Europe went to War', Penguin Books.

Culpin C and Henig R:(1990) 'Modern Europe 1870-1945' Longman.

Fergusson, N:(2014) BBC 'History Magazine' 30.1.2014

Fischer, F:(1967) 'Germany's Aims in the First World War', London.

Fischer, F: (1973) 'War of Illusions', London.

Glancy,R, *The Times*, 16 06 13.

Hardie, M : (2015) 'A finger on Tommy's Pulse', accessed 23.4.

Hasek, J: (1921) 'The Good Soldier Svejk', Penguin Classics, 1974.

Hastings, M: (2013) 'Catastrophe: Europe goes to War 1914', Collins.

Junger, E:(1961) 'Storm of Steel', Penguin Modern Classics.

Keynes, J.M. (1919) 'The Economic Consequences of the Peace'.

Knightly, P., 'If People only Knew', accessed 23.4.2015.

MacIntyre, B., *The Times*, 1.6 13.

Mallinson, Allan: (2014) '1915. Fight the Good Fight – Britain, the Army and the Coming of the First World War', Bantam Press.

Owen, W(1988) 'The War Poets, An Anthology', Marshall Cavendish.

Remarque, E. M.(1929) 'All Quiet on the Western Front', Putnam.

Sassoon, S:(1930) 'Memoirs of an Infantry Officer', Faber and Faber.

Sheffield. G. Professor of War Studies, University of Wolverhampton, The Times, 1.2.2014.

Traynor, J :(1992) 'Europe 1890-1990', Nelson,

Treaty of Versailles, Annex 4, 6. Accessed June 29 2015.

Chapter 6

Whose history? Coming to terms with the past

Germany's changing view of the Second World War

Roger Moorhouse

A generation ago, the English comedy character Basil Fawlty neatly summed up the differences between the German and British attitudes to the Second World War. After a bang on the head, the proprietor of *Fawlty Towers* (the hotel after which the classic BBC TV show is named) went to take a lunch order from a group of German guests, and proceeded – while ostensibly trying to be sensitive – to serve up every Freudian slip and anti-German stereotype imaginable, culminating in a flamboyant goose-step around the hotel foyer. "Don't mention the war!" he warned his baffled staff: "I mentioned it once, but I think I got away with it."

The joke is on the British, of course. It is their sometimes crass insensitivity, their casual triumphalism, that is being shown up, to hilarious effect. German views of the Second World War were – and *are* – something rather distinct from that, and for obvious reasons.

The dominant British view of the Second World War is, in part at least, an expression of patriotism: a subconscious celebration of that country's 'finest hour'. With its 'Dunkirk Spirit' and its 'Keep Calm and Carry On', it is a nostalgic wallow in an era when the United Kingdom bestrode the world; a period when Britain did the right thing in standing up to tyranny and oppression and, by its endeavour and sacrifice, enabled justice and the free world to triumph.

Like all national myths, this reading of events is much simplified and rose-tinted – it takes little notice, for instance, of Britain's less glorious moments – and ignores the uncomfortable fact that in combating one brand of tyranny, it was obliged to ally with another, that of Stalin's Soviet Union. But it is nonetheless fundamentally persuasive and is a large part of the reason that Britain is still fascinated with the Second World War. For all its horrors, the war makes Britons feel good about themselves; it reminds them of what they like to see as their nobler qualities – dogged determination, ingenuity and a strong moral compass.

The German view of the war is naturally rather different. There is certainly precious little to celebrate, but contrary to some popular assumptions, the subject is not ignored – not any more at least. Rather, it is confronted; actively wrestled with. The title of this essay 'Coming to terms with the past' is one of the best-known composite words in the German language

– *Vergangenheitsbewältigung* – which literally means an 'overcoming' of the past. It neatly sums up the modern German approach, and it is telling that the 'past' that is referred to is only ever the past of 1933-1945.

Modern German awareness of the Second World War is certainly no less than that of the British. Indeed, it is arguably all the greater, all the more urgent and all the more present. Through aerial bombing and military defeat, Germany felt far more of the material and human consequences of the war than Britain ever did. Every ton of bombs dropped by the Luftwaffe on the UK provoked 26 tons in response, for instance, German civilian and military losses are fully 20 times those of the United Kingdom.[1] For all their heavy symbolism to the British, the bombing of Coventry or the defeat at Dunkirk simply cannot stand comparison with the likes of Hamburg, Stalingrad or Dresden.

The effects of the Second World War are all around in Germany, even influencing the geography. Almost all German cities and towns still bear the material scars of the war, in their pock-marked buildings, their empty spaces and their 'rubble mountains'. The highest hill in Stuttgart, for instance – the Birkenkopf – is a pile of wartime rubble. The same is true of Berlin and of Frankfurt. Most German cities in fact – Krefeld, Leipzig, Munich, Cologne, Pforzheim, Nuremberg, to name but a few – have at least one rubble mountain. Berlin has no fewer than eight, comprising of over 75 million cubic metres of rubble.[2]

Unsurprisingly, given the magnitude of the human and material destruction that was wrought, Germany was – for a time, at least – simply unable to face the subject of the war head-on. For a generation of Germans, the recent past with all its personal and collective tragedies was effectively taboo. Germany had been broken, rendered lame; its people killed, maimed and humiliated; and unspeakable suffering had been inflicted on others in the name of Nazism. Also, post-war Germany had more pressing problems to deal with than its own recent past: a shattered economy and the division of the Cold War, to name but two. To cap it all, as a succession of Nazi functionaries filed through courtrooms in the late 1940s and 1950s, the German people were perennially reminded of the toxic ideology that had once held them in its thrall. Little wonder, then, that most Germans of the post-war era preferred to look forward rather than back. For many of them, the Second World War was a subject that was simply too painful to discuss.

Of course, it was not ignored by everyone. A generation of post-war writers and dramatists bravely engaged with the topic and *Trümmerliteratur* – or 'Rubble Literature' as it was known – began to emerge in the immediate post-war years, addressing the trauma of refugees, survivors and homecoming soldiers; their shattered lives and their dashed dreams.

Perhaps the most famous of the genre was the dystopian 1947 play *Draussen von der Tür* ('The Man Outside') by Wolfgang Borchert. It is the grim tale of a soldier named 'Beckmann' – described as 'one of many' – who returns home from imprisonment to find the life that he had left behind destroyed; his wife with another man, his parents having committed suicide. What follows is a dark nihilistic journey in which Beckmann tries, and fails, to find meaning in his suffering. Tellingly, perhaps, though he tries, he is unable to take his own life, and his humiliation is thereby complete. Though Borchert subtitled his piece 'a play that no theatre will want to stage, and no audience will want to see',[3] it proved remarkably popular, graduating from radio to the stage following its author's premature death in 1947, at the age of 26.

Another salient example of the genre is that of Gert Ledig. Himself a *Wehrmacht* veteran, who had been severely wounded on the Leningrad front, Ledig wrote two books in the 1950s, drawing on his experiences: *Der Stalinorgel* – or 'The Stalin Organ' – which deals with the horrors of combat and *Vergeltung* – 'Payback', which is set on the German Home Front. Yet, unlike the rather more thoughtful Borchert and despite his evident writing prowess, Ledig did not enjoy commercial success. His brutal, visceral narratives did not endear him to German readers of the 1950s and he gave up writing to pursue a career as an engineer. With few exceptions, *Trümmerliteratur* was far too raw for most Germans of the period; too close to the bone, too brutally true.

By the 1960s, however, something of a shift had taken place. Time had healed some of the scars, memories had faded, and a new generation was expressing an interest in the period of the war. It was an interest that had been spurred by a number of factors. Firstly, such was the taboo that surrounded the period that it was quite possible for those of the post-war generation to have grown up having been taught or told *nothing* about the war or the Third Reich by their parents and teachers. Secondly, a number of events in that watershed decade caused that ignorance to be suddenly cast into sharp relief. In 1961, for instance, Adolf Eichmann was brought to trial in Jerusalem for his role in the planning of the Holocaust, amid a blaze of publicity that provoked a round of agonised reflection in Germany. Five years later, in 1966, the release from imprisonment of Albert Speer; the most high-profile of Hitler's surviving paladins, once again brought Germany's recent past – and the questions of complicity and contrition – to public attention.

The growing curiosity of the younger generation was further evidenced by the events of 1968, in which political and civil protests spread across the country. One of the many wellsprings of the protesters' anger was the inter-generational tension that had been spurred over the previous decade; the feeling among the younger generation that their parents had never been entirely open and honest with them, and that their teachers had told them little.

In addition, for many of that '68 generation' – the famed *acht-und-sechziger* – it appeared that not much had changed in German post-war politics. They could point to a number of senior figures in German political and economic life and claim that 'the Nazis' were still in charge. Kurt Kiesinger, for example, the German Chancellor from 1966 to 1969, was a former Nazi Party member and deputy department head in the wartime foreign ministry, who had specialised in radio propaganda. When he was publically slapped by the 'Nazi-hunter' Beate Klarsfeld in 1968, with the shouted accusation that he was a Nazi and should step down, it was a sentiment that would have found a ready echo among large sections of German youth.

Another example was that of Hanns Martin Schleyer, a senior Mercedes-Benz executive who would later become president of the German Confederation of Industry. In 1968, however, Schleyer was targeted by the student movement for his wartime past. As a former officer in the SS, he had served in the defeat of France in 1940 and had subsequently been active in the wartime German occupation of Prague. For many of the *acht-und-sechziger*, Schleyer was a stereotype; an ugly reminder of the dark continuities that they perceived in modern Germany.[4]

So, the question 'what did *you* do during the war, Father?' was on the lips of many of that younger generation in 1968. It was no longer an innocent enquiry, however; it had become an implicit accusation. In the circumstances, it was little wonder that the question was often evaded or simply went unanswered. Clearly, in the domestic sphere at least, far from being 'overcome', German history was barely being talked about at all.

By the 1970s and 80s, that greater curiosity about the war and the Third Reich had begun to have a cultural resonance. On one level, historians and intellectuals engaged in the so-called *Historikerstreit* – or 'Historians' Quarrel' – a protracted and sometimes bitter series of exchanges via the specialist and mainstream media. At its heart was the natural desire to salvage a 'usable history' from the horrors of the 20th Century, with the right broadly seeking to compartmentalise and relativise Nazism and the Holocaust, while those on the left fought to resist any downgrading of the perceived lessons of the era or its supposed uniqueness. It was telling that the quarrel began with a speech – by historian Ernst Nolte – entitled 'The Past that will not go away'.[5]

Though the educated public watched this intellectual squabble with considerable interest, they also witnessed much more prosaic developments. In place of the *Trümmerliteratur* – which had concentrated mainly on the social after-effects of the war – there came a greater focus on the war itself, albeit still approaching the subject rather obliquely. The best examples of this were the *Heimat* series, concentrating on the experience of the 20th century for one rural Rhineland family, and the excellent *Das Boot* of 1981, which via a novel and a film brought the story of the submarine war during the Second World War to a world-wide audience. Such was the international success of the latter that, for the first time, British audiences found themselves in the peculiar situation of rooting for the plucky Germans. Few, on either side, would have imagined *that* in 1945.

Yet, despite such televisual forays, the issue of wrestling with that difficult past was mainly confined to the sometimes arid musings of intellectuals in the opinion pages. For the majority of Germans, it was still a subject that was too thorny to address with any genuine introspection. A salient date in the story is 8 May 1985, the fortieth anniversary of V-E Day; the end of the war in Europe. On that day, the West German president, Richard von Weizsäcker, addressed the Bundestag in Bonn, and in the process gave an important lead on the complex issues of German guilt and German suffering. It has been called the most important speech on the subject of the war and the Nazi period that has ever been given in Germany.[6]

The 8 May, Weizsäcker said, was a "day of liberation" for the Germans too, a liberation from the "inhumanity and tyranny" of the Nazi regime, but also from the "aberration in German history" that it represented. There was no such thing, he went on, as "the guilt or innocence of an entire nation. Guilt, like innocence, is not collective, but personal". Everyone who experienced that period, he said, had to examine their own conscience but – importantly – no-one expected the generation born after 1945 to "wear the penitential robe" just because they were Germans. Nonetheless, he warned, it was not a question of simply "coming to terms with the past" – that was not possible; the past could not be wished away. Their forefathers had left them a "grave legacy", he said. "All of us, whether guilty or not, old or young, must accept the past. We are all affected by its consequences, and take responsibility for it. Young and old can and must help one another to understand why it is essential to keep the memory alive."

Weizsäcker went on to address that crucial question, the issue of what kind of 'usable past' could be rescued from totalitarianism, genocide and war. He did so with characteristic clarity and elegance, suggesting to his audience that remembering the Nazi persecution of the mentally impaired will inspire the modern Germany to prioritise the care of the mentally ill. "If we remember how people persecuted on grounds of race, religion and politics and threatened with certain death often stood before the closed borders with other countries, we shall not close the door today to those who are genuinely persecuted and seek protection with us." And, where Nazi Germany exacted penalties for free thinking, the Federal Republic would "protect the freedom of every idea." In short, modern Germany was to define itself as the very opposite of the Third Reich. Only in that way, Weizsäcker concluded, could the country "look the truth in the eye".[7]

It was powerful stuff, praised in later years by Chancellor Gerhard Schröder as having forged "a new historic identity and set a new collective norm".[8] But, while considerable progress had undoubtedly been made, the grand shift in German attitudes to the war came after reunification in 1990. By that time, not only had a couple of generations passed, but the most visible geo-political consequence of the war – the division of the country itself – was healing. Germany was finally approaching what the rest of the world might call 'normalisation'. In the 1990s, therefore, though the more immediate economic and social requirements of reunification quite rightly dominated the political and media agenda, there was a new tone in the country's treatment of its past.

This new era took many forms. For one thing, long neglected subjects, such as the history of Prussia, enjoyed seasons of renewed popularity, with cultural retrospectives, television documentaries and museum exhibitions. A wave of war memoirs and diaries also emerged, often penned by ordinary Germans, which told of their everyday experiences of the war. Remarkably, the novels of Gert Ledig, which had shocked audiences when first published in the immediate post-war period, were re-released to popular and critical acclaim in the 1990s. Clearly, that which could scarcely be talked about in the 1950s could now be openly discussed.

The second major trend in the 1990s and early 2000s was a spate of publishing and documentary-making about the thorny issue of German victimhood. This arose, in part, as a result of the ongoing process of 'normalisation', but was also a consequence of that slew of memoirs, which for the first time had highlighted the wartime suffering of ordinary Germans.

In truth, there had always been voices that were keen to trumpet German victimhood; whether the grim fate of the nation's 500,000 civilians killed in the air war, or the harsh treatment meted out to its millions of post-war expellees from eastern and central Europe. Yet, while Germany was divided and the Cold War threatened, such voices tended to be confined to the extreme right of politics and consequently shunned by the mainstream. With re-unification and the end of the Cold War, however, it finally became possible to discuss such views in polite company, and – through a number of books and television documentaries – the vexed issue finally (and quite rightly) became an essential part of the German national narrative of the Second World War.

This trend led to some excesses, however. In 2002, for instance, German historian Jörg Friedrich published *Der Brand* – published in English in 2006 as 'The Fire' – which suggested that the wartime Allied bombing campaign against Germany had been a war crime and clumsily juxtaposed the bombing with the Holocaust. Despite some trenchant criticisms from academics and commentators, it is notable that Friedrich's book was well-received within Germany itself, thereby suggesting that it at least found some resonance with the German public. As the author explained at the time: "The bombing left an entire generation traumatised. But it was never discussed ... It is only now that they are coming to terms with what happened."[9] In this, at least, he was absolutely correct.

There have been other shifts. In the sphere of town planning, for example, Germany has finally found a satisfactory solution to the problem posed by the toxic locations most closely associated with Nazism. In many cases, new museums – or 'Documentation Centres' – are established on the sites, which then serve to place the war and the Third Reich into their historical context and engage with a new generation of Germans, for whom it might otherwise all appear to be so much ancient history. So it is that the empty lot on what was once Prinz-Albrecht Strasse in Berlin – the former SS and Gestapo headquarters – has become, since 2010, the acclaimed 'Topography of Terror'. Similar museums have also been built in the vast Congress Hall on the Party Rally Grounds in Nuremberg, on the Nazi 'playground' of the Obersalzberg and on the site of the Nazi Party Headquarters: the Brown House in Munich.

Perhaps the best example of this conscious detoxification of Nazi sites – is that of Hitler's country residence – the 'Berghof' above Berchtesgaden – which was long one of the most historically-burdened locations in all of Germany. After the war, the ransacked ruins of the building were dynamited, trees were planted on the site and all traces of this former epicentre of Nazi power were systematically erased, leaving only a small overgrown section of a retaining wall. For over half a century thereafter, the site was hidden away in the woods, ignored and virtually forgotten. Then, in 2008 – remarkably – an official information board was erected on the site, informing visitors of the building's history and its infamous former occupant.

Such moves, like the placing of an information board at the site of Hitler's bunker in Berlin, are in tune with the very best tradition of *Vergangenheitsbewältigung*, that of confronting and overcoming a difficult past. In both examples, the primary motive was a practical one. Both sites had become so clogged with dubious tales and mythology that an information board was the easiest way of restoring a factual narrative for visitors. Yet, it is hard not to imagine an underlying philosophical motive; that of taking ownership of that toxic history, rather than – as had previously been the case – attempting to simply obliterate it and wish it away.

In addition, Germany's difficult relationship with nationalism itself seems to have shifted. For a long time, post-war Germany positively eschewed appeals to patriotism, preferring to actively subsume Germany into the European project and leave such vulgar flag-waving to the tiny, despised minority on the extreme right. Yet, with reunification and the new millennium, even *that* taboo seemed to gradually lose its power. Proof of the change came in 2006, with the FIFA World Cup in Germany, when many commentators were pleasantly surprised to see a generation of young Germans proudly wrap themselves in their flag and paint the national colours on their smiling cheeks. To any other nation, this would have been entirely normal and expected, but for the Germans it was something like an epiphany. Germany, it seemed, had come of age; the past had been overcome; normality was finally beckoning.

Of course, there are limits to the process – and one can certainly *not* conclude that German and British attitudes to the war are converging. For one thing, German 'acceptance' of the past should not be confused with any sort of enthusiasm, however innocent. When RAF conservation teams raised the last surviving Dornier Do-17 bomber from the sands of the Channel in 2013, for instance, German commentators were resolutely unimpressed and the dominant view was that the half a million Euros that the operation had cost had been a monumental waste of money.

Germany is still resolutely pacifist, which – for a nation that had suffered so much from warfare in the 20th century, and had inflicted so much suffering on others – should come as no surprise. Consequently German participation in the operations in Kosovo and Afghanistan was profoundly controversial, particularly when the latter resulted in Germany's first combat deaths abroad since 1945. Even support for the 2011 NATO intervention in Libya caused controversy, though the German government stopped short of offering any material assistance.

Yet, though pacifism still broadly holds sway as an article of faith amongst the country's political and media elite, even these sands have begun to shift as the consensus is increasingly put under pressure from a new, more interventionist and hawkish generation; those less burdened and less inhibited by the country's past. And, as calls grow both domestically and internationally for Germany to once again play a more active role in world affairs, this is an argument that seems set to run and run. The shadow of the last war is still keenly felt by some, but its presence is slowly fading.

While attitudes are shifting and the old norms are being challenged, some things remain unchanged. Though sympathy might now be legitimately expressed for German 'victims' of the Second World War, and the Holocaust might now be legitimately contextualised, there is still – quite rightly – no revision in the attitude towards the ideology of Nazism and its geo-strategic and racial aims. Neo-Nazis remain utterly beyond the pale in German politics and Hitler's ideology is more despised than ever. Though much has changed and will continue to change, it is hard to imagine any shift in this respect. Hitler, thankfully, is not about to be rehabilitated.

Though a political rehabilitation of the erstwhile *Führer* is most certainly not in the offing, there has nonetheless been a profound and significant shift in the way in which Adolf Hitler is portrayed in the German media. This was most visible in the 2006 German feature film *Downfall*, in which the film's makers were confident enough to present a very 'human' Hitler; a man who was largely rational, charming to his secretaries and felt betrayed by his closest followers, a man – somewhat alarmingly – with whom the viewer could momentarily sympathise. This would not have been remotely remarkable were it not for all that had gone before. In German cinema, Hitler had traditionally been presented as peripheral or two-dimensional, while western screen depictions had tended to present Hitler only as a ranting, carpet-biting psychopath.[10] It was a shift that, unsurprisingly perhaps, was considered unacceptable by some. According to one German viewer, the film 'went too far in making [Hitler] human … If you show someone like this as a human then people might be tempted to forgive him.'[11] Troubling though it may have been, it was, nonetheless, another significant shift in Germany's process of 'coming to terms' with its past.

This cinematic shift has recently found a literary counterpart. Serious historians have traditionally eschewed Hitler's personality in favour of a focus on his political significance and consequences. Indeed, the landmark biography by British historian Ian Kershaw opted to shed very little light on Hitler's character, considering such aspects to be rather tangential to the wider political considerations. 'The task of the biographer,' Kershaw wrote in his introduction, 'is to focus not upon the personality of Hitler, but squarely and directly upon the character of his power.'[12] For all its brilliance, the result was a 2,000-page biography in which the human subject was curiously absent.

However, a recent German biography has finally addressed the issue of the 'Human Hitler'. The book, by historian and journalist Volker Ullrich, is an attempt, as the author puts it: 'to place the personality of Hitler once again centre stage.'[13] This might, at first glance, seem a minor point of historiography, but it marks something of a seismic shift. Treating Hitler as a human being – a charmer as well as a sociopath – is another step along the road to 'normalisation'.

More significantly perhaps, even Germany's reflexive sense of collective guilt has also come in for scrutiny. The sentiment of *mea culpa*: donning the hair shirt for Nazi crimes, is – of course – still very much the default line of the German establishment and is assiduously propagated. But some have recently dared to question its ubiquity and the forms that it takes. Most famously perhaps, the novelist Martin Walser made his feelings plain in 1998, when accepting a German literary prize. Though he spoke of

Germany's "everlasting disgrace" and the heavy "burden" of its history, he nonetheless railed against what he saw as the increasingly ritualistic marking of Germany guilt, which he felt was in danger of becoming reflexive and thereby meaningless – even, as he noted, a "banality of good". He focused much of his criticism on the controversial 'Memorial to the Murdered Jews of Europe' in Berlin, which he described as "a nightmare the size of a football field" and "the monumentalization of shame" representing the "institutionalisation of negative moral emotion and the raising of historical guilt to a state creed".[14] He had a point, but he was also challenging one of post-war Germany's most sacred taboos.

More recently, the public debate about collective guilt was spurred once again by a television series. *Unsere Mütter, Unsere Väter* (Our Mothers, Our Fathers),[15] was a big-budget, three-part, wartime drama which aired on mainstream German television in the spring of 2013. For those whose expression of collective guilt had become, as Walser complained, rather reflexive and platitudinous, or had lazily subscribed to the comforting idea of *Opa war kein Nazi* (Grandpa was no Nazi), the programme came as something of a shock.

Following the experiences of five young men and women through the war, *Unsere Mütter, Unsere Väter* charted their personal compromises and their gradual corruption as the Nazi regime reached into every corner of their lives. The message, which was made very explicit by the programme's title, was that almost the entire generation had been made complicit in Nazi horrors, even those that were never Nazi Party members and had personally committed no crimes.

The programme was generally well-received, with positive reviews from much of the press and public, though some historians complained that it glossed over the Holocaust or was unfair to the Poles, or that by showing ordinary Germans as victims, it became an exercise in self-pity. Nonetheless, despite its faults, it did mark a significant turning point in its unflinching examination of the thorny issue of everyday complicity.[16] As such, indeed, it highlighted the emergence of a new front in Germany's ongoing confrontation with its past: that of genealogy.

One German reviewer of *Unsere Mütter, Unsere Väter* noted that: 'The history of the Third Reich has been examined down to the level of Hitler's dog, but our own family history is a deep dark crater.'[17] He was right. Generations of silence have meant that, for many Germans, the last unexplored chapter of recent history is that within their own families. As I have discovered from my own work on wartime Berlin,[18] the memories of survivors from the Nazi period – however innocent they may be – are rarely shared with younger family members. It may be that fear of an angry, judgmental response – as in 1968 – prevents full disclosure; or that the older generation does not wish to burden the younger one with its most troubling memories, but the result is that many surviving Germans of the wartime vintage would rather share their stories with a foreign historian than with their own children and grandchildren. Genealogy, which is widely enjoyed as a harmless hobby in the UK, is a decidedly minority interest pastime in Germany; but it is nonetheless the final frontier in the country's ongoing battle with its past.

German attitudes towards the Second World War are complex and ever-evolving. As in the UK, the subject still looms large and forms a central strand of the national psyche and of national identity. Yet, that is where any similarity between the two ends. In short, while the Second World War reminds Britons of their noblest national qualities, it confronts Germans with their most egregious human failings. While Britain appears to bask in the rosy, self-congratulatory glow of endless TV repeats and a merry-go-round of rehashed histories, Germany – through its sometimes agonised process of *Vergangenheitsbewältigung* – has arguably arrived at a rather more considered, more mature relationship with its profoundly difficult past.

German history may never be completely 'normalised'. Even after the remaining few of those who directly experienced the events of 1933-45 have passed away, the cultural and political resonance will remain. In spite of Richard von Weizsäcker's elegant words in 1985, Germany's sense of collective guilt for the depredations of Nazism and the Holocaust will take decades to fade. This was something that – remarkably – was even predicted at the time. In 1941, Henning von Tresckow, a Wehrmacht colonel and mainspring of the German military resistance noted what German atrocities on the Eastern Front would mean for the future. "This will still have an effect in hundreds of years", he told a colleague, "and it will not only be Hitler who is blamed, but rather you, me, your wife and my wife, your children and my children, that woman crossing the street and that lad kicking a ball."[19]

Yet, though that guilt may yet prove durable, Germany has nonetheless made tremendous strides in engaging with and – yes – overcoming its hideous history. Through its own efforts and the passage of the generations it is now able to address its recent past with an ease and an objectivity that was not only unthinkable four decades ago, but should be the envy of its less encumbered neighbours. What is more, it has achieved the remarkable feat – advocated by Weizsäcker – of forging a 'usable history' from the most harrowing chapter of its past; developing a narrative of human rights, liberal democracy and equality as a counterpoint, and a retrospective antidote, to fascism and genocide.

If the much-vaunted normalisation is a chimera, then objectivity at least may be close at hand. In a recent study, it was shown that Germany's younger generation, less encumbered by the past, was comfortable with learning about its country's darkest period and found 'no contradiction between keeping the memory of Nazi crimes alive and at the same time seeing Germany as a normal country.'[20] Basil Fawlty would doubtless have been thoroughly baffled, but it seems that modern Germans are often happy to 'mention the war'; they are only concerned that it should be done with the seriousness and solemnity that the subject deserves.

References

1   Collation of statistics from John Ellis, The Second World War Databook, (London, 2003), pp. 233-236 & 253-4.

2   See, for instance, Michael Meng, Shattered Spaces, (Harvard, 2011), p. 1.

3   See the title page of 1947 first edition, at upload.wikimedia.org/wikipedia/commons/5/5b/Borchert%2C_Drau%C3%9Fen_vor_der_T%C3%BCr%2C_first_edition_%281947%29%2C_title_page.jpg

4   Schleyer was kidnapped and murdered by the Red Army Faction during the 'German Autumn' of 1977.

5   Ernst Nolte, "Die Vergangenheit die nicht vergehen will", in Frankfurter Allgemeine Zeitung, June 6, 1986.

6   www.spiegel.de/politik/deutschland/weizsaecker-rede-1985-8-mai-war-eintag-der-befreiung-a-354568.html

7   Abridged English text is in Hywel Williams, Great Speeches of Our Time", (London, 2013), pp. 217-223, original German text is at www.bundespraesident.de/SharedDocs/Reden/DE/Richard-von-Weizsaecker/Reden/1985/05/19850508_Rede.html

8   Quoted in www.spiegel.de/politik/deutschland/weizsaecker-rede-1985-8-mai-war-ein-tag-der-befreiung-a-354568.html

9   Quoted in Luke Harding, "Germany's Forgotten Victims", in The Guardian, 22 October, 2003. www.theguardian.com/world/2003/oct/22/worlddispatch.germany

10 Kate Connolly, "Germany breaks the Hitler taboo", in The Daily Telegraph, London, August 24, 2004.

11 Quoted in Roger Boyes, "Sympathetic film portrayal of Hitler leaves Germans baffled" in The Times, London, September 17, 2004.

12 Ian Kershaw, Hitler: 1889-1936. Hubris, (London, 1998), p. xxvi.

13 Volker Ullrich, Adolf Hitler: Biographie, (Frankfurt am Main, 2013), p. 14.

14 Quoted in Bill Niven, Facing the Nazi Past: United Germany and the Legacy of the Third Reich, (London, 2001), p. 189.

15 The programme aired in the UK in 2014 under the title "Generation War".

16 Jeevan Vasagar, "German TV drama confronts a nation's wartime guilt", in The Daily Telegraph, London, 22 March, 2013.

17 Christian Buß, "Glaube, Liebe, Hitler", at Spiegel Online Kultur, 13 March, 2013 www.spiegel.de/kultur/tv/zdf-weltkriegs-epos-unsere-vaeter-unsere-muetter-a-886932.html

18 My book "Berlin at War" (London, 2010) used interview material from around 35 Berliners of the wartime generation.

19 Tresckow quoted in Roger Moorhouse, Killing Hitler, (London, 2006), p. 183.

20 Christian Staas, "Was geht mich das noch an?", in Die Zeit, 45/2010, 4 November, 2010.

Bibliography

Thomas Elsaesser, German Cinema - Terror and Trauma: Cultural Memory Since 1945, (London, 2013).

Bill Niven, Facing the Nazi Past: United Germany and the Legacy of the Third Reich, (London, 2001).

Peter Reichel, Vergangenheitsbewältigung in Deutschland: Die Auseinandersetzung mit der NS-Diktatur von 1945 bis heute, (Munich, 2001).

Gitta Sereny, The German Trauma: Experiences and Reflections 1938-1999, (London, 2001).

Harald Welzer, Sabine Moller & Karoline Tschuggnall, Opa war kein Nazi: Nationalsozialismus und Holocaust im Familiengedächtnis, (Frankfurt am Main, 2010).

Chapter 7

Whose history? Whose painting?

Making the invisible visible

Richard Caston

As an artist and educator, my interest in history has always been fostered by my passion for art, particularly for the art of painting. I am equally at home in my art studio and in art museums; in fact one sustains the other. I cannot imagine creating in my studio without the inspiration and context of the history of painting and the riches found in art museums.

Looking at paintings takes time and it is best done with my workbook and pencil. To draw I need to look hard and the drawing eventually is a record of what I see and what I understand. This chapter traces my journey across the interface between two cultures with strong painting traditions, European and Japanese, and tries to map the exchanges made between painters. Uncovering these exchanges indeed leads to the question, whose painting is this? The painters ... and who else's?

I have kept the background historical facts brief and in separate boxes, allowing the paintings and my observations, where possible, to do the talking.

July, 2004, Tokyo Metropolitan Museum

In 2004, my wife Beatrice and I visited Tokyo and remember seeing posters of Vermeer's *The Art of Painting* hanging all over the city. It had recently been restored at its home base in Vienna and was on tour for the first time. Almost 750,000 people came to the Tokyo Metropolitan Art Museum to see it. We did too. It took some time before we finally entered a darkened room where the painting was hanging. Although it was crowded, we could catch glimpses of it from several rows back, peering over shoulders and between heads of those in front. Why was this painting, familiar to us but less so in Japan, literally moving masses?

Vermeer's painting shows several realist techniques we would consider European, such as linear perspective, chiaroscuro, a single light source and verisimilitude. What we could see best was the upper part of the painting where, hanging on the back wall, Vermeer depicts a historical map of the Netherlands. It was designed by the graphic artist Claes Fischer in 1610 and shows the 17 regions of the country and illustrates several of the major cities. What caught my attention was the access to the sea and the ships sailing off shore. The Netherlands were a seafaring, trading country with galleons capable of reaching far off countries, including Japan.[1]

July, 2004, The Modern Art Museum, Tokyo

The following day we went to see works by Japanese masters from the 20th century and discovered the panel paintings by Yokoyama Taikan.

Workbook page with the poster for Vermeer's The Art of Painting *in Tokyo.*

The scale of the work *Red Maple Leaves* was stunning. It was painted on 12 panels in sets of four; each set over 3.60 meters wide. I had expected panel paintings, but this was more like the dimensions of a mural.[2] To view the entire painting, one would need to stand far back, which is not the intention, as the fine details, such as the ripples on the ocean, need closer attention to be enjoyed. I stood close enough to feel engulfed by the wide panorama. But, in fact, it was best seen in motion, not from a fixed point of view, but by absorbing while turning one's head, or by walking slowly along.

Could this be a 'Japanese' response to showing both time and space 'in motion'?

It reminded me of David Hockney's painting of the Grand Canyon, and later his Yorkshire landscapes. As many western artists have discovered, it is not possible to construct a panorama view on a large scale with a single point perspective without creating distortions in the wide areas. Hockney tried to solve the problem by using multiple canvases, each showing a slightly different view, rather like a panning shot in cinema. He said that he wanted to be inside the paintings, moving close to the subject and turning his head left and right to take in the side views.[3, 4] This is exactly what I did with the Taikan.

One can achieve a similar effect simply by opening ones' eyes wide and taking in the entire visual field to the very periphery of vision. One striking feature of this wide view is the small size of objects in the world. Tiny figures and buildings in a huge landscape are a common feature of many early Japanese paintings, especially from the Kano School, which developed from Chinese painting. To avoid a fixed view point, buildings were painted in depth with a fixed 30 degree orthographic projection.[5]

The meditative Buddhist philosophy behind much of Japanese painting since the eighth century was later influenced by Taoism and the inspiration of nature. It shunned realism in painting, instead focused on the underlying reality rather than the surface appearance of things. This meant that the viewer needed to feel detached from the physical world, so there was no need to create the perspective space that we saw in the Vermeer, with its fixed viewpoint. The viewer was not meant to be in a specific physical location in relation to the painted image, rather at one with the spirit of the work, like Hockney's *Grand Canyon*; inside the painting as it were.[6]

Workbook drawing of Yokoyama Taikan's Red Maple Leaves *1931.*

October, 2010, The Church of Santa Maria Novella, Florence

In 1428 a nail was hammered into the wall at 1.72m above the floor of the church of Santa Maria Novella in Florence, the beginning of a fresco painting that would change and help define Western painting for the next 500 years and longer. The painting was the *Trinity* by the painter Masaccio.[7]

Unlike in other churches, one enters the church of Santa Maria Novella through a gate to the right side of Alberti's façade first, and then walk into a close and through the small cemetery of the Avelli, eventually reaching a door on the north wall. At this entrance one sees Masaccio's fresco *Trinity* on the opposite wall of the nave right away.[8]

Even with the aging of colours and plaster, the painting shows incredible spatial depth. My documentation says that, at first, many thought that a new chapel had been built, so convincing was the illusion. At the time, nobody had seen anything like it.

The nail marked the vanishing point for the construction of a single point perspective, probably the first in painting in modern times. By attaching string to the nail, the perspective geometry of the design was marked out with scratches onto the plaster wall and by snapping the string onto the wet plaster to make guide lines, which are still visible today.

The geometry for linear perspective had been formulated a decade earlier by the architect Filippo Brunelleschi and it is thought likely that he had assisted Masaccio with plans for the design.[9]

The painting creates the illusion of an architectural space, a triumphant arch and a barrel vaulted chapel in a classical style. Inside the perspective space, Masaccio painted the holy figures of the Trinity, a Christian subject never seen quite like this before. Well-proportioned and occupying a believable space, the figures were solid, balanced and to most eyes looked realistic.[10]

I noticed that Masaccio had painted the front of the arch, *trompe l'oeil* style, on the plane of the church wall, so that it looked like part of the church architecture. At the base he painted a sarcophagus and skeleton, a *memento mori*, which seemed to come forward towards me into the space of the church.

The vanishing point of the perspective, the point where the nail was hammered in, was at my height. It meant that I was physically attached to the perspective construction of the painting, sharing a spatial relationship. There was a continuity of space between the illusion of the perspective in the painting and me standing in the church. I was part of the painting! To be in the same space as *Trinity*?

I needed to look at the holy figures again to try to imagine how this must have felt in the 15th century and the implications it must have had for the followers of the faith.

Traditionally the spiritual and earthly worlds were separate and if anything, devotional paintings were like two way mirrors, to see and to be seen by the holy figures. In Masaccio's painting humankind suddenly became part of the picture.[11]

Workbook drawing of Masaccio's Trinity, *1428.*

April, 2012, Kunst Historisches Museum, Vienna

This day was a 'day-at-the-museum' day and I spent most of it looking at the Velasquez paintings and other treasures, saving Vermeer until the end. Somehow I must have made a wrong turn and arrived prematurely at the exit. After some help from the staff I eventually found the painting in a large room some way off the main galleries. Nobody was there – just Vermeer and me. I thought of Tokyo years ago and just thoroughly enjoyed this special chance to examine every centimetre of the painting.

The painting depicts the artist at work in his studio with his model, representing Clio, a daughter of Zeus and the Muse of History. History was considered a noble subject for painting and probably Vermeer wanted to elevate the status of painting to become a liberal art. Most painters know this intention.[12]

Looking at the painted tiled studio floor, with the aid of my pencil to sight the angles, I could find the position of the vanishing point. It was to the lower left, making the eye level beneath that of the painted artist. If he had been drawing or painting this view from direct observation, he would have been sitting on the floor. Would this be the height of a projection machine – a camera obscura?[13]

I could find other clues, such as the relative sizes of the objects, through foreshortening, including the large chair in the foreground, which is cropped by the frame of the painting, something we are used to seeing in photography. Here Vermeer has used the cropped objects as compositional elements for the design of a painting.

The use of lenses would have been nothing new for Dutch painters in the 17th century and they were especially useful for mapping out perspective angles without using rulers or nails and string. They had been in use from the time of Jan van Eyck, and other northern Renaissance painters.[14]

Apparently it had not, after all, travelled well and some restoration was required after the journey back from Japan to Vienna. Looking closely I could see the layers of oil paint and the wooden panel, aware of the fragility of this magical painting that is still travelling with us through time, hundreds of years after it was made. This was the real object, in the flesh, not just the image.

Could this painting, in its fragility, one day, disappear? Be lost for humanity? What is it that would be lost?[4]

At the time *The Art of Painting* was created in Delft, Japan was isolated from much of the world, during the Edo Period. The only Western country allowed to trade was the Netherlands. Although the contact was strictly limited to the island base of Dejima, the impact on Japanese culture was widespread. Many scientific objects, including lenses and even the camera obscura, reached Japan from the Netherlands and the isolation was not a stagnant time for painting.

Trade included printed books on a wide range of subjects, mostly scientific. What interested the Japanese artists were the engraved illustrations, which showed perspective and chiaroscuro to render objects real and solid. The illustrations of plants, birds and animals, appealed to the Japanese sense for nature. Other books on medicine, anatomy and mathematical perspective

Workbook drawing of Vermeer's The Art of Painting, *1666-67*

were eagerly taken and some were published with a Japanese translation. Together with engravings of European paintings, these images helped to develop a Japanese School of Western style painting called *Akita Ranga*; Akita being the region and Ranga meaning 'Dutch painting', part of a samurai intellectual pursuit of Dutch learning (rangaku).

Although the paintings from the *Akita Ranga* school used western techniques and styles, such as the horizon line between the earth and the sky and reflections in water, to most European eyes they still look Japanese.[15]

November 2014, Folkwang Museum, Essen

With the opening up of Japan to trade in the 19th century, the influence of Japanese culture on the West was immediate. Many European artists were fascinated by the works of their Japanese contemporaries, such as Katsushika Hokusai and Utagawa Hiroshige, and consciously or unconsciously adopted some of their styles, compositions and subjects.

The art works that arrived in Europe from Japan were mostly wood block prints. These were inexpensive and collecting Japanese prints became a vogue in many European cities, especially Paris.[16]

When we attended the exhibition 'Monet, Gauguin, Van Gogh... Japanese Inspirations' at the Folkwang Museum in Essen, we realised the extent of it. Not only did we see Japanese prints, but also a wide variety of Japanese arts, crafts and other objects. The influence on European art and design was clear and immense. All that we had seen in Tokyo started to make sense in this broader context.

Workbook drawing of Katsushika Hokusai Under the Waves off Kanagawa *1830-31.*

Amongst the artwork was Hokusai's *Under the Waves off Kanagawa*, one of our all times favourites. As is often the case when in the presence of an original – in this case a hand-made print – it was a new discovery and a moment of connection with the artist.

In Hokusai's *Under the Waves off Kanagawa*, he describes depth by three planes rather than a continuous linear perspective. The first two planes depict waves, including the giant wave and the third depicts the small Mount Fuji in the distance. In other prints, Hokusai plays other perspective tricks, such as mixing eye-levels and perspective with orthographic projection.[17]

To express the power of the great wave, Hokusai uses the geometry of nature, a golden spiral. In fact he uses two, one on the outside edge of the wave and another smaller spiral on the inside edge. The two spirals are related in the ratio of the golden section.

This was the same geometric form that had fascinated Renaissance artists such as Leonardo da Vinci and Albrecht Dürer and had underpinned Masaccio's *Trinity*.[18]

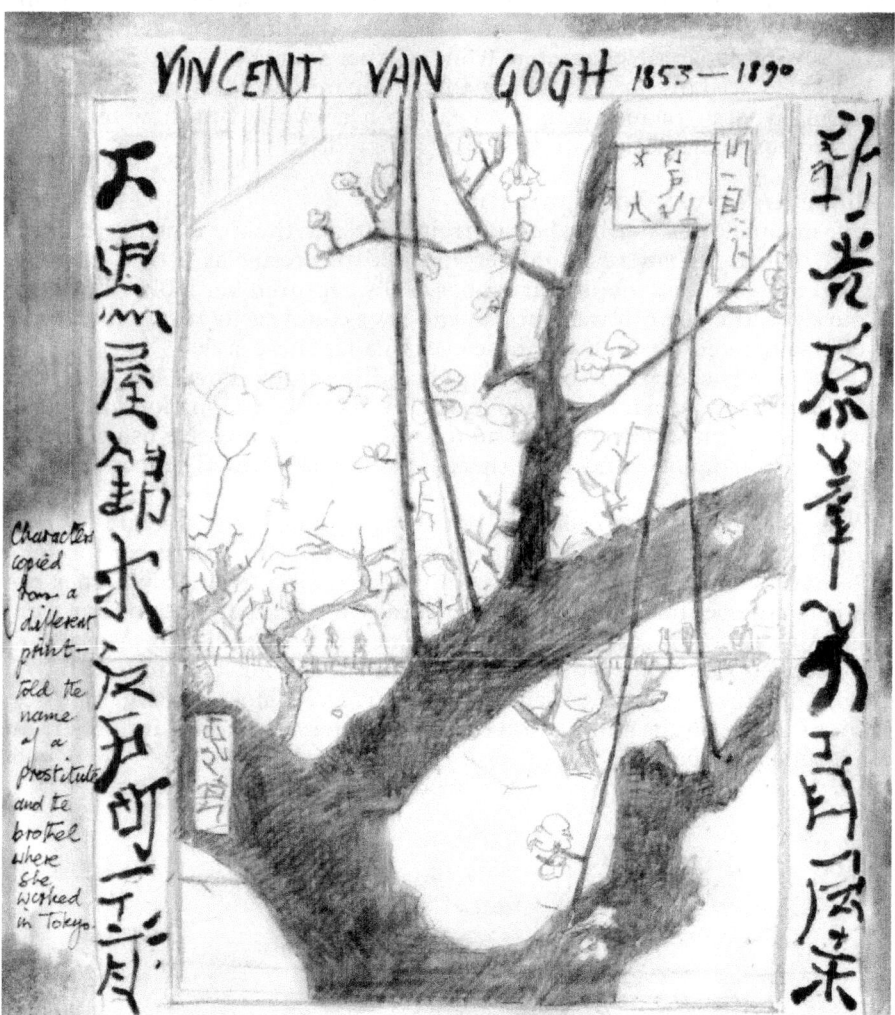

Workbook drawing of Vincent van Gogh's Flowering Plum Tree *(after Hiroshige), 1887.*

The many wood block prints illustrate 'the floating world' (*ukiyo-e*) of landscape, urban pleasures and everyday life. The idea of a fleeting, ephemeral world appealed especially to the Impressionists who themselves tried to capture the moment. Today it is hard to think of artists such as Monet without immediately having the Japanese bridge in his garden coming to mind.[19]

For an artist like Vincent van Gogh, this was the breakthrough he was looking for: the even values; pure colours; close up objects; high horizons; surprising perspectives; flat two dimensional areas of colour. He owned several prints, mostly by Hiroshige, which often appear on the background wall of his paintings. Van Gogh also made his own painted versions of some of the prints, such as *Flowering Plum Tree*. He painted it in his vigourous style, adding Japanese characters from another source.[21]

It was so striking and touching to see Japanese and Western painters adopting what attracted them from each other's work. But, how much did they project of themselves in what they adopted?

Whose history, whose painting

While in Japan, Beatrice had her portrait painted in the street near the Tokyo Tower. All the Japanese bystanders praised the result as a true likeness, saying, more or less, that the artist has really captured her looks. However, to our eyes, the portrait was not a likeness we could easily recognize. It was of course painted through Japanese eyes in a Japanese style.[22]

Do we really see people or the world so differently? There is a universal visual language in painting, such as the harmony of proportion and form; mastery and synthesis of media and technique; the expressive use of colour to create mood, *etc*... and then there is culturally formed perception and expression.

Picasso said that "good artists borrow and great artists steal"[23] which suggests that by stealing one can take possession and incorporate a different form or style into one's own work. Taking from others does not override an essentially unique and culturally formed perception. Far from being simply technical innovations, Vermeer's verisimilitude, Masaccio's perspective, Taikan's panorama, Hokusai's spatial constructions and Van Gogh's openness to Japanese culture, have triggered new creative impulses. Painters thrive on the stimulation of other painters, including art work from other times and cultures.

So, when we look at a painting ... whose painting are we seeing?

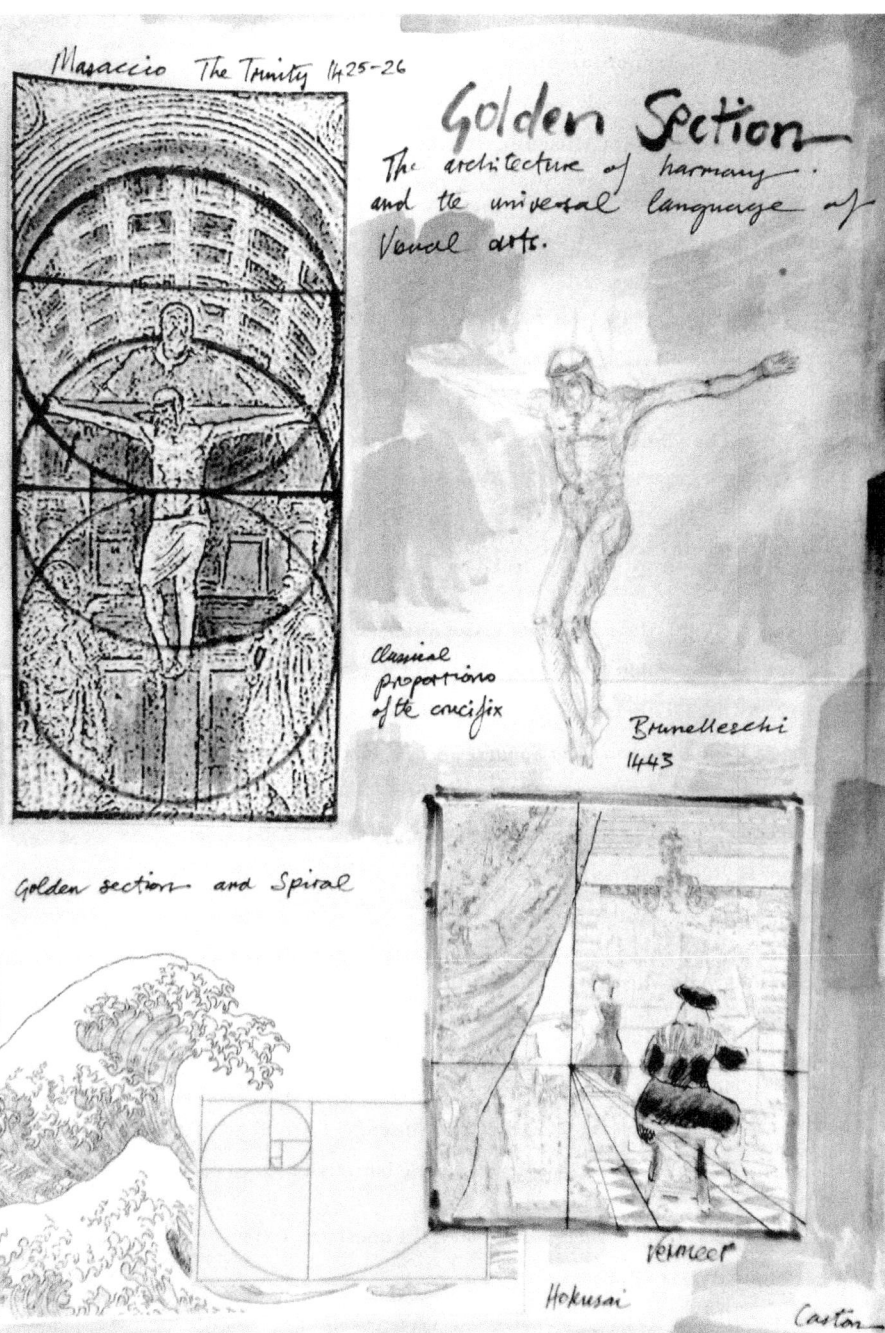

Wookbook drawings of the Golden Section.

Select bibliography

July, 2004, Tokyo Metropolitan Museum

1. Netta I. (2001), *Vermeer's World*, Prestel, Munich, London, New York.

July, 2004, The Modern Art Museum, Tokyo.

2. Matazo,K., Misao, Y. (1987), *Yokoyama Taikan, Takeuchi Seiho*, Art Gallery Japan, Shueisha.

3. Livingstone, M., (2012), *David Hockney: A Bigger Picture*, (pp. 24-37), Royal Academy of the Arts, London.

4. Gayford, M. (2011) *A Bigger Message*, Thames and Hudson, London.

5. McKelway, M.,(2014) *Art in Time*, (pp.297-298), Phaidon Press Limited, London.

6. Stanley Baker, J., (1984), *Japanese Art*, Thames and Hudson, London.

October, 2010, The Church of Santa Maria Novella, Florence

7. Cole Ahl, D., (2002), *The Cambridge Companion to Masaccio*, Cambridge University Press, Cambridge.

8. Tarquini, A., (1987) *Santa Maria Novella*, Becocci Edition, Florence.

9. Vasari, G., (1987), *Lives of the Artists (Volume 1)*, Penguin Books, London.

10. Goffen, R., (1998) *Masaccio's Trinity*, Cambridge University Press, Cambridge.

11. Drury, J., (1999), *Painting the Word*, Yale University Press, New Haven and London.

April, 2012, Kunst Historisches Museum, Vienna

12. Rüger, A., (2001), *Vermeer and Painting in Delft*, National Gallery Company, London.

13. Steadman, P., (2001) *Vermeer's Camera*, Oxford University Press, Oxford.

14. Hockney, D., (2001) Secret Knowledge, Thames and Hudson, London.

15. Johnson, H., (2005) *Western Influence on Japanese Art*, Hortei Publishing, Amsterdam.

November 2014, Folkwang Museum, Essen

16. Michiko, M., (2014) *Monet, Gauguin, Van Gogh ... Japanese Inspirations*, (pp. 21-27), Edition Folkwang Museum/Steidl, Göttingen.

17. Forrer, M., (1991), *Hokusai*, Prestel-Verlag, Munich.

18. Hemenway,P., (2005), *Divine Proportion*, (pp. 127-132), Stirling Publishing Co. New York

19. Trede, M., (2010) *Hiroshige*, Ota Memorial Museum of Art, Tokyo, Taschen, Cologne.

20. Homburg, C., (2012) *Van Gogh Up Close*, Yale University Press, New Haven and London.

21. Kodera,T., (2006) *Japanese Prints*, Waanders Publishers, Zwolle.

Whose History, Whose Painting

22. Gombrich, E.H.,(1962), *Art and Illusion*, (pp.73-74), Phaidon Press, London.

23. Picasso quotation, (2015), Quotations, www.painterskey.com.

Part two

Whose history do we teach?

Chapter 8

Whose history? Whose culture?

Teaching history as an inter-cultural experience

Terry Haywood

There are many good reasons to study history, but there are essentially just two good reasons for teaching it, at least in the compulsory curriculum. One is to open young people's minds to the understanding that things have not always been the way they are today, which is closely related to recognising that the actions of each generation, including ours, have implications that ripple through the future. The other is to contribute to the learner's development of a personal sense of place, identity and values.

Both goals can be contentious in the sphere of national education, but in the context of an *international* or *multicultural* school they make history perhaps the most critical subject in the curriculum. It is the litmus that indicates how seriously an institution is reflecting on its international aspirations and how effectively it is striving to develop young people with an 'international mindset' encompassing values and attitudes as well as knowledge and skills.

Neither of the learning goals introduced in the opening paragraph is exclusive to the teaching of history, of course, and every subject can claim a special role in the formation of international minds. However, in most of the other taught subjects there is a recognised terrain on which the value curriculum is developed. In mathematics and science, for instance, teachers work with a largely conventional and well-defined subject matter that is rarely controversial apart from occasional references to the evolution/ creation debate or certain aspects of sex education. The creative energies of these teachers can be focused on pedagogy and on making authentic connections to global themes or international values.

The study of literature, on the other hand, offers numerous opportunities for exploring values, relationships and identity from multiple perspectives, often delving into the learner's personal cultural baggage. The fact remains, though, that for the vast majority of a student's life this exploration will be carried out in the context of the literature of one specific language. The obsession with 'original language' literature can sometimes go so far as to require an explicitly 'national language' content and there is a smouldering debate in the UK as to whether American authors should be studied in English Literature courses. Yet even without these extreme views there are inherent constraints on how inclusive the study of literature can ever be and on how wide the teachers of this subject can be expected to throw the net when they select texts that will be examined in their courses[1].

These constraints do not apply in history, though, where the content can (at least in theory) be chosen from any period or place from the human experience on our planet, with a consequent range of temporal, geographic and linguistic diversity that makes it impossible for any single teacher or department to be knowledgeable about the whole. The most basic decisions about what to include and to exclude risk communicating a political motivation about what is important to know and to study and what we can ignore.

The choice of subject matter in history has implications beyond deciding when to teach the laws of thermodynamics in physics or which of Shakespeare's plays we will explore with Grade 10. What is more, almost all of history's knowledge base is open to critical appraisal from diverging perspectives that can make virtually every topic contentious. There is nothing wrong with controversy (otherwise known as multiple perspectives), of course, but given the strength of feeling that some topics can engender there needs to be a carefully nurtured pedagogical climate in class to be truly conducive to a constructive and respectful dialogue. This is what sets history apart and for the remainder of this brief chapter I will look at three areas of learning in which the history department and the history teacher make a difference as to how students interpret their place in the world. I did not write 'can make a difference' because the question is not whether a difference will be made but whether it will be positive or negative and whether it will be conscious or accidental.

Content

> *Who controls the past controls the future. Who controls the present controls the past.*

(George Orwell, *1984*)

Although the traditional approach to history teaching that was lampooned in *1066 and All That*[2] has not completely disappeared, contemporary pedagogies usually prefer to highlight learning outcomes that are based on skills drawn from historiography rather than the stress the rote learning of facts and dates. The Cambridge International Examinations IGCSE syllabus makes explicit reference to 'the development of historical skills, including investigation, analysis, evaluation and communication' and expects that 'learners' knowledge' will be 'rooted in an understanding of the nature and use of historical evidence'[3]. Concepts also feature prominently in contemporary learning goals. The IGCE history syllabus aims to 'promote an understanding of key historical concepts: cause and consequence, change and continuity, and similarity and difference'.

The International Baccalaureate (IB) perhaps goes even further. In its Middle Years Programme (MYP), history appears as one of the components of the 'Individuals and Societies' area of the curriculum where there is a specific emphasis on 'change, global interactions, time, place and space, and systems'[4] while the IB Diploma history syllabus has recently been reviewed to give 'a greater focus on the key concepts of change, continuity, causation, consequence, significance and perspectives'[5].

The terrain on which these generic skills and concepts are developed still remains to be allocated, however, and this poses the question of 'whose' history should be the reference frame as regards content. There is an understandable expectation, sometimes perhaps even an imperative, for national schools to establish this terrain as the history of the national experience as this can be a legitimate contribution to the formation of a national identity.

Even when this outcome is not posed explicitly, it is likely to be an inevitable consequence when the teaching of history focuses on periods and themes that, over the course of compulsory schooling, are drawn primarily from one nation's past. In some democratic societies, this albeit legitimate component of national education can become controversial when the goals are framed in a form that seem to encourage jingoistic indoctrination rather than a critical examination of the nation's story. Michael Gove, the UK Secretary of State for Education, provoked widespread debate in 2014 when he proposed a new history curriculum centred around British ideals and achievements:

> British Empire, Wolfe, Clive of India, the Jacobite rebellion, the American Revolution, the Enlightenment, the French Revolution, the Napoleonic Wars, Nelson, Wellington, Peterloo, the slave trade, the abolition of slavery, the High Victorians, the Industrial Revolution (including all of our great inventors), the role of women, the Scramble for Africa, Rowntree, the welfare state, Ireland, the Suffragettes, World War One, the Great Depression, Edward VIII, the Second World War, retreat from empire, Attlee, the Commonwealth, social reform after the war, Thatcherism and the fall of communism[6].

In a similar vein, Japanese history textbooks often come under critical scrutiny both within Japan and from neighbouring states on account of the tendency to promote a 'patriotic' perspective. Recent textbooks, apparently encouraged by Prime Minister Shinzo Abe who led the Japanese Society for History Textbook Reform in the 1990s, created protests from South Korea and China by appearing to claim disputed islands and by playing down Japanese responsibility for mass killing during the invasion of China in 1937 in referring to the Nanking Incident rather than the Nanking Massacre[7].

Even if we want to avoid historical indoctrination, there are significant advantages in giving national histories a central place in curriculum. Besides forging a sense of common identity, there are likely to be greater opportunities for using original sources in the national language, enabling students to explore questions such as bias and reliability in more authentic settings than when they are approached through secondary sources or documents in translation. But in multi-cultural or multi-national classrooms there is always likely to be an inquisitive inner voice prompting some students to reflect that 'this is only part of my history' or asking 'why do we never talk about my history?'

These observations are worth examining under the lens that is increasingly used by teachers working in second language acquisition. Over the past two decades, these teachers have taken a refreshingly critical look at the role played by mother tongue languages not only in enhancing language learning and cognitive development in general, but also in the child's perception of the way their cultural background and heritage is perceived. At least in many international schools, though not always in national frameworks, they have engineered the shift from full-immersion-one-language-only environments to learning contexts that are languages-rich and where the mother tongue is given equal recognition.

Eithne Gallagher (2011) has repeatedly pointed out that 'when students' language, culture and experience are ignored or excluded in classrooms they are immediately starting from a disadvantage'[8] and the political extrapolation of this exclusion goes much further. Argued extensively in the works of Cummins, Carder and Gallagher is the persistent warning that exclusion of the mother tongue language in school sends a message to the child about the lack of value given to that language and to its cultural heritage for the school community and maybe even for society as a whole.

Some of the established curriculum formats for history, like those mentioned earlier in this chapter, make a conscious effort to be 'selectively inclusive' when choosing themes and topics for their syllabi. The new IB Diploma Higher syllabus makes obvious attempts to ensure that students have the opportunity (although interestingly not the obligation) to study topics across a wide range of time periods and geographical areas.

In this kind of 'selective inclusion' the teacher or the curriculum designer chooses to expose students to a variety of topics or themes from what s/he considers to be 'important moments' of global history. In some ways this is an extension of earlier methods for teaching world history, especially in American schools, and it suffers from the same risks. Writing in 1990, Donald Johnson expressed the view that:

> World history as taught in most of our schools is still the old Whig history, which plots all human development from the ancient Middle East to modern Europe and America as the inevitable march of human liberty and freedom

and

> the curriculum and the texts that support it give the West a history, while China, India and Africa are studied as *cultures*[9].

I hope that we have gone a long way to breaking down the notions of history/culture to which Johnson refers, but implicit in the decision of what to teach and what not to teach is the question of value. There are many regions and peoples of the world whose histories are never included in our curricula, even though young representatives of these histories may be sitting in our international history classes.

Perhaps this 'selective inclusion' format is inevitable in specialised history courses for advanced classes (even if only because of external examination requirements) but in primary and middle schools a more flexible approach could be used. The challenge is to develop pedagogies that are not 'selective' of content but that allow for 'authentic inclusion', encouraging every student to bring to the classroom contributions from their own national or cultural heritage.

There is no shortage of ways that this can be done and many contemporary curricula have formats that are flexible enough to cater for it. Examples could be inquiry themes that can refer to history in any national or cultural context, open projects where students can critically examine topics from national textbooks in their mother tongue, or family history projects with projections back to experiences (real or imagined) at the limits of the actual family record.

Displays can encompass sources in the mother tongue languages of students in the class. Of course, for equal dignity to be awarded to each project, equal opportunities for presentation and sharing must be provided. But in answer to the question 'whose history should we teach' the answer has to be not only the big themes and topics that teachers think are important but also the history that the students themselves bring to our classes.

Empathy (perspective)

> *The past is foreign country.*
>
> L P Hartley, *The Go-Between*

Recognising diverse histories is only a gesture towards equal dignity and inclusion: it is not in itself an inter-cultural experience although it can become one following collective discussion in the classroom. Developing a sense of historical empathy or perspective is most definitely an inter-cultural experience but it is one of the hardest historical skills to acquire. Indeed, although it's values were widely extolled in the 'new history' that came to the fore in the 1980s it has now struggling to find a place in the way we view history education today.

Almost all of us are guilty of projecting our perception of contemporary ways of thought onto the protagonists of historical events and some of history's actors appear to be well suited to this way of interpreting their actions and their motivations. We think we can understand why Julius Caesar crossed the Rubicon or why Martin Luther pinned his 95 theses to the door of All Saints Church in Wittenberg.

The same applies in literature, where characters in Boccaccio's *Decameron* likewise seem to be no different from typical personalities in 21st century Europe. The huge success of Philippa Gregory's books about Lancastrian, Yorkist and Tudor women has been ascribed to the way she makes them recognizable to popular readers today because she makes these historical figures think and act like women we can understand[10]. In terms of intercultural competence, this most certainly places learners in the ethnocentric section of Bennett's progressive scale, described as denial, defence or minimization. The learner takes a superior stance, other cultures are romanticised rather than respected and differences of mindset and outlook are minimized.

Professional historians know that this is only part of the story and that the mindset of medieval and early modern princesses was significantly more complex than this projection of modernity implies. The truth is that we can't really understand Tudor times and Tudor women unless we accept that alongside some apparently universal characteristics of the human psyche (such as, perhaps, ambition, pride, doubt, fear and sexuality) there are some very context-specific components in the way we see the world that derive from the cultural environment in which we live.

This is where coming to terms with the Tudors and the English Reformation can be as much an inter-cultural experience as preparing to live and work in a foreign country today. Recognising these inter-cultural considerations is essential if we are not to reduce history to a description of the past delivered for popular television. Reaching this conceptual level of understanding is one thing, though, while actually having time to explore all that it implies every time a history class encounters a new topic is an altogether different matter.

There are also some significant differences between interacting with the past and interacting with another culture in the present. For a start it can be conceptually difficult for young people to appreciate how much mindsets within their own culture have changed over time. Multinational, multilingual and multicultural classrooms should have an advantage over more homogeneous school communities in this respect because the students may already be attuned to working with multiple perspectives on a daily basis, maybe even more so than a monolingual or mono-cultural teacher.

Indeed, students who operate naturally in multiple languages and have friends from different cultural backgrounds have to deal with questions of empathy in their own personal lives on a daily basis. It is not uncommon for their home culture to have different expectations of thinking and behaviour than their school, so extending their developing awareness of diverse ways of thinking to the Tudors may not be conceptually problematic *per se*. But what are the pedagogical implications? How much time can we realistically devote to trying to understand a past culture? And what kind of sources and resources can we refer to from Tudor times that are accessible to young people without making the exercise as complex (and potentially dull) as a cryptic crossword instead of bringing history to life by getting on with the constantly surprising to-and-fro of events in 16th century England?

The term itself (whether empathy or perspective) does not always lend itself to this kind of study because it can be confused with the alternative meaning of a word that is in more common usage. In the study of history there are some occasions when questions of 'empathy' can emerge naturally from the topic under consideration. Empathy with the Aztecs encountered by Cortez can be relayed either through *sympathy* with the citizens of an incredibly successful civilization which was about to suddenly collapse at the height of its power or *mystery* (maybe even horror) in confronting a world view that demanded regular human sacrifice to keep the cosmic machinery in motion.

If we are not careful, references to empathy in these cases could easily end up as exercises in creative writing with little authentic historical value. These boundaries of history and anthropology are full of pitfalls as the impossibility of reaching an appropriate level of understanding for middle school students might only end up encouraging stereotypical and simplistic assertions about others, something that needs to be avoided as much in the past as in the present. The dilemma for the historian is that if we shy away from questions of empathy completely then not only do we fail to use our subject for its inter-cultural potential but we fail to do it historical justice, too.

Although the use of empathy can be fraught with dangers, interacting with another culture today or another culture (even in our own tradition) in the past *is* an inter-cultural experience, so the opportunities for internationally minded schools would seem to be evident. Moreover, many international schools have adopted curricula that utilise pedagogies of inquiry founded on constructivist principles, an approach to learning that requires students be given appropriate tools to make sense of their inquiries into past events. We cannot expect students to explore accurately for themselves if we fail to provide a language guide to help them interact with the people they will encounter in the new territory.

Over the past 40 years Peter Lee has written extensively about empathy (and other conceptual challenges in history teaching) and in one of his recent articles he and Denis Shemilt call it 'the concept that dare not speak its name', asking 'should empathy come out of the closet?'[11] Their article takes a critical look at how the use of empathy has declined in the UK after being promoted extensively before the 1990s and they argue for a tentative reintegration into the history teachers' toolkit. Interestingly, they refer to a six-level progression model that describes how students become more proficient in their use of empathy. It would be interesting to explore the analogy with Milton Bennett's six levels of inter-cultural sensitivity, and although this is beyond the scope of this chapter it could be an interesting project for another history specialist[12].

Since it is difficult for empathy in school to go beyond the shallow stereotype, there is a risk that students will reach inaccurate conclusions and make simplistic cultural judgements. Rather than enhancing historic understanding and inter-cultural learning, this kind of outcome is detrimental. The problem for history teachers is that they cannot shy away from it. In the skills-based and concept-driven courses that we work with today, students must be exposed to the complexity of empathetic interpretations. The role of the teacher is to accompany this with inter-cultural sensitivity that supports the students' creation of meaning in a way that does justice to both historical reality and to their developing international minds.

Values

To know what is right and not do it is the worst cowardice.

Confucius

Neutral or objective interpretations of history are not an option for adults and it is even harder for young learners to approach the subject without constantly making value judgements. In their narration of history, like the novels they read and the movies they watch, the past is populated by 'goodies' and 'baddies' and passionate students can feel the same kind of moral outrage about incidents that occurred long ago as they do about current events. Unlike fiction, though, there is no moral written into the story by a conscious author so evaluating who got to have the last say leaves us with another dilemma about the kind of lessons we can draw from our study of the past.

Values are present as thorny questions in the evolution of inter-cultural competence and this is exactly the same for students of history. They push learners into the ethno-relative positions of Bennett's scale, described as acceptance, adaptation and integration – but progressing to these levels of competence means recognising diversity and dealing with inner controversy. In coming to appreciate another society (present or past) and in becoming empathetic with the motivations of its protagonists, we sooner or later face the dilemma of evaluating the extent to which we can appreciate and take on board its values. This has been called the 'ethical paradox'.

> Taking historical perspective demands that we understand the differences between our ethical universe and those of bygone societies. We do not want to impose our own anachronistic standards on the past. At the same time, meaningful history does not treat brutal slave-holders, enthusiastic Nazis, and marauding conquistadors in a 'neutral' manner[13].

This kind of risky dilemma is actually inherent in any approach that encourages the use of multiple perspectives. Many teachers claim to adhere to constructivist principles and try to engage students in looking at contentious issues from different standpoints to explain the actions and behaviour of individuals and groups. When this is effective the learners become skilled at understanding the complexity of authentic situations where multiple groups have competing demands, each of which can appear to be justified when examined in isolation.

The educational value of this process cannot be denied as a first step towards recognising the value and integrity of other mindsets and as a precursor for any meaningful resolution to the contention. The ethical dilemma emerges when the process is so successful that it becomes a purely relativistic exercise and students are able to identify (or empathise) with groups whose moral position we would not normally want them to associate with at all.

We all know that the more distant we are from events then the easier it is to take a relativistic perspective. Standard descriptions of the ancient world describe the rise and fall of civilisations which all seem to be imperial, militaristic, monarchical and expansionist in nature. Even the Athenians, who are always taken as the pinnacle of cultural achievement in antiquity and who seem distinctly akin to contemporary liberals when compared to their rivals in Sparta or Persia, maintained a slave economy that would be horrific to modern eyes. But apart from rare cases (maybe the Athenian world is one of them) there is often no easy way for young people to evaluate historical events of so long ago in moral or ethical terms. The same can be said about the beginning of European imperialism. Both the Spaniards and the Incas were examples of societies where war had become a central component of the state to extend influence or regain territories that were felt to be their just rights.

At the heart of this dilemma is the kind of lesson we want history to teach us. On the one hand we have the Machiavellian interpretation of history and its justification of the winner. In his lessons to the Prince, the Italian philosopher-politician (and teacher) continually utilises historical references to explain and justify the way a virtuous leader should behave. His use of the term 'virtuous' does not have the moral meaning we expect today, however, since virtue to Machiavelli more often than not means coming out on top and maintaining or extending one's influence in a world where vicious competition and constant danger are the norm.

Machiavelli's lessons from history have stood the test of time to the extent that they are widely read and admired today. One can argue that Abraham Lincoln's abolition of slavery and Martin Luther King Junior's epic struggle for civil rights owed as much to the way these two leaders showed a pragmatic appreciation for political reality that Machiavelli would have admired as they did to purely idealistic and humanitarian proclamations about the human right to equality and dignity for all.

Contrasting with Machiavelli's emphasis on the winner, we can examine history not simply to seek guidance for survival strategies, but as a moral compass to help us to find orientation in the complex decisions that we have to face in society today. This approach requires students to go beyond the success stories to ask whether action was right or justified. The Spanish settlement of Mexico was certainly successful but would its methods be justified to contemporary minds? Henry VII established a successful dynasty but how justified was his claim to the throne? Were the Opium Wars a high or a low point of British imperialism? Was the Jewish settlement of Palestine a legitimate way of responding to the search to find a homeland for the diaspora?

Beyond these questions we have to face the responsibilities that knowledge about the past poses in today's world. Why are we obligated to remember the fallen soldiers of World War I? Do we remember the soldiers who fell on all sides of the conflict or only our own? Do we owe reparations to the aboriginal residential schools? For how long should the fallen colonial powers feel responsible for their actions of conquest, exploitation and cultural manipulation in their liberated colonial territories? 'In other words, what responsibilities do historical crimes and sacrifices impose upon us today?[14]'

Although these ethical questions emerge naturally in the teaching of history, the subject itself is not explicitly about values but simply about understanding the past. This means that in most circumstances the teacher will have to initially count on values that the students bring to the classroom themselves. The role of the teacher can be compared to that of the inter-cultural mediator and mentor, who guides the learner through the challenge of dealing with an uncomfortable exposure to a contrasting world view and leads them towards a more profound realisation that an alternative interpretation or reality might be equally legitimate.

At the same time the teacher is a moral role model who cannot always take a relativistic perspective but needs to have a clear ethical position to stimulate appropriate reflection by the students. This is especially the case because a great deal of contemporary history is taught in our schools and some students may have strong feelings about the impact of recent historical events on their own family or national experiences.

The teacher needs to be able to challenge learners to question their preconceptions and take a critical perspective in examining rival claims to the moral high ground of what is right or legitimate. S/he needs to have a pedagogy that enables questions to be debated openly with equal dignity awarded to contrasting interpretations. Such is the hallmark of a genuine inter-cultural encounter. But there also have to be parameters about the ultimate limits to which we can pursue arguments that lead into moral quagmires. History is, after all, about reality and is not a creative writing exercise. Slavery, Nazism and genocide are not fictional dystopias but actual phenomena that can only be abhorred and never justified in the international mind.

Conclusion

History is not simply the objective study of the past but rather the way that we interpret the past from our unique perspective in place and time. It is not a purely rational discipline like physics and maths, and its characters are not fictional like the actors in a play or a novel – they are real people whose decisions and actions impacted on our world to make it what we have today. History education is about us – and inter-cultural learning is an integral component of its methodology. However we decide to teach history in our schools the students will take away lessons about themselves.

This may be about their personal sense or place or identity or it may be about the role that their national or cultural heritage has played on the global stage. It will teach them to evaluate claims of what is right, wrong, legitimate or justified regarding events in the past and in dealing with contentions in the present. This chapter is an appeal for us to recognise that these learning goals are just as significant as the skills and concepts that are expected by curriculum designers – and in the long run they may be what matters most of all in the students' futures.

References

1   26 May 2014.

2   Sutherland, J., The 10 American writers that English children should study for GCSE, *The Guardian*,. Sellars, W.C and Yateman, R.J., 1066 and all that, Methuen, London, 1930 (latest edition 1998).

3   www.cie.org.uk/images/128388-2015-syllabus.pdf

4   International Baccalaureate (IBO), Individuals and Societies guide, May 2014.

5   International Baccalaureate (IBO), History Curriculum Review: Update for Teachers, 2014.

6   Antony Little, "Gove, The History Teacher's Friend", *The Daily Telegraph*, 4 February 2014, www.telegraph.co.uk/education/educationopinion/10616152/Gove-the-history-teachers-friend.html

7   *The Guardian*, 7 April 2015, www.theguardian.com/world/2015/apr/07/japan-south-korea-china-protest-textbooks

8   Gallagher, E. "Many Languages One Message: Equal rights to the Curriculum", ECIS Conference 2011, edmundo.ecis.org/new/conference/esl/Documents/Gallagher%20II.pdf

9   Johnson, D (2007) "US Schools Need an Integrated World History", New York Times, 28 February 1990, www.nytimes.com/1990/02/28/opinion/l-us-schools-need-an-integrated-world history-880490.html

10   Suzannah Lipscombe, Is the past a foreign country?, St Paul's School TEDxSPS, www.youtube.com/watch?v=VfKWd7iXMSo

11   Lee, Peter and Denis Shemilt. "The Concept that Dares not Speak its Name: Should Empathy Come Out of the Closet?" Teaching History 143 (2011): 39-49.

12   Bennett, M.J., A Developmental Model of Intercultural Sensitivity, www.idrinstitute.org/allegati/IDRI_t_Pubblicazioni/47/FILE_Documento_Bennett_DMIS_12pp_quotes_rev_2011.pdf

13   Centre for the Study of Historical Consciousness, The Historical Thinking Project, Ethical Dimensions, historicalthinking.ca/ethical-dimensions

14   Centre for the Study of Historical Consciousness, The Historical Thinking Project, Ethical Dimensions, historicalthinking.ca/ethical-dimensions

Chapter 9

Whose history? Whose nation?

National and international interpretations

Caroline Ellwood

To consider the changes in relation to the education of young people and history in the curriculum is to be a single rider trying to control a tandem. For simultaneously two movements are in process. On the one hand there is evolving historiography, the way history itself is interpreted, and on the other there are new attitudes to pedagogy. Thus methodologies are on the move simultaneously, challenging older attitudes and accepted ways of thought not just in what history you teach but in how it is taught.

Illustrative of the seismic nature of this change is the contrast between Goldsmith's' *History of England from the invasion of Julius Caesar to the death of George 11, with a continuation to the present time* published in 1764 and revised and reissued until the end of the 19th century, and Bill Gates' and David Christian's *Big History Project*. Goldsmith's history was limited to the political record from the point of view of one country within a fixed period, the narrative of a nation abridged from a larger four-volume work with set questions at the end of each chapter to test memory, the only skill involved. The *Big History Project* is a framework bringing together the sciences, humanities and social sciences within a historical context; starting with the origins of the universe it then covers interlocking global concerns. Multiple skills are developed, in particular the ability to explore concepts, test the evidence and think for yourself (Gustafson 2014).

These two widely differing approaches demonstrate the dilemma of deciding what and whose history to teach. Indeed why teach history at all? For centuries history, often transmitted by memory, or written down by chroniclers, was the record of the great deeds of the tribe. By the 16th century, for a selected group of Europeans, the main history that was learned was through the texts of Latin and Greek origin that formed the basis of a classical education.

A certain amount of biblical historical knowledge would be picked up from religious studies and services and, for younger children, there were primers that told stories of national history intermingling factual events with folk heroes such as Robin Hood and Fra Diavila (guerrilla Michael Pessa, who fought against Napoleon). The main purpose however was to preserve national pride and identity.

It is when the teaching of history has a purpose and becomes a message related to the creation or preservation of a culture that history becomes mixed with ideas of values and missionary fervour. At the basis of all history teaching is an act of selection. Who makes the selection that becomes what is taught in schools has enormous power. Any history teacher who encourages discussion is involved in the making of ethical judgements. There are moral dilemmas in the teaching of peace studies, comparative religion, revolution and counter revolution, which is why governments get involved in the writing of history textbooks.

Indeed the study of history can be so dangerous that in the dystopian novel *Brave New World* no history is taught, and a major theme of Orwell's *1984* is control of the past:

> If all accepted the lie which the Party imposed – if all records told the same tale – then the lie passed into history and became truth.
>
> (Orwell, *1984*)

Totalitarian states, nations with a desire to cover up, mitigate past misdeeds or reinforce claims to territory can encourage patriotism by what is left out just as much as by what is included. Nor is it only totalitarian states that gloss over unpalatable aspects of their past or give an interpretation that supports their own view of, say, progress and democracy. This is particularly evident in the way 'the West' treated the history of Islam and the Middle East.

Certainly until fairly recently for many European and English speaking history students contact with Islam came only when 'our' history bumped into 'theirs' – 'the Crusades', 'the sick man of Europe', colonisation and 'spheres of influence'. Maps were drawn, land allocated, kings put in place, military bases established, petroleum commandeered. Little attention was given to the religion, the culture or the history of nations that 'we', the countries of the West, influenced or indeed created. Telling the 'national story' created heroes and legitimatised actions.

However the telling is not as simple as it sounds. A country is not an isolated unit, 'my' version of what happened may not be 'yours'. It has become clear that what can be called 'white man's history' is very different to that of a colonised world. Until relatively recently the study of history, like other humanities subjects, was 'led' by scholars from the West. Indeed it was assumed that the European mind was somehow superior to that of other races. As Lord Cromer put it:

> The European is a close reasoner, his statements of fact are devoid of any ambiguity, and he is a natural logician ... the mind of the Oriental, on the other hand, like his picturesque street is eminently wanting in symmetry. His reasoning is of the most slipshod description.
>
> (Said, 1978).

As Europeans controlled vast areas of the globe they assumed to study 'them'. 'We' interpreted 'their' history, indeed often assumed there was none worth recording until 'we' arrived and discovered 'them'. George Combe summed this up in 1823: 'The history of Africa, so far as it has a history, exhibits one unbroken scene of intellectual desolation.' The European powers of Germany, Britain, Belgium and France took upon themselves to sort out this 'desolation' by drawing boundary lines across the region and thus creating 'nations' in their own image.

Only as these nations gained independence from their colonial masters did their pre-colonial histories emerge, now interpreted in post-colonial terms. When President Nyerere of Tanzania convened a conference in 1963 for the purpose of 'a rediscovery of our own history' he was asserting the right of his nation to not just political independence but independence of thought, and its own interpretation of the past. Rejecting 'Tanganyika', 'Tanzania' would rely on its own historians, not the view of the West:

> The primary sources are here, in Africa, and the primary interest is not really other people's desire to understand us, but our own desire to understand ourselves and our societies, so that we can build our future on firm foundations.
>
> (Nyerere 1963)

Nehru had done the same thing for the new Indian nation in 1947, leapfrogging the history of the British Raj and claiming an India shaped at the 'dawn' of history:

> At the stroke of the midnight hour, when the world sleeps, India will awake to life and freedom. A moment comes, which comes but rarely in history, when we step out from the old to the new, when an age ends, and when the soul of a nation, long suppressed, finds utterance... At the dawn of history India started on her unending quest, and trackless centuries are filled with her striving and the grandeur of her success and her failures.
>
> (Nehru Independence Speech, 1947)

Africa and India were not the only countries to throw off the idea of Western culture and its interpretation of the past. Nations of the Middle East (itself a European concept) that in many cases had also been Western constructs also asserted the right to their own past.

These changes of emphasis, from national to global, from colonial to post-colonial, are a result of seismic shifts in perception of political and social change, revolutions, wars economic developments and movements of populations. As focus has moved from Cold War politics to the Middle East, there has been a realisation that oil-rich Islamic countries have not just grown in political power but also have an intellectual inheritance not only as rich as that of Europe, but often were themselves a part of that very foundation of ideas.

The realisation that history is multifaceted – not just a universal frame of reference based on developments out of Europe and the establishing of empires – means that perceptions have to change. So history can become not 'my' history or 'yours' but 'ours'. Hamid Dabashi, in his study of aspects of orientalism *Can Non-Europeans think?*, analyses the changes in attitude over the last 50 years or so that have resulted in the dismantling of the notion of 'West' and 'European'.

Tragically it has taken the terrorist bombing of ordinary citizens in the West, and a turbulent war torn Afghanistan and the Middle East, to change perceptions and perspectives of history in the region. These, together with the presence of large groups of immigrant Islamic families across Europe, have alerted both politicians and educators to the need for a greater knowledge and understanding of Islamic history and religion. Teaching in schools now includes units of study of Islamic culture, religion and history often with specialist examinations available.

> Europe has much to teach the world. But this will now take place on a far more level and democratic playing field, where its philosophy is European philosophy not 'Philosophy'. Its music is 'European music' not 'Music'.
>
> (Dabashi, 2015).

A major source for changes in attitude from a myopic view of history as being just 'our history' can be traced to efforts after the Second World War to create a better attempt at world government than the League of Nations. The horrors of war, and in particular the revelations of the holocaust, brought about a number of changes in attitude. As the old colonial empires were breaking apart, disparate forces across Africa, India, the Middle East and the USSR were forming a new world order. It was to try to contain extremes and inculcate a feeling of communal global responsibility that the United Nations was formed and the Declaration of Human Rights proclaimed.

Add to this that a specific part of the work of The United Nations Education, Science and Cultural Organisation (UNESCO) and the Organisation of Economic Cooperation and Development (OECD) was educational, and there is the opportunity to extend history teaching beyond the national to a universal view of people as 'world' citizens. 'Global Education' can now be found involved in making students socio-politically aware, culturally sensitive and, on occasion, politically active.

Harriet Marshall analyses the complexities of provision and intent in her article 'The Global Education Terminology Debate: Exploring some of the Issues' (Marshall 2007). She describes a long and confused evolution of a mixture of intent and process. Historical exemplars become the basis for discussion in relation to values, citizenship, peace studies and democracy. John Godfrey goes so far as to dismiss the concept of 'global citizenship' altogether as essentially ill-considered and meaningless:

> I am arguing for a more rigorous alternative which is a deeper understanding of national citizenship and a more sophisticated understanding of the international world as it actually is ... there is a real task for internationally minded schools in thinking through carefully what citizenship skills we need to teach our students for them not only to survive but also to thrive in the 21st century.
>
> (Godfrey, 2014)

To track some of these changes in attitude towards the purpose of, and what should be included, in a history curriculum and the side growths that are now available, the development of two particular examples will be examined in detail. One is a response to national pressures and the other an attempt to produce an international programme for students of any nation.

History as part of the National Curriculum 1970-2015 – United Kingdom (England and Wales) Key Stage 3, 11-16.

The history component of the International Baccalaureate Middle Years Programme 11-16.

The United Kingdom (England and Wales)
Developments in the teaching of history from 1970- 2015

In 1933 Dr Olive Shropshire, an American, produced a report on her study of The Teaching of History in English Schools. She found little consistency of approach,

> whether it should be national, European or world history or a combination of all three. The syllabus maker is confronted also with the problems of reconciling the various phases of history, political, social, economic, constitutional, naval and military, religious and local to which are added the history of science, art and architecture.
>
> (Shropshire, 1933)

She noted that original documents were being used in some classes, simple dramatisations, time charts, debates and visits to museums but the basis of most history teaching was the oral lesson, reinforced by the text book and 'the emphasis both in the text books and in most of the teaching observed by this writer is political and military' (Shropshire, 1933). History teachers could live a quiet life using any method and material that they wished so long as they bore in mind the eventual requirements of examinations for the clever and future employment for the rest.

Move on 20 years and history teaching, its content, skills and purpose are part of what became known as 'The Great Debate' on education. Initiated by an address at Ruskin College by James Callaghan, this created an immediate response as traditionalists opposed reformists. In the case of history it became both heated and divisive as the proponents of the 'new' history battled their case against the traditionalists. Left wing and right wing clashed over ideas for integrated studies, use of evidence-based themes, projects, empathy, expansion of subject area, study of contemporary issues, national testing and how much the government should be involved. It seemed there was little about history teaching that did not produce a variety of responses.

How this situation arose is due to a number of changes in attitude that came after World War Two and the reforming zeal of certain politicians and influential educationalists, a movement that included the replacing of the grammar schools by comprehensive education. Teachers who had very successfully gone their own way with the classroom door firmly closed now had to respond not just to change in their own area but change everywhere. Suddenly the whole rationale as to why history was being taught, how, and what was up for discussion – the old comfortable days – were over. And not just in the classroom: the oil crisis; economic decline; loss of empire; 'erosion of standards'; all demanded a 'return to basics' on the one side and a 'radical reappraisal' on the other.

The Plowden Report in 1967 had promoted child-centred education and a number of government reports looked at not so much what was taught but how it was taught. HMI published the working paper *Curriculum 11-16* in 1977, defining a series of 'eight areas of experience' which should be the foundation and common core of every child's education. These were the aesthetic and creative; ethical; linguistic; mathematical; physical; scientific; social and political; and the spiritual.

History was considered as relating to a number of subjects but specific skills concerned the nature of evidence, sense of change and continuity. cause and effect and empathy. Recommendations for content are not specific but should include a local component, some regional and national studies and some world history. Taking this into consideration the choice of content was still left to the school.

> Final decision on content will inevitably and rightly, vary with the locality of the school, the availability of books and other resources, the accessibility of local archives, public libraries, experience of the teachers and their pupils.
>
> (Curriculum 11-16, 1977)

There was an immediate response from the right at not just changes in methodology but the overwhelming trust in the teachers and criticism of the way history was taught rumbled on for the next decade. A focus to the unease at what was seen as teaching nothing but a random and pointless search for clues to evidence from the past was presented by Sir Keith Joseph, then Education Secretary in 1984. He felt that children should be taught shared British values in order to unify the nation by emphasising its distinct character and institutions. Clutter such as 'world history' should be removed.

> For the child brought up in this country British History has something to convey that cannot, however expert the teaching, be conveyed through Roman History, American History or Caribbean History.
>
> (Joseph, 1984)

It is against this background that a series of suggestions for discussion were made by Her Majesty's Inspectorate and recommendations put forward by The Historical Association. Protectors of British heritage such as Alan Beattie (*History in Peril*) accused the left of teaching a history that was not real history but 'creative imagining'; genuine history teaching had nothing to do with multiculturalism or peace studies. Nevertheless the 'National Criteria' that eventually were proposed owed more to the skills-based ideas of the left than the 'heritage lobby' of the right. Ideas of change, causation and continuity are given importance but so also are communication and interpretative skills. Assessment objectives include the ability to separate fact from opinion, to detect bias and inconsistency, and extract information from all kinds of evidence and evaluate it

At last in 1988 the National Curriculum was introduced. No longer would state schools be free to create their own curricula – all now had to follow an orderly system based on three key stages.

Reception   age 5

Key Stage One   age 6-7

123

Key Stage Two   age 8-11

Key Stage Three   age 11-16

Clear Attainment Targets were set out for the study of history. Core study units included a solid background in British history, a number of topics involving European and World history, and choice could be made from a selection of supplementary units giving a wide spectrum of social, cultural and local history topics. This curriculum, with some adjustments, stayed in place until 1999, when a major review that reduced the amount of prescribed content was undertaken. Further adjustments were made in 2005 with the promotion of cross-curricular themes and personalised learning and in 2007 when another major review was announced.

Even allowing for minor criticisms, the attainment targets and content could be considered as an admirable programme which would produce a student with an excellent range of historical knowledge and skills by the age of 16. Unfortunately the reality is somewhat different, as history was not made a compulsory subject during secondary education and a great many students dropped history at 14.

Added to this, the last two years of Key Stage 4 became, in most schools, totally devoted to passing the final examination, the General Certificate of Education. Indeed testing and assessment have been a major point of discussion in relation to the development of the curriculum. The ambitions of all governments to 'raise standards' led to 'an educational arms race where children were 'tested to destruction' (Turner 2015). Whilst history as such was not included in the programme of assessment, the importance given to the nationally regulated and published Standard Attainment Tests (SATS) that are taken at 7, 11 and 14 have unbalanced the curriculum. Focus is given to the demands of tests in math, English and science with a narrowing of the curriculum as a result.

Controversy over what was taught and how was the background when the next major review of the National Curriculum was announced and the first formal consultation on proposed changes began in 2013. The proposals for the history curriculum proved to be highly controversial and generated intense debate. There was general approval of the aims:

> Key Stage 3 Pupils should extend and deepen their chronologically secure knowledge and understanding of British, local and world history, so that it provides a well-informed context for wider learning. Pupils should identify significant events, make connections, draw contrasts, and analyse trends within periods and over long arcs of time. They should use historical terms and concepts in increasingly sophisticated ways. They should pursue historically valid enquiries including some they have framed themselves, and create relevant, structured and evidentially supported accounts in response. They should understand how different types of historical sources are used rigorously to make historical claims and discern how and why contrasting arguments and interpretations of the past have been constructed.
>
> (National Curriculum, 2013)

In planning to ensure the progression described above through teaching British, local and world history, teachers were told to combine overview and depth studies to help pupils understand both the long arc of development and the complexity of specific aspects of the content.

However the rest of the proposals caused an eruption of criticism from all quarters. The programme for history recommended a chronological approach starting a child off at seven with feudalism and then a brisk trot through time to end up (if you were still taking the subject) at WW2 at 16. The aim was to give children 'an idea of what it is to be British and – the concept of a nation and a nation's history, heroes and heroines'. Letters flew off to *The Times* and eminent historians joined the debate in articles to the press. The then Education Secretary, Michael Gove, was criticised for proposing a patriotic view of history more suitable for the 19th than the 21st century. A typical response was that from Richard Evans, Regius Professor at Cambridge:

> The proposals ... look set to replace the existing breadth and ambition of coverage, critical method and historical debate with rote learning of the patriotic stocking fillers so beloved of traditionalists in both main parties. Out goes the drive to cover a broader canvas, taking in European history and other civilisations. In comes a narrow-minded focus on British history alone – to the exclusion of everything else.
>
> (Evans, 2013)

The Historical Association weighed in with all the power they could muster – 'we represent 6000 schools, teachers and academics with a further 2000 branch associates ... and 19,000 history teachers registered with our website'. With only 4% of a poll of members thinking that the curriculum was a positive change, the Association's criticisms had impact. They considered the curriculum over-prescriptive, the chronological approach unhelpful for understanding, the topics for the primary school a complete mismatch with how children learn and the whole programme too narrow in focus and Anglo-centric (Consultation Response Form, 2013).

However there were some defenders, as John Burrows from Ipswich says in his letter to *The Times*: 'Can you imagine any other country regarding it as wrong to teach children the nation's past achievements?' It is not difficult to trace the roots of the government's desire for a common and binding cultural history to the rapid changes that were occurring in British society through immigration. In fact the proposals were considerably adjusted after the consultation period, resulting in a compromise that went some way to answer its critics. The Historical Association responded:

> We are particularly pleased to see world history reintroduced to the curriculum alongside the opportunity to study local history at all key stages. The revised curriculum removes much of the prescription giving greater scope for choice and respect for teachers' expertise. Overall this revision presents a curriculum that will help the aims become a more realistically achievable goal.
>
> (The Historical Association, 2013)

125

A diet of British history was thus avoided; however the idea of history as a purveyor of right attitudes was not abandoned. The new Education Secretary, Nicky Morgan, sidestepping the 'patriotic' pitfall, proposed that 'British values' should be woven into the whole curriculum. Challenged as to what this meant, Morgan said "tolerance and respect for other people's views" (Morgan 16.10. 2014). Certainly a possible start for teaching history in a multicultural society.

For many historians, as important as bickering over what was taught and how was the fact that most pupils had at the most 80 minutes a week exposure to history and that only until the age of 14.

Conclusion
The teaching of history in the schools of England and Wales is in many ways a continued shift between the patriotic right and the progressive left. However, whichever is preferred, both approaches are using history to carry a message. Whether the history that is taught is seen as part of a cultural programme to unify an increasingly disparate population or as the basis for independent thought in a global context it has a purpose. The devolution of government in the United Kingdom, together with the rise of Scottish Nationalism, could create a further impetus for a national history but ironically not one promoting unity but independence. There is no such thing as innocent history.

The history component of the International Baccalaureate Programmes
International schools are diverse in origin, size and location. Finding a common description is like trying to put fog into a box. However there are commonalities and possibly the most unifying process has been the evolution over the last 50 years of the programme for international education – The International Baccalaureate (IB). The initial IB Diploma was founded in 1968 to provide a curriculum for the growing number of international schools and facilitate ease of student movement from one institution to another.

As anything from 30 to 80 nationalities could make up a school community it was obvious that, since a 'national' point of view was not the answer, a new educational philosophy was required. From a modest beginning the IB has become an established curriculum choice for both national and international schools. Starting as a diploma to be awarded after the final two years at school the success of the programme meant that a whole school curriculum was soon discussed.

Four programmes are now available from age three to 18. The IB is presently implemented in over 4200 schools worldwide (IB statistics). From the start there was awareness that in an international setting the study of history would be

> one of the most problematic subjects in an international context ... how were students to get a general education, not in the sense of acquiring general information in order to forget it, but in experiencing ways of

thinking in order to understand? To learn history not in order to know some specific 'facts' but to learn to think historically?

(Peterson, 1987)

Thinking 'historically' would, according to the IB, mean engaging with multiple perspectives, appreciating the complex nature of historical concepts and issues, having a sense of chronology and context and being able to deal effectively with sources – a skills list very similar to that of the UK National Curriculum. What was different was the search for an overall mindset that would cut across nationality, but not erase it. A 'melting pot' was not the answer; schools did not have to aim at all being the same or produce the same answers. IB history was to train the mind to look globally, across cultures, not be a training ground for a particular nation's idea of citizenship. Hill sums this up:

> It was not the content of the contemporary history course that was to differentiate it from its national counterparts, it was its pedagogical approach. The fundamental premise required students to analyse, explore and appreciate the different interpretations of the same event by various historians operating in diverse cultural contexts. Understanding the complex reasons why a particular interpretation exists, without necessarily agreeing with it gives legitimacy to other points of view.

(Hill 2010)

What did evolve was an attitude towards not just history but to the world. It became known as 'international mindedness'.

> An education for international mindedness; an education designed to break down the barriers of race, religion and class; an education that extolled the benefits of cultural diversity, above all else an education for peace.

(Walker 2011)

This constructivist approach assumed a role for history far beyond the learning of facts or even the development of the ability to think. It assumes that thinking is for a purpose. Just as the National Curriculum has grappled with the sub theme of the creation of good citizenship, so the IB is aiming at world citizenship and a 'transnational perspective' (IB, 2014). It also sees history as one part of an holistic approach to learning which is promoted not just through individual subjects but by a core component of the Theory of Knowledge (TOK) programme.

This encourages students to reflect upon the nature of knowing. Thus history is not only a subject for the diploma: it is also one of the eight areas of knowledge at the centre of TOK's exploration of certainty. Furthermore, the internal assessment of TOK requires students to reflect on 'the role of methods used by, and challenges facing a historian' in relation to a chosen historical investigation (*ibid*).

Thus all students, not just those taking history for the diploma, are involved in consideration of the importance of history in relation to our understanding of ourselves in the present. Indeed history, far from being 'problematic' as Peterson described, has emerged as an essential part of the structure of the whole programme. Finding a programme for those 30-85 nationalities became an exciting challenge and one always open to new developments as global events could be viewed trans-nationally.

However idealistic intentions, or what Paul Tarc has termed 'Global Dreams' (Tarc, 2009), did not always become the reality. In practice it is not just the Western bias of text books and predominance of teachers of western origin (Ellwood 2001), but also what topics are chosen from the carefully balanced syllabus. Cambridge points out how the history curriculum was adapted in the US to serve the needs of the Goals 2000; Educate America Act (Cambridge, 2013). He also quotes research by Lewis (2006):

> ...of 18,712 students throughout the world who sat for the May 2005 IB Higher Level History examination, 98%... pursued either the history of the Americas or the history of Europe as their optional topic. In other words, less than 3% of all higher Level History students concentrated upon Asia, Oceana, the Middle East or Africa.

Early awareness of the imbalance in the history programme resulted in the evolution of a programme on the study of Islamic history. Introduced in 1989 to offset western bias, The History and Culture of the Islamic World was as a stand-alone diploma option. Whilst not being aimed solely at Islamic students, it would show a recognition of the growing importance of the spread of international schools in Islamic countries. Never attracting great numbers, it continued until 2009 when it was discontinued as part of a total revamping of the history programme.

Responding to criticism that the history curriculum could be seen as leaning too heavily on a western interpretation of history and acknowledging that world history is also Islamic history, it seemed desirable to abandon the fig leaf of one not very popular option for the thorough integration of Islamic history into the whole syllabus (Ellwood, 2012). The other leaning of the history programme to modern European history would also be balanced by covering not just Islamic but also European history c300-1600. The marketing of the IB programme to the rapidly growing number of international schools in the region must also be taken into account.

Teaching about Islam is an interesting example of the problems faced by the history teacher in an international school. In a period of intense turmoil, wars, terrorism, and religious extremism, the roots of which go deep into the past, virtually no classes will be untouched by recent events. Teachers in Islamic countries, Islamic students, students with a Jewish background, the growing number of students and indeed teachers affected by terrorism, will all react according to selection of topic and method of approach.

The challenge, according to US National History Standards, is to maintain perspective by avoiding 'present mindedness, judging the past solely in terms of present norms and values' (Spice, 2003). Whose norms and values is of course the inevitable question when anything from 30-80 nationalities could make up the school community.

In the 1990s a Primary Years Programme (PYP) and a Middle Years Programme (MYP) were added to the Diploma. The teachers who worked on the evolution of these curricula (and it was mainly teachers who did the pioneer work) started not from the point of the content of a discipline but the needs of the student. It was obvious that since a 'national' point of view was not the answer, just as for the Diploma programme an educational philosophy was required that would link the programmes as a continuum.

What emerged as common to all three programmes was a concept-driven approach aimed at helping the learner construct meaning through enquiry, critical thinking and an awareness of connections. Thus the learner was the starting point, not the subject. Central to all three programmes is the idea of international mindedness and the 'Learner Profile' for all students who should be

Inquirers.

Knowledgeable.

Thinkers.

Communicators.

Principled.

Open-minded.

Since each part of the IB continuum was developed separately, the first models did not always present a clear pathway connecting the three parts. The Primary curriculum was based on the exploration of trans-disciplinary themes with a very clear route through the curriculum to guide, but not prescribe. The MYP was based on five interlocking circles representing Areas of Interaction: central was Approaches to Learning; then Community and Service; Health and Social Education; Environments; and Homo Faber (human ingenuity). On the outer edge were the subject areas – languages (mother tongue and others); technology; humanities; physical education; science; the arts; and mathematics. This programme aimed to show that, given the information revolution, skills and attitudes are more important than the massing of knowledge and knowledge is holistic.

The early years of this programme encouraged diversity of approach and were heady with enthusiasm and experimentation. However, whilst for many teachers it was an opportunity to explore their craft through the freedom of the framework, others were lost. Since many of the secondary teachers who set up the MYP were also Diploma teachers, there was a link to the higher level but virtually no connection to the PYP. There was need for revision from the points of view of rigour and assessment, but also in relation to continuity between the three parts of the IB curriculum.

A period of consultation and analysis produced a number of changes to promote consistency, ease of implementation, a clearer programme of assessment and congruence across the whole curriculum. The MYP, innovative and enterprising as it was, did not lead smoothly from PYP to

Diploma. Indeed, because of that very exciting spirit of innovation, it was interpreted in very different ways across the international spectrum. In 2010 a review was undertaken to provide not just a clearer structure that would lead to the Diploma but also make it more acceptable to national/ state systems (IB, 2011). The Learner Profile was adopted across all the programmes and the areas of interaction became specified global contexts that were a progression from the PYP's trans-disciplinary themes (see Harrison, 2015, for a detailed analysis of changes).

In 2014 a two level structure of conceptual understanding including key concepts and related concepts was introduced 'which identified certain ideas, complexes as having not only special relevance or relevance for the subject, but the power to connect across the disciplines' (*ibid*, 2015).

Aesthetics	Change	Communication	Communities
Connections	Creativity	Culture	Development
Form	Global interactions	Identity	Logic
Perspective	Relationships	Systems	Time, place and space

MYP 2014 Key Concepts (Harrison 2015)

The history teacher is presented not with fact and knowledge but with interesting topics, 'big ideas' to explore and debate. History is seen as interconnected with other subject areas and open to interpretation. Such an attitude to history teaching is in no way unique; most history teachers would claim such methodology as part of their teaching. However what is different is the stated aim to develop inter-cultural understanding through global contexts and establish international mindedness as the core of the curriculum framework.

MYP global context explorations encompass inter-cultural understanding, multilingualism and global challenges that exist in the realms of conflict, rights, environment, development and cooperation and governance.

> ...Combining concepts and contexts, the MYP is located securely
> within a strand of curriculum theory that emphasizes the importance
> of engaging students with real-world applications and relevant
> connections with (or challenging expansions of students' personal
> interests).

> *(ibid)*

Within this philosophical framework the IB history teacher has tremendous freedom to develop skills through a wide choice of topics, and subject matter that can be (and sometimes has to be) related to the location of the school. However, in spite of developments such as that described in Islamic studies, what can become the challenge and what is still a major criticism of the programme is that it sets forth a western interpretation and view of the past.

As one young Australian student said on being asked to write about her country in the Middle Ages (another western construct), "I can't do that, I hadn't been discovered." Teaching in English, using text books with origins in either Britain or the US, with a large proportion of history teachers coming from English speaking nations, the danger is always that history teaching regardless of the topic can become a view from the west, an interpretation based on the Enlightenment. It is here that the IB is dependent on the teacher's own will to overcome this and include post-colonial attitudes, global issues and also be willing to think international-mindedly.

It is important to note that as the IB programmes develop and spread there is an awareness of a constant need to adapt and react to changes both in education and in society. Change is not always seen as in the spirit of the original programme. The curriculum and its aims are in constant review. The introduction of examinations in order to firm up of methods of assessment is in process and not popular with all stakeholders. In 2006 George Walker stated that 'much of what we do is not really international education, it has been developed from a very influential Western humanist tradition of learning' (Walker, 2006). The emphasis on 'international mindedness' is one response; discussion of 'cultural awareness' is another.

A shift to considering history in relation to 'global studies' is an indication of the post-colonial thought aptly summed up by Conrad Hughes when he maintains that it is necessary for 'international education in practice to transcend its theoretical limitations' (Hughes 2009). This is possible in all the IB programmes, not just because an international school gives the teacher an opportunity to use the rich resources existing in the students in the classroom, but the curriculum demands that they do this.

Such pedagogical responsibilities require a special kind of teacher. An acknowledgement of this is present in the exploration of new methods of teacher training in Finland outlined by Professor Räsänen in chapter seven.

Conclusion

The National Curriculum of England and Wales illustrates how national pressures impact on curriculum and specifically on the teaching of history. The International Baccalaureate in contrast shows an attempt to produce an international programme for students of any nation. Yet these programmes can be complementary in a number of ways. That a great many schools across the world now have classes containing multiple nationalities with diverse histories has increased awareness that writers of text books and history teachers can no longer present a single view of the past.

Whilst international mindedness and a global view may bump up against the desire to give meaning to a national story and relate that to the idea of good citizenship, this need not be an either/or. If history is more than a narrated story but based on the skills of the historian to sift evidence, analyse outcomes and discuss a variety of interpretations, then there is the opportunity to include the 'mine' of a national message whilst acknowledging the 'ours' of a global view. It is possible to be a discerning historian as well as a good citizen.

References

Cambridge, J. (2013) 'Dilemmas of International Education: A Bernsteinian Analysis' Chapter 10 in International Education and Schools Ed, Pearce, R. Bloomsbury.

Consultation Response Form, Historical Association, Department of Education, 16.4.2013.

Dabashi, H.: (2015) Zed Books, *Can Non-Europeans Think?*

Ellwood, C.: (2012) *Learning and Teaching About Islam: Essays in Understanding*, John Catt Educational.

Ellwood, J.: (2001) unpublished PhD research survey.

Evans, R., Little England Folly at the Heart of History; *Financial Times* 7.2.2013.

Godfrey, J., 'Does 'global citizenship' really exist ?' *IS* Magazine Vol 17. Issue 1, John Catt Educational, September 2014.

Gustafson, L.S., 'The Big History Project', *International Schools Journal*, Vol. XXX111 No 2. April 2014, John Catt Educational.

Harrison, R. 'Evolving the IB Middle Years Programme :Curriculum'. *International Schools Journal* Vol.XXXIV No 2 2015, John Catt Educational.

Hill, I.: 'The International Baccalaureate: Pioneering in Education', *International Schools Journal Compendium*, John Catt Educational. 2010.

Hughes, C.: 'International Education and the International Baccalaureate Diploma Programme 'Journal of Research in International Education ' Vol 8 No 2, Sage.

Huxley. A.: *Brave New World*, Vintage Classics, 2004.

IB, MYP: Next Chapter Project Report, Cardiff International Baccalaureate, 2011.

IB, MYP: From Principles to Practice, Cardiff International Baccalaureate, 2014.

IB: Fostering Interdisciplinary Teaching and Learning in the MYP, Cardiff International Baccalaureate, 2014.

Joseph, K.: Address to Historical Association Conference, *TES*, 17.2.84.

Lewis, C.: 'International but not global; How international school curricula fail to address global issues and how things must change', *International Schools Journal*,Vol XXV No 2, John Catt Educational, 2006.

Lloyd Parry, R.: 'History is rewritten for Japanese Pupils', *The Times*, 8.3. 15.

Marshall, H.: 'The Global Education Terminology Debate: Exploring Some of the Issues', in *The Sage Handbook of Research in International Education*, London, Sage Publications Ltd. 2007.

Morgan, N.: Commons Education Select Committee on Education, 15. 10.2014.

Nehru, J. L.: 'Tryst with Destiny', Independence Speech en.wikipedia.org/wiki/ 7.9.15.

Nyerere, J.: Speech to Conference on African History, 1963.

The National Curriculum 2013. www.gov.uk/government/collections/national-curriculum accessed 15.8.15.

Orwell, G.: *1984*, Penguin Books, 2008.

Peterson, A D.C.: 'Schools Across Frontiers', Open Court. 1987.

Said, E.W.: *Orientalism*, Penguin Books. 1978.

Shropshire, O.: *The teaching of History in English School*, Columbia University, 1936.

Tarc, P.: *Global Dreams, Enduring Tensions: International Baccalaureate in a Changing World*, New York, Peter Lang. 2009.

Turner, J.: 'Our children are being tested to destruction', *The Times*, 18. 5.2015.

Walker, G.: *Educating the Global Citizen*, John Catt Educational. 2006.

Walker, G.: 'The Changing Face of International Education, Challenges for the IB', International Baccalaureate. 2011.

Chapter 10

The Cambridge approach to supporting history instruction and assessment in schools

Rebecca Conway & Jack Higginson

In 1858 candidates in England sat the first University of Cambridge local examinations. History formed a compulsory part of the assessment (Shaw and Cooke, 2010). The questions tested knowledge of the English monarchy ('Give a list of the sovereigns of England from Richard I to Richard II, inclusive, stating the title of each monarch to the throne'), wars and political events ('Name some of the chief battles in the wars between England and Scotland, with their results. When was the Act of Union passed?') and figures from English history ('In what reigns did the following persons live, and for what were they famous: Sir Thomas More, Chaucer, Titus Oates, Edmund Burke, John Hampden, Sir Walter Raleigh, Thomas a Becket') (UCLES, 2010, pp. 27-28, 70-71). Candidates were expected to recall knowledge but not explicitly required to demonstrate any other historical skills.

These early examinations were developed in a period when history was beginning to emerge as an academic discipline in Britain with only a handful of undergraduate degree courses available, no professional organisations for historians nor history teachers and no formal guidance on what should be taught (Cannadine, Keating and Sheldon, 2011). An 1889 article by Oscar Browning, the education reformer and former schoolteacher, discussed how history should be taught for success in Victorian examinations. He decried the apparently common practice of working through a textbook, learning by rote, as 'the very worst method of teaching history' (Browning, 1889, p. 70).

Instead Browning called for history teaching to be delivered with 'less minute attention to individual facts, and with more regard to the sequence and connection of the facts' (1889, p. 79), a prescient statement in support of developing chronology and narrative. Examiner's reports from the 1890s show a gradual change in expectations, from recital of factual knowledge to construction of historical explanation, and even critical assessment of events.

In 1899 examiners commented that 'It was noticeable that few candidates attempted explanation of the *reasons for the importance* of the reign of Edward I', though these reports suggest an inconsistent approach with comments elsewhere critiquing candidate's factual recital, 'excellent *short biographies* of Beckett were written; the *chief facts* of the life of Wiclif (*sic*) were less well known' (UCLES, 1900, own emphasis).

A school in Trinidad became the first overseas centre to offer Cambridge examinations (Watts, 2010). In 1867, six students were recorded, answering questions on Henry II, George I and II, the history of Ireland under British rule and the 'principal outbreaks of the lower orders of society in England' (UCLES, 1868, p. 38). Questions with local content were not set. Entries by overseas centres grew slowly, with approximately 370 candidates by the end of the century, and their names suggest that they were principally the children of British expatriates (Shaw and Cooke, 2010).

In 1918 the School Certificate was introduced in Britain. Candidates attempting the School Certificate were offered a broader choice of papers – Modern European History, Greek History, Roman History and The History of the British Empire. This choice reflected a growing understanding of the differing needs of candidates engaging with the assessments in different geographical areas. A Joint Committee for Overseas Examinations was established in 1933 to further consider the requirements of international candidates.

Initial steps into localisation were also taken with the development of schemes in Nigeria and Malaya to set and mark examinations locally (Watts, 2010). At the same time, some of the questions on the examinations reflected a growing understanding of the importance of historical skills. For example, one question from the Modern History paper in 1926 asked learners to evaluate a statement about the reputation of Napoleon I: 'Napoleon I has been described as the "enemy of mankind". Do you consider this description to be justified? Give your reasons' (UCLES, 1927, p. 37).

The School Certificate was phased out in Britain after the Second World War in favour of the new GCE O Level (first assessed in 1951), but the Certificate was retained for the international market. Cambridge made some changes to enable continued comparability with British qualifications and, crucially, to ensure that they were suitable for candidates based in different geographical areas (Lacey, 2010).

By 1955, candidates could choose six different history papers as part of the School Certificate: British and European History (1066-1920), British and European History (1871-1939), History of the British Empire and Commonwealth, Indian history, Indo-Pakistan history (for candidates in Pakistan), the Development of Tropical Africa (UCLES, 1956). Cambridge generally produced the syllabuses and examination papers and sought specialist input from local schools, ministries or other educational institutions to ensure their appropriateness for overseas markets (Minutes of the Advisory Committee for Overseas Examinations).

A 1961 summary written by the Secretary of the Local Examinations Syndicate provides a snapshot of the early Cambridge localisation projects in West Africa, the Sudan, Malaya, and India. The earliest of these was the West African Examinations Council, founded in 1952 by governments in the Gold Coast (now Ghana), the Gambia, Nigeria and Sierra Leone. At the time of writing, the Council was on target to complete one-third of the marking for the qualification and one-quarter of the setting, but conducted the West African School Certificate jointly with Cambridge (Notes on the Formation of the Oversea Examination Council).

An alternative type of localisation developed in India with the establishment of the Council for the Indian School Certificate in 1959. Rather than seek to take on the responsibility for setting and marking assessments, this organisation advised Cambridge on the examinations taken in different Indian states, set up committees with representatives from schools, established subject panels and performed administrative work on behalf of Cambridge (Notes on the Formation of the Oversea Examination Council).

Cambridge gave training on assessment processes including marking and administration. The Syndicate's 1966 Annual Report outlined training events that had been conducted over the preceding 12 months for examiners and ministry officials from Nigeria, Ghana, Malaysia, Hong Kong and the Sudan with additional support on standard setting and awarding provided in Khartoum. This mixed-economy approach to localisation continues today with some partners requiring on-going support in setting and marking assessments, while others join Cambridge with the intention of building their own awarding organisation to create and mark their own assessments.

The development of the International General Certificate of Education (IGCSE) for first teaching in 1988 coincided with the development of GCSE and the National Curriculum in England, Wales and Northern Ireland. Some features of IGCSE history furthered developments already introduced in the O Level during the 1980s, such as the use of pictorial sources, but in other ways IGCSEs presented a radical departure from what had gone before.

Candidates were awarded marks for evaluating source material and determining what a historian might learn from it. Questions were scaffolded into sub-questions that tested particular skills, and the assessment was marked using a 'level of response' mark scheme with strands representing different skills. At the highest levels, candidates were awarded marks for discussing competing historical interpretations.

The 'new history' approach that assessed candidates skills and understanding of history as a discipline was controversial when it was introduced in the UK. The idea that that school-aged learners could be assessed on their ability to interpret evidence and question historical interpretations, rather than learning about accepted interpretations, was seen as inappropriate and even dangerously relativistic by some observers (Sheldon, 2011). Despite a perceived change in emphasis on learning established historical facts, chronology and views, the IGCSE still tested knowledge in practice.

The developments introduced by Cambridge through the IGCSE were intended primarily for British-pattern international schools, with IGCSE papers having different content and topics, but the same scheme of assessment as the GCSE. However, Cambridge recognised that it was not appropriate to assert this approach to delivery and assessment on overseas partners, such as government ministries. The O Level would 'continue to be offered in and after 1988' (UCLES, 1985, p. 1).

At first, it was thought that the IGCSE would provide '[a] syllabus appropriate for a wider ability range ... while maintaining Ordinary Level standards of the more able candidates' (UCLES, 1985, pp. 8-9). However, the skills and approach to history first assessed by Cambridge in the IGCSE have subsequently been cascaded into other qualifications. Localisation since 1988 has resulted in some countries such as Lesotho and the Bahamas operating their own versions of the IGCSE. These qualifications assess content on international history in a similar way to the Cambridge IGCSE but with the addition of questions focussing on content pertinent to those countries, so as to protect the teaching of national histories. O Level History itself has been redeveloped to include a second component, requiring critical evaluation of sources.

The sense that Cambridge exports an understanding of the purpose of history and an implied pedagogy is, in part, conscious. It was felt at the time of the introduction of IGCSE that 'there is a desire for a system of assessment that is in step with developments in the UK' (UCLES, 1985, p. 2). However, the approach to history and the content of history curricula for countries with which Cambridge works in partnership with government ministries is not unidirectional; the development is a cooperative effort. Within a history syllabus, it is the aims and content that determine the teaching, whereas the assessment objectives determine how those aims and that content will be examined.

In many cases, the aims and much of the content are written by partner organisations, whereas Cambridge provides more input on assessment objectives. History specialists in-country provide input about the appropriateness of the assessment and syllabus coverage from the beginning of the development. Nevertheless, an awareness of the pedagogical, political and cultural implications of syllabuses is required. Sometimes these relate to content: during the development of an American history syllabus, attempts to include the study of influential immigrant groups were difficult because of the impossibility of naming every such group and the possible offence caused by not doing so, as well as the impossibility of subsequently assessing or teaching the material. Questions related to disputed areas of the world, such as Kashmir or Israel/Palestine are set, but care is taken in questions to avoid making political judgements, whilst retaining assessment standards.

In other cases the challenges faced are more subtle. During the development of a syllabus for an Asian partner, Cambridge responded to concerns that an examination on the history of south-east Asia had previously featured mainly Western sources, such as American newspapers' comments on south-east Asian affairs. These sources viewed the affairs of south-east Asia through a prism of Western priorities, such as the Cold War. Inclusion of such material on examination papers effectively required candidates to be taught about these concerns in addition to the syllabus content, though the concerns of the partner were with regard to fairness of the assessment, rather than implicit hegemony of historical narrative. The partner agrees that the history examination should assess skills such as critical evaluation of sources in addition to learning about the events of the past of that nation and others in the region.

In other instances the challenges have revolved around different definitions of what is meant by 'history' and the function played by history teaching. Redeveloping a history syllabus with an African partner, Cambridge suggested improving the reliability and scope of the examination by including source analysis and an increased focus on international history in addition to the events of the history of the nation concerned. The partner was concerned that this would diminish learners' knowledge of their national history, and was not keen on source analysis, with which their teachers had no experience.

The difference in approach between Cambridge and this partner is perhaps explained by differing conceptions of the definition and function of 'history'. The partner was concerned that pupils have a working knowledge of the historic events of that country. The perceived function of this was limited but focused around the growing heritage and tourism sectors in that country, and to a lesser extent, fostering a sense of national unity. In promoting skills development and the teaching of history as a process and a discipline, Cambridge was presenting an approach that has its origins in the economic and political priorities of a developed nation. Nevertheless this does not mean that such an approach is not valid; there is a fine line between the promotion of good practice and pedagogical imperialism.

References

Published sources

Browning, O. (1889). The Teaching of History in Schools. *Transactions of the Royal Historical Society* 4, 69-84.

Cannadine, D., Keating, J., & Sheldon, N. (2011). *The Right Kind of History: Teaching the past in twentieth-century England*. Basingstoke, UK: Palgrave Macmillan.

Hunt, T. (2011). The Importance of Studying the Past. *History Workshop Journal*, 72 (1), 258-267.

Lacey, G. (2008). International Examinations after 1945. In S. Raban (Ed.), *Examining the World: A of the UCLES* (pp. 106-130). Cambridge: Cambridge University Press.

Raban, S. (2008). Introduction. In S. Raban (Ed.), *Examining the World: A history of the UCLES* (pp. 1-11). Cambridge: Cambridge University Press.

Sheldon, N. (2011). *The National Curriculum and the Changing Face of School History* 1988-2010. *History in Education Project*. Retrieved from www.history.ac.uk/history.../history.../a_history_of_school_history_1988- 2010.doc

Shaw, S. and Cooke, G. (2010). The Evolution of International Examinations: An analysis of history question papers for 16 year olds from 1858 to the present. *Research Matters* 9, 11-18.

UCLES. (1868). *1867 Examination Papers*. London: Cambridge University Press.

UCLES (1900). *42nd Annual Report*. London: Cambridge University Press.

UCLES. (1927). *1926 Examination Papers*. London: Cambridge University Press.

UCLES. (1957). *1957 Examination Papers*. London: Cambridge University Press.

UCLES. (1966). *108th Annual Report*. London: Cambridge University Press.

UCLES. (1985). *Discussion Paper: International Certificate of Education*, Cambridge Assessment Group Archives, JSH/RL/S6/JSH1/A.

UCLES. (2008). *1858 Examination Papers*. Cambridge: UCLES.

Unpublished Sources

Cambridge Assessment Group Archives.

Minutes of the Advisory Committee for Overseas Examinations, C/ACOE 2/1.

Notes on the Formation of Oversea Examination Council, PP/TSW 4/11.

Minutes of the History Subject Committee, 1947, S/H2/1.

Chapter 11

Dangerous interpretations in post conflict history teaching

Paul Regan

The contemporary world of geopolitics is a mess of contradictions; the nation state is both supreme and ubiquitous on the one hand, but vulnerable to sabotage and terrorism on the other; whilst new technologies promise a brave new world on the cusp of an information-based and genetically enhanced golden age, divisive and sometimes primitive ideologies are causing misery and chaos and have never seemed so active or so powerful. Superficially, at a global level, we seem to be moving closer to each other in values, behaviours and norms, but we are also regularly confronted by ancient appeals to nation, creed and race.

The pursuit of difference dominates our political debates. The global citizen, cosmopolitan and tolerant, cannot, nevertheless, be confident in the status of her citizenship and may not always be able to identify who are her co-citizens. As wars between states become rarer, conflicts inside states become the new norm. If the study of the past can guide us to future action then educators in areas of conflict or post conflict have the role of peacemaker thrust upon them whether they are willing or not.

It is important for historians to try to understand why the world is simultaneously drifting apart on one level and coming together on another level, and whether one direction will take precedence over the other. An understanding of how conflicts break out in the first pace is the first step towards preventing similar conflicts from repeating. Conflicts within states tend to be more vicious and costly in relative terms than wars between states. This is principally because all sides often attack personal and shared values, and even identities, rather than merely interests. This can result in a zero sum game when the dominance or superiority of one is based exclusively on the inferiority or repression of the other.

The Ancient Greek city-state of Sparta was an early example of an utterly exclusive caste which was able to hold military dominion for more than two centuries thanks to its enslavement of an entire population of fellow Greeks called Helots. The terrifying return of caste-based politics in the 20th century in the form of Nazism in Germany (Arians), Communism in Russia and China (the Proletariat), Apartheid in South Africa and the Southern USA (Whites), for example, has given way to a growing demand for inclusion and acceptance which has come to define the age we now live in. Because issues that divide peoples may not relate to negotiable interests such as land, economy, or resources, there is often little room for negotiation to prevent violence and less room later for peaceful resolution. Appeals to different historical interpretations, when not based on a mutual desire for truth and reconciliation, may dredge up myths and symbols rather than evidence and proof.

History as a study of past events is rarely approached dispassionately even by seasoned historians. How tempting must it be then to use history to appeal to emotions, and passions and to stoke fires of hatred and suspicion rather than of shared reflection? In fact, as we shall see, it is possible for a person to adhere to two competing narratives simultaneously, the one to satisfy one's place in the community and the other to satisfy a desire for truth. This is a trap of sorts for all history teachers.

Our current patchwork of global conflicts is proof that whilst theoretically the struggle for independence, recognition, enfranchisement or equality is a noble one, in reality diplomacy and dialogue are too easily set aside for the apparent quick fix of terror and violence. We are daily witnesses also to the evidence that whilst the fear of change and of loss of status which confers privilege is also understandable, it is becoming increasingly improbable that violent repression can ever get things back to what they once were. The prolonged war in Syria for example is so mindless because it lacks any hint of compromise from any party, or willingness to settle for intermediate goals or to search for common interests.

Whilst it appears the case that so few are able to heed the lessons of history, we do need to examine the rare successes, the little battalions of peacemakers, the concepts and terms that frame the conversations and negotiations, that permit opposing sides to begin to comprehend, and to share at least some common space. If we can do this, then we should apply them relentlessly wherever possible. The big picture, our *zeitgeist*, is that not only does the majority across the world now want its place in the sun (that has always been the case), but that the many also know where the sun is and how strongly it is shining. As a socio-political phenomenon it can be compared to the struggle for the franchise and for self-determination that continued throughout the 19th and 20th centuries.

The conflicts that defined many of the now developed modern nation states, the Thirty Years War in Germany (ended 1648), the Civil Wars in England (1641-1649), the USA (1861-1865) and Russia (1918-1921), are now being enacted in different ways over a huge swathe of land stretching across Saharan Africa through the Middle East to Afghanistan and Pakistan, its tentacles spreading southward to Nigeria and the Horn of Africa. Even prosperous Europe is not immune, and the recent war in the former Yugoslavia between 1992 and 1995 contained all the usual ingredients of intra-state violence. These included genocide, rape and torture, mass displacement, and population exodus. Much of this is being copied with depressing regularity at the present time elsewhere. The number of such conflicts is rising, casualties are also rising and humanitarian crises proliferate. Depressingly, there is a loss of nerve or will to fix the causes both from within and without borders.

It is fair to note that, for the most part, conflicts have been brought to an end in Central and South America (if we discount drug wars and gang violence), the Far East in Indonesia, Vietnam, and Cambodia, and in South Asia in Sri Lanka. Additionally, peaceful revolutions have been achieved against the odds in the USA and South Africa to end racial segregation. Conflicts that once seemed interminable in their day (Bosnia and Rwanda in the 1990s for example) were ended and have not broken out again. But to be complacent about this would be to miss the point.

It is not sufficient to end any one conflict or to be content with peace in one region. The enormous challenge for our current generations is both to end all conflicts and to prevent all future conflicts. If that bar seems to be impossibly high, historical precedents can be invoked. Who now, other than the criminally disturbed, would approve even in their hearts of the slavery of even one individual let alone the millions who were legally enslaved right up to the time of our great grand parents? The ISIS group operating in Syria and Iraq have distinguished themselves for barbarity and for amongst other things espousing and practising the slavery of subjected non Muslim populations such as the Yazidis, and the monetization of captured women. In this they are unique even amongst other terrorist organizations such as Al Qaeda.

Religious difference and prejudices, and especially different interpretations of Islam by Shia and Sunnis now dominate the field of human conflict and are often conflated with less intractable difference caused by territorial disputes or claims to resources. This new (for our time) phenomenon has arisen not only because of deeply held religious beliefs *per se* but equally because of power vacuums, and socio-political uncertainty in the wake of war or insurrection. The Soviet invasion of Afghanistan, in 1979, the USA-led invasions of Iraq and Afghanistan in 2003 and the dethroning of Gadhafi in Libya have opened up wounds in much the same way as the collapse of Communism and the Soviet Bloc did to the communities in Yugoslavia. They seem to be interminable and, to outsiders at least, incomprehensible. History informs us that eventually there will be a peace of sorts due to a victory of one side over the other, international interventions, exhaustion of all parties, a peace agreement, or a combination of all of these.

But what happens then? Numerous studies of societies in conflict, emerging from conflict or post conflict, once local peculiarities are taken into account, converge on a small number of common conditions that will determine the likelihood of a return to hostilities within ten years. Unsurprisingly, a key factor is whether one or more sides continues to harbour grievances or to feel oppressed. This might be due to an incomplete peace process, a lack of commitment from one or more sides to maintain the peace or indeed a lack of means to maintain the peace where there is a will to do so.

Given this, what is of most interest to educators is the degree to which education in general can play its part in the promotion of security, resolution of continuing grievances and peaceful co-existence. A commitment to quality education where that is taken to mean access to a school up to at least secondary level, reform of textbooks, teacher training, adequate resources and common approaches to teaching and learning, is shown in all cases to mitigate the possibility of future conflict.

Conversely, where any one of these factors is not in place, or where education is divisive either in terms of its provision, administration or its content, then the opposite will prevail. Unsurprisingly, it is the different approaches to the teaching of the social sciences, languages, literature and history which are more likely to have an effect on attitudes towards former enemies than the teaching of natural sciences and mathematics which are to a much greater extent value neutral. Teachers, and especially history teachers, have to accept that they have a role which goes way beyond the classroom in terms of impact.

It is not an exaggeration to state that history can be manipulated more than all other disciplines to affect young minds. Even the most advance democracies (the UK as an example), have until fairly recently, regarded the subject as fair game to inspire patriotism and allegiance and to promote a one-sided narrative of progress and superiority. Although that approach has largely been set aside in favour of a more balanced and broader narrative in addition to a more forensic examination of the facts, there are frequent accusations from politicians and some sections of the press alike that a more nuanced skills-based pedagogy leads to relativism and decline.

Of course, all democracies wish to promote democratic values, theocracies wish to promote religious values, and all successful states wish to present their histories in a positive light. Even were it the case, as in Germany, that there is no attempt to deny the darkest periods in its past, there is still room for the values or trends of today to be reflected in the lessons from yesterday. But what both mature democratic states and weaker or failed states have in common is the degree to which some of its own citizens are excluded or made to feel excluded from their own history. Whether states are successful or not in confronting alienation, the degree of removal will have a directly proportional influence on political instability in the future. This may not of course necessarily be in the form of open conflict as much as individually based acts of protest as we see happening today across Europe.

There clearly is not a single template that can be applied to any region or state emerging from conflict, nor will there ever be. Empirically, there are huge differences. Some states, like South Africa and Rwanda, initially abolished the teaching of history altogether while wounds were given time to heal through various processes of peace and reconciliation. At a later date, history teaching was reintroduced. There are also factors that affect even the best and most inclusive history teaching. How long after the end of a conflict is it safe or practicable for students to discuss or study it? Five to ten years is probably too early since students will retain some direct memories. Even after ten years, whilst memories of the events will not be fresh, there will be latent prejudices handed down from parents and communities. What is the best age for students to be encouraged to study a recent conflict?

Evidence is emerging that very young students can be the most receptive. In Northern Ireland, emerging from the Troubles which lasted from 1979 and were brought to an end with the Good Friday agreement in 1998, where textbooks were being comprehensively revised even before the conflict had been resolved, attitudes are now slowly changing a generation later. In Finland, which experienced a brief civil war in 1919, it is unthinkable that such a conflict could be repeated. Finland developed early on a methodology of history teaching which encouraged students to make judgments about the most plausible interpretations based on the facts as they were discovered rather than on appeal to emotion and bias. In this, it has been a pioneer in successfully allowing all parties to a previous conflict to see themselves as equal players in the national story.

Whilst it is instructive to look at successful approaches to history teaching, it is equally instructive to look at failures, deliberate or otherwise. The post conflict context to education in Bosnia and Herzegovina in the years following the 1995 Dayton Peace agreement serve to illustrate the latter.

Bosnia and Herzegovina today is still a divided country. It is not at war and it seems increasingly unlikely that it will return to war, but it is hardly a successful state or even a normally functioning state. Under the terms of the Dayton Peace Agreement, brokered by the USA, which brought the wars in Serbia, Bosnia and Croatia to an end in 1995, Bosnia itself was split into two entities, the Bosnian Federation and the Serb Republic. This settlement imposed an institutional freeze on the ethno-religious separation between Serbs and Bosniaks (Bosnian Muslims) on the one hand and acknowledged the political fracture between Bosniaks and Croatians (Catholics) on the other.

But ten years after Dayton, Bosnia remained a deeply divided nation permanently on the edge of disintegration and economic collapse. The fact that it had received more international funding than any other state in history per unit of population is indicative of serious errors in the settlement and its objectives. As late as ten years later, its bombed-out cities were a physical reminder that not only the political divisions ran deep but so did individuals, their communities and institutions. The failure to prioritize the importance of education in 1995 followed by a second failure to revise it in 2001 was a tragic mistake and with hindsight quite inexcusable.

In fact, so keen were the peace brokers to cement the *status quo* and to allow the cantonal administrative structure to remain in place, they nodded through the very educational framework most likely to keep the divisions festering into the future. It is important to remember that until the outbreak of War in 1992, Yugoslavia had been a more or less united country. Regardless of religious or ethnic affiliation, people spoke the same language (Serbo-Croat), went to the same schools, studied the same curricula, (and the same history), supported the same football team, intermarried, and generally got on well together. The Post War Tito period came to be seen as a golden age, all the more remarkable after the internecine atrocities of the Second World War in which Serbian partisans (Chetniks) and Croat collaborators (Ustaze) had fought viciously against each other with the Bosniak Muslims forced to choose which side they were on.

After 1995, schooling came to reflect the reality of the settlement that acknowledged that Bosnian Muslims, Orthodox Serbs, and Catholic Croats would always stay disunited. In the predominantly Bosniak and Croat Federation, schools catered to one or the other affiliation and students who lived in the 'wrong area' would need to travel long distances to find the right school. Even in well meaning initiatives promoted by the Organization for Security and Cooperation in Europe (OSCE) such as 'two schools under one roof', which was an attempt to bring schools close together, students from different communities entered and exited through different doors, learned in different classrooms, and rarely if ever met socially.

Over the years, attempts have been made to mitigate the situation, and slow progress has been made. Increasing attention has been paid to the constitutions of mixed student councils, youth parliaments, mixed sessions in citizenship and human rights, but most of these are set up by outside agencies such as OSCE, sponsor governments, and NGOs. This begs the question of whether the real task of building local civic and institutional capacity would ever be achieved without international assistance.

Most seriously, the separate schools taught a separate curriculum. Education reform was put back by decades, teacher training, such as it was, was de-prioritized, and most forms of outreach were frowned upon. Text books were initially xenophobic, separate languages became mother tongues (Bosnian, Croatian and Serbian), and three distinct separate histories were taught in one country. Both sides adhered to the understandable fear that their history, culture, language, value system, and religious beliefs might be undermined by contact with the other side in the classroom.

Most empirical research focused on educational priorities in conflict scenarios agree that it is wise not to broach discussion of any recent conflict for at least a few years afterwards, and not until at least five years have elapsed since the end of hostilities. Attempts to do so could backfire when passions were still raw. However, some new history textbooks in Bosnia and Herzegovina used divisive and inciting language to describe the role of the other side during the conflict. Books aimed at teaching Croatian students were especially negative in their views of the other side. Religious and ethnic hatred, manipulated by a partisan press and politicians on all sides, which had helped to cause the war in the first place, were allowed to remain, and attempts to impose lawful change from outside by the Office of the High Representative were only partially successful.

Completely divergent versions of the war, sanctioned by the politically partisan education authorities, became the truth for the next generation. Bosnia and Herzegovina was a client state and head teachers were political appointees. Stories of atrocities, genocide denial, refusal to admit guilt, or to offer forgiveness were rampant. In the absence also of any context for reconciliation or truth other than the steady stream of cases passing through the International Criminal Court for former Yugoslavia based in Sarajevo, attitudes froze.

In a city like Mostar, the provincial capital of Herzegovina, which had an active Croatian minority, the town was completely divided along the front lines occupied at the end of the hostilities there. Mostar had experienced a war within a war in 1993, which had been fought for six months between Bosniaks and Croats whilst the bigger war against Serbia raged elsewhere: 1500 lives had been lost. The 1995 *status quo* was reinforced by the division of educational administration into 11 ministries of education, each with autonomy for devising curriculum content.

Amongst the international initiatives to undo some of the damage of the Post War settlement and to start at least some process of intergroup dialogue, the United World College, of which I was Founding Headteacher, was established in Mostar in 2006. Supported financially by pubic donations from governments (notably the Netherlands, Finland, Germany and Norway) by a handful of NGOs and private donations, and backed by OSCE, the school's specific aims were to enrol students from all three former Yugoslav national groups, in addition to students from other conflict areas (Rwanda, Palestine, and former Soviet bloc for example), and peaceful countries so that they could live and learn together in mixed residences, study the IB Diploma programme together over two years, and learn history together. It was a brave experiment in Post War education reconciliation. It was variously described as a lighthouse, a beacon and an oasis in a barren desert of division and suspicion.

A research programme carried out between 2008 and 2009 identified four main areas that were influential in promoting integration within the student body:

> Learning together in class.
> Shared student residences.
> Interacting with others from different cultures.
> Shared extracurricular activities.
> (Hayden and Thompson, 2011; Hayden and Thompson, 2012)

It found that the college had met with some notable successes in changing attitude of students, although the caveat must be made that the students themselves were self-selected and may not have been typical of their contemporaries. Still, it was a good start. Unsurprisingly, success was more limited when it came to influencing wider communities of parents, students of other schools, the media, other educational institutions, and the education ministries themselves.

The school became the third school in the Mostar Gymnasia that had been one of the 'two school under one roof'. The financial sponsors had attached numerous naïve time-limited expectations to their generous grants. They failed to see the limitations of trying to influence and change attitudes from outside, or to sufficiently acknowledge the stubborn nature of prejudice, once it has been allowed to fester. This may be less true today than it was in 2006 when the first generations of students would have been alive during the conflict and would have been raised to vivid stories from their parents and other relatives and community figures, not to mention their media and previous teachers.

Importantly, history was taught as a discrete subject on the curriculum, but in effect, the unique and to some extent experimental situation created a sense in which students and teachers were not only living through history but also interpreting it on a daily basis. According to the 'contact hypothesis' of Alpert (1988), prejudice between groups may be reduced where a number of key conditions are present: equal group status as perceived by the members of all of the groups; common goals, shared across and between groups; inter group cooperation, involving collaboration rather than competition; and the support of authority. All of the above were present in the school as it tried with varying degrees of success to foster at least a willingness to listen and to learn from views that may be opposed to one's own.

The school also grappled with three philosophical objectives; to pursue the truth; to think critically; and to be open to alternative perspectives of historical reality. These three concepts, critical thinking, truth, and multi-perspectivity, are intrinsically problematic however. All of them would be explicitly reinforced as part of the history discipline, without being used necessarily to address the events of the 1992-1995 conflicts. The Spanish Civil War, the Versailles Agreement, the Cold War and other modern aspects of war, received the same forensic treatment as would be applied to any future discussion of the Bosnian conflict. History came to be seen therefore as the teaching of a range of higher order skills such as analysis, evaluation, scepticism, ordering of facts, and selection from a range of alternatives interpretations on the basis of the evidence rather than on personal ideology or conviction.

Critical thinking involves all of these tasks, but all of us know how conveniently we can set it aside if the occasion demands, deciding to think critically (and therefore objectively), when the occasion suits us. In fact we can all hold two alterative interpretations simultaneously without feeling in any way upset by ambiguity. Whilst accepting that one action or another will probably have contributed to a specific atrocity, (the 1995 massacre of Srebrenica for example), students could hold tenaciously to the more emotional (*ie* subjective) view that the atrocity did not take place, or not in the way it was portrayed by the other side.

In fact most of us are capable of this kind of woolly thinking when it suits us. How many times do we become emotional and excited by the outward symbols of nationhood or religious practice such as national anthems, raising of flags, stories of battles won, and victories against the odds, prayers and invocations, and choose to temporarily set aside the alternative perspectives of those who might be excluded by those same symbols and fictions. Such is the raw material of propaganda, benign or otherwise! The true critical thinker treats each knowledge claim with scepticism not as a nihilist in order to deny the truth but as a philosopher who wishes to find it.

Equally problematic is the concept of multi-perspectivity. Whilst it seems uncontroversial that students of history should approach each period, event, or trend, with a mind open to all possibilities, in fact this can rarely be the case. Just as a scientist, whose observance of experiments affects the outcome of those experiments, historians and teachers and students of history will approach most topics already primed with a context or a personal view of history. This might be in the form of a national story, a belief in human progress, belief in cyclical events, adherence to a current ideology or religious belief, or just some vaguely connected bits of prior knowledge.

Furthermore, it is easy for opponents of this more open approach to accuse its proponents of relativistic thinking leading in many cases to the charge of moral relativism. But multi-perspectivity, if it is properly understood, does not equate to relativism since it makes no prior claims to the truth nor does it give equal weight to opposing views. On the one hand, it encourages discussion, and a more open frame of mind. On the other, it allows for the development of skills as set out above to enable the student to make judgements based on evidence of bias and biased evidence.

Both critical thinking and multi-perspectivity rely on the truth and on some shared agreement about what the truth actually means. This is where misunderstanding can easily occur. Common sense and intuition tell us that there can only be one truth. For some the truth may be out there waiting to be discovered either though religious revelation or scientific progress. In applying this to the study of history, it seems obvious that, regardless of individual perspectives, all of them will be wrong except the one that is true. (Or they will all be wrong until the truthful one is discovered?) If one adheres to this idea of the truth, then even a multi-perspectival approach to history will be limited to at least listening politely to what someone else has to say, There will still be one correct history and only one possible correct interpretation.

Another way to address this is to argue that there is no truth at all. Any perspective, if argued well and based on evidence can aspire to the truth, in which case all claims to the truth are equally valid. If there is no truth, then there is no falsehood and that is clearly not right. So the history teacher is therefore trapped between the Scylla of absolutism, leading to the kind of prejudice whereby there are only winners and losers, and the Charybdis of relativism, wherein different schools can teach their own version of history as the truth regardless of other claims.

'We cannot really search unless we admit we are really lost' (John Caputo, 2013). Removing the claim to certainty may be the first step to knowledge and understanding and this might be a good start for the first history lesson. There is of course a middle way and one that can be more easily adapted to the situation in the history classroom. This is to agree with the class some reasonable definition of the truth that works. Students easily accept scientifically derived laws of nature mostly without protest because they are seen to work and to be evidently correct. Mathematics likewise possesses accepted truths that work every time, and so appears to be necessary and fixed rather than contingent and local. It seems that numbers cannot have happened otherwise, It is not possible to envisage 2+2 ever coming to anything other than 4.

We could all agree that what we believe to be truths are in fact interpretations. Of course there is the plain fact that a fact is a fact. If 8000 people were killed at Srebrenica, and the corpses of the dead have been found, then it is foolish to deny the fact. The more that students can become experts at judging the plausibility of explanations, then the more they will be able to understand other perspectives. History teaching therefore comes down to creating the thinking and critical skills needed to make those judgements and to get the evidence as close as possible to the certainties that are familiar to mathematicians.

But is that enough? Evidently not, since those judgements may, as stated earlier, sit alongside other kinds of judgements based on different criteria. How then can a multi-perspectival approach to history teaching, based on a shared notion of the truth however limited in scope, lead to a change in attitudes and eventually to peace?

The early experience of the United World College showed that it was very difficult but not impossible to modify attitudes through dialogue. Does the experience of studying in the same room with the child of your parent's former enemy do enough to open up minds to a different interpretation? Can more than one interpretation be allowed to co-exist without creating animosity and sowing the seeds for further conflict? Which lessons can be learned?

First, it is clear and evident that time plays the key role. As memories of conflict recede, attitudes can harden one way or another. Schools that remain divided and teach different histories will only make matters worse. Since the time is not being used to soften or to acknowledge nuances of interpretation, blame and enmity remain and can lie dormant until the next opportunity to break out into factionalism and violence whether on the football field or on the front line. On the other hand, if the time can be used to encourage dialogue in a shared, safe place, then there is at least a chance that prejudice will start to break down over time.

Secondly, teachers can never assume that discussion itself is enough. It is necessary but not sufficient. Discussion must be guided, terms must be set, and agreements made on ways of speaking and listening which are acceptable or not. Resorting to stereotypes, negative and insulting phrases, jokes, and broad judgements should always be forbidden by the agreed rules of engagement.

Thirdly the teacher must be a role model. Teacher training should be aimed not just at methodology and content but also at character. If the teacher is seen as being committed to fairness, to listening, to slowness to judge, and a readiness to listen and include, then students will take their cue from that. This is especially difficult for history teachers who may resent the added expectations placed upon them.

Fourthly, students do better to look at historical conflicts other than their own. The UWC in Mostar was able to hold discussions about other conflicts (for example between Israel and Palestine) and between students from those countries. Once students can see the generic nature of conflict and the role of history in manipulation or in reconciliation, they are more inclined and able to stand back and make better sense of their own conflicts.

Fifthly, teachers should never underestimate the emotions that colour our judgements especially when the memory is raw and recent. Rather than ignore them they would do better to utilize and manage those passions, to give them their day and to bear witness to what students have to say. This is the stuff of reconciliation. Invariably, when such risks are taken, tempers my flare up, but fear of this happening should not prevent the attempt since the rewards can be great.

And finally, the pursuit of truth itself, though noble, is laden with uncertainty and confusion. Given that no two persons are likely to agree on a definition of truth that will suffice in all places and circumstances, it is better to continually return to the notion of truth and to how it has been viewed through the ages. How can a historian discover the truth if she does not have a firm idea of what truth is? Philosophy should be taught alongside history since one cannot exist let alone flourish without the other.

Conclusion

It would seem naive to foresee a time when we will have placed all conflicts behind us. Certainly not in the biological age of man will this be achieved since the roots of conflict lie in the dazzling complexity and range of our mental universe. However, almost all of those civilians who have experienced any form of conflict will wish for peace for the rest of their lives. Therefore educators owe it to those people to make that possible since education can be the key to peace and resolution. History does have a special role to play in this, since it is the subject with the greatest potential to guide young minds either way. It can lead towards lasting prejudice or towards openness, fairness and readiness for dialogue and diplomacy.

Whist the current conflicts in the Middle East and parts of Africa now seem interminable, in reality they are not. In time they too will end, and educators will have the role assigned to them by peacemakers to build consensuses. The great work that has been done by history teachers in many parts of the world is little appreciated. Their expertise will be sorely needed in the years to come.

References

Allport, G (1988) : The Nature of Prejudice. Reading:Addison-Wesley.

Hayden, M. C. and Thompson, J. J., (2010): Student Integration in Bosnia and Herzegovina: A Study of the United World College in Herzegovina.

Mostar.Reading: CfBTEductionTrust Online:www.cfbt.co./evidenceforeducation/pdf/06_Bosnia_Report.pdf

Hayden, M. and Thompson, J. J., 2012. Improving intercultural understanding: a case study of the United World College in Mostar. *In*: Ellwood, C., ed. *Learning and teaching about Islam: essays in understanding.* Woodbridge: John Catt Educational Ltd, pp. 45-57.

Chapter 12

Past present: drama and theatre strategies for bringing the past to life in the history classroom

Dinos Aristidou

Introduction

Drama is a powerful tool for inquiry-based learning. This art form gives students the opportunity to examine the world, develop their conceptual understandings and express their ideas and learning. Its value and power lies in the fact that it brings abstract concepts and ideas to life and makes them concrete and tangible. Drama and theatre cannot help but address the human condition and the world around us – what it means to be of the world, to live in the world and to live with each other. In addition, and relevant to the use of drama and theatre in history, is the fact that because theatre is *live*, it takes place in the present, *as if* it is happening now. It therefore has the power to bring the past into the present, transforming the *then* into the *now*.

History, like drama, also deals with humanity, our actions, interactions and the impact these have had on the world. Among the many skills required of the historian is the ability to look at the world through different perspectives – be they of another time or another place – in order to piece together a narrative that will provide us with insight and understanding into events we have not been part of or witnessed.

One of the most obvious and most commonly used forms of drama is the re-enactment or reconstruction of particular events in history. These may be battles, or scenes showing the everyday lives of people in the past. Though these may be useful, especially in giving students a physical sense of a past situation, they run the risk of encouraging playacting, a form of performance which focuses primarily on the external and the superficial.

Playacting is enjoyable but has more in common with play than it does with acting. It is often a good way to start, especially if the aim is to give students a sense of the spatial (dimensions) or the physical (movement) of, for example, the medieval hall, the battlefield, the prison cell. However because it focuses on the physical and the external this is not the most effective drama form for developing conceptual understandings or giving students alternative perspectives of a situation.

Theatre is the creation of alternate realities. By alternate I mean fictional worlds that sit within and are presented in our world. In terms of live theatre the two worlds co-exist and by doing so reference each other. Experiencing two worlds simultaneously gives us the ability to come to a better understanding of each by viewing each from the perspective of the other. This theatrical model, it seems to me, provides us with a wonderful strategy for the study and understanding of history. In theatre, we reach understanding through the experiential, the experience of being an audience member. By using elements of drama to study the past, the history teacher gives students the opportunity to encounter the past as an experience – a particular, living story which, like all good theatre, is also our story. It allows us to perceive the past as an alternate world, running alongside our own, the one giving insights into the other.

In this article I present two approaches to turning learning about history into an experience through drama. I am drawing a distinction between drama and theatre. I see drama within the history classroom as an educational tool that helps learners to actively explore concepts, ideas and the world around us. Theatre, on the other hand, is the presentation of these ideas or of a play text to an audience. Theatre also incorporates the study of the art form, sites of performance and the socio-historical, cultural context in which theatre is created and presented.

The drama approach uses elements of the art form to bring the past to life and is what I am calling classroom drama. The theatre approach uses the examination of a play from the perspective of a production team (director, designer, dramaturge, performer) as a way of understanding a time, its people and its cultural life. This is what I am calling staging history, the consideration of how plays from the past can be authentically staged.

I would like to begin by sharing some drama exercises and approaches that can be used in the history classroom. They are designed to bring history to life, helping students to develop both an affective and a cognitive relationship to material that promotes deeper and longer lasting understanding. In classroom drama the students are both the agents and creators of the drama, the experience, ('I am making it happen') and the recipients, the spectators, observing themselves within the drama and learning from that ('it is happening to me'). Where the affective, through play and experiential learning, develops a genuine engagement with material, the cognitive develops understanding. Understanding, augmented by the affective, gives students an experience that helps the learning to be meaningful, authentic and life-long.

1 Classroom drama strategies
The positioning and timing of the following exercises is dependent on the learning objectives of the unit of work. The exercises can be used

> To introduce a topic or a particular concept.
> To engage students with a particular concept or idea.
> To review or check understanding.
> To revise.
> To gather ideas.
> As an assessment.

The use of stills
A still, also sometimes referred to as a tableau, is a stationary image presented by students using their bodies. The use of stills is particularly

effective in examining and investigating moments or particular concepts or ideas. Because the images are still, freezing time, they give the class time to look, think and discuss. They can be easily recorded as photographs or as drawings.

Structures

The students are asked to use their bodies in a frozen stance to create 3D structures that can be viewed from all angles, allowing viewers to look at them from 360°. The students can create any of the following:

A 360° structure of a period or event – this allows students to look at one particular event in detail and from different angles and perspectives, *eg* the signing of a treaty.

A 360° structure depicting a concept, *eg* revolution, justice, tyranny – this gives the teacher the opportunity to look at key concepts and relate these to particular moments in history as well as looking at the meaning of certain concepts in particular historical contexts.

A 360° monument to commemorate, honour or glorify a particular event or particular people in history. This is useful as an introduction to different perspectives or the way a nation state presents history or current events to its people. It Is also a useful way to look at propaganda, *eg* the end of WW2.

Recreating paintings

Students use their bodies to recreate a pre-existing visual or a series of visuals (visuals can be paintings, drawings, cartoons, photographs) in three dimensions. I tend to try to find paintings from different periods as this also engages students with style and asks them to consider how different contexts, historical and cultural, can affect the interpretation of the past. This allows them to examine a particular historical situation or to examine a series of events through their visual representation, *eg La Morte di Cesare* by Vincenzo Camuccini (1804-5).

Installations

This is similar to the structures exercise described above, but this time students create a 3D installation for an art gallery or museum depicting a particular period or aspect of the history programme. Students should also write a catalogue entry which gives an interpretation of the installation.

The idea of the installation is to turn events, movements, periods or moments of history into abstract depictions from the perspective of the present. It is the idea of the past as interpreted and perceived by the present. The installation exercise, therefore, asks students to view and make comment on the past from the perspective of the present, *eg* an installation of the Battle of the Somme.

Juxtaposed installations in front of projections

Students create an installation with their bodies in front of a projected pre-existing visual or image from a particular period. They also provide a written caption to accompany their image. The installation should be something that somehow comments on and gives a perspective of the image. This is particularly useful as a way of looking at contesting sources or ideologies, *eg* use the painting *Liberty Leading the People* by Eugène Delacroix and create an installation in juxtaposition to it.

The moment...

This exercise can be used to focus on either a particular significant moment in history (for instance when an army crosses a border), a moment of experience (when a landowner evicts a peasant family from their land) or a moment depicted by a visual (such as a representation of a sitting of the Roman Senate: Cicero attacks Catilina, from a 19th century fresco in Palazzo Madama, Rome).

It can also be developed into looking not only at 'the moment when...' something happens but also 'the moment before...' and the 'moment after...' This gives students the opportunity to examine a sequence of events in detail. In addition students can create an image of 'life before' and 'life after' to explore the origins of an event, the event itself and its consequences or impact.

Animations

Stills can be further developed and given more depth through animating, captioning or thought tracking.

Animating

This requires students to bring a still picture to life, using words and movement. To stop students' tendency for lengthy improvisation or playacting, it is advisable to restrict the number of spoken lines or to give a time limit. I tend to favour a set number of lines, usually six to ten lines, with a line being any length of uninterrupted speech. This encourages students to select their words carefully and to think about the significance of word and gesture. Alternatively students may be given a selection of sources or transcripts and asked to select lines from these.

Captioning

Students are asked to devise a caption to any of the stills they have created. These should **not** be descriptive but should guide the viewer to the concepts within the material or to a particular interpretation. Captions can be written on paper to accompany the still or be spoken by one of the students. These are useful in encouraging students to look for meaning and it develops their ability to look for significance and express ideas and deductions concisely.

Thought tracking

Thought tracking is the process whereby someone speaks their thoughts or describes their feelings out loud so that we can hear them. The teacher taps each person in a still and they say what they are thinking or make a statement about the situation/concept/image. This is a good way of getting the student to consider how someone in a different period may have thought or what their responses would have been. The thoughts we hear provide a good starting point to discuss whether we can ever get inside the head of someone in the past or how the study of history enables us to see and understand someone else's perspective. Thought tracking is also useful if students are representing a visual such as a painting, as it can encourage students to think beyond the image.

Atmospheres
The senses
This is a strategy I use to bring a period to life in the imagination through the senses. It is particularly useful as an introduction to empathetic exercises or assignments which ask the student to imagine themselves in a different time or place. The exercise requires the students to note down responses to the following questions. Teacher gives students a countdown of 30 seconds to respond to questions:

When you think of __(period)____what do you *see*?
When you think of __(period)____what do you *hear*?
When you think of __(period)____what do you *smell*?
When you think of __(period)____what do you *taste*?
When you think of __(period)____what textures do you *feel*?

Machines
Creating a human machine, using repeated gestures and sounds/words, is a good way to capture the spirit or the key elements and ideas of a period, historical situation or event. One person comes up and presents an action that can be repeated and that epitomises the period/situation/event being examined. They can also add sound/words that can also be repeated. The next person comes up with their own action and positions themselves in relation to the first person and does their action and sound and so on until the group forms a machine. This works best with no more than ten students at a time. For instance, create a Russian Revolution machine.

Roleplay
The Professionals
One of the most powerful ways to engage students with material is to get them in role as experts. Inspired by 'Mantle of the Expert', developed by Dorothy Heathcote, I use an exercise that I call 'The Professionals'. I begin by thinking about the different types of professions that may be associated with history or with the investigation of historical sources or ideas, *eg* archaeologist, forensics specialist, historian, publisher, detective, archivist, museum curator, documentary film maker, explorer.

Students are put into groups and assigned a particular communal role. The whole class is given the same role, but the students are divided into small teams and asked to create a professional identity for their team. For example, as a team of archaeologists they are asked to give themselves a company name and logo. Before the students as professionals are given a brief it is important for them to build belief in their role. Though the brief is make-believe, the success of this exercise relies, as with any game, in the group having a purpose and a context that they believe in.

This should involve some research into what the role does and the skillset of the role. These are some of the exercises that can be used to build belief and to give students a sense of the professional nature of the company's work:

Building belief through thinking about role's expertise
Write company CV.
Create a presentation introducing us to the role's expertise
Present the company's achievements.

Building belief through thinking about role's skillset
Write a job description for the role.
Write a skillset for the role in bullet points.

Building belief through thinking about role's training
Write the elements of training the role has had to prepare them for their job.
Simulate the training of the role using mime and narrative.

Building belief through giving the role a professional identity
Come up with a name for your company.
Design company logo.
Create the company website/brochure.

Building belief through thinking about the work life of the role
Show us a day in the professional life of the role.
Develop a documentary that informs people about the role's job.

Building belief through communal mapping and drawing
The class as a whole group draws a plan of a place. This helps the whole class to inhabit the same fictional place/context when they are subsequently put into their smaller groups.

Once the teacher is confident that the students have belief in their roles, the teacher then gives the brief. The brief may be:

To create something (*eg* a magazine or documentary).
To investigate something (*eg* an unsolved mystery).
To arrange something (*eg* to curate an exhibition, arrange a display).
To present (*eg* to make a presentation to other professionals, to run a workshop for schools).

Through the adoption of 'The Professionals' role, students have the opportunity to look at material from a different perspective. It also, through the make believe, motivates students and gives them a strong sense of purpose for their research. This activity makes for authentic learning and gives a sense of real life activities that have to do with the study of history.

156

The Representatives

This is similar to 'The Professionals' and requires a similar approach to the building of belief. In this instance, however, the students are in role as representatives of a particular country, movement, initiative *etc*. This is particularly useful if you want to get different perspectives of a particular situation. Students may be given sources or a particular brief appropriate to the country or people they are representing. It is an effective approach for looking at particular moments, agreements, treaties or meetings and examining them from different perspectives. Alternatively it can be used as a way of engaging students with particular historical problems or contemporary political challenges by getting them to consider how the perspective changes depending on your context, national circumstances and political agendas.

2 Staging history

Using play texts from particular periods and approaching them from the perspective of a theatre production team is another effective way of engaging students with particular periods of history.

Similar to 'The Professionals' roleplay described in the previous section, the students adopt the role of theatre specialists who are tasked with the authentic staging of a play text, authentic in that it needs to be produced and presented as it would have been during the period when it was written or the period in which it is set. This requires the students to research the playwright, the role of theatre, the type of performance space, the costumes and set, the audience, the purpose of the piece and its impact on audiences. The artistic team can be made up of:

Director – Responsible for the organisation of space, the interaction of performer and audience, the communication of the story and/or meaning of the play.

Designer – Responsible for the costumes, set, lights, sound, props.

Dramaturge – Responsible for historical accuracy, providing research regarding the socio-political context of the play, the stage action and design, performance space, role of theatre.

Performer – Responsible for the portrayal of a character through voice, movement, gesture, use of space, delivery of text

The four Cs: Context, Content, Characters, Creator, are good starting points for research and provide the students, through the brief of staging the play, with:

Insights into how people lived, moved, spoke, interacted.

Insights into the politics, preoccupations of the period and key issues.

Insight into cultural life of the time and the role of theatre in people's lives.

Students can work on both the play as a whole or on key scenes. Actually staging these scenes or moments of the play provides students with a practical focus and provides authentic research opportunities and a purpose for their research.

In addition there are plays that can be categorised as historical plays. These include:

> Plays that were written in a particular period which are about that period or the preoccupations of their time (Shakespeare, *Henry V*).

> Plays that are set in the past which shed light on the historical context (Shaffer, *The Royal Hunt of the Sun*).

> Plays that take the past as their subject matter (Littlewood, *Oh What a Lovely War*).

> Plays depicting particular historical events (Bolt, *A Man for all Seasons*).

> Plays of speculation that imagine historical events and encounters that we have no access to (Sophocles, *Antigone*).

> Plays that are based on oral history or on transcripts (Christine Bacon, *Ice and Fire* exploration of human rights).

> Verbatim theatre that dramatises events using the exact words of witnesses or of people involved, (Hare, *Fanshen*).

These plays, created either by a playwright or a company, whilst being works of fiction, present a particular historical perspective. They provide a rich resource for the study of history because they engage young people with historiography. They encourage them to research the history being presented and compare it to its dramatic representation. Historical plays can be explored by examining:

> Provenance: when the play was written.
> Subject: the period/event the play is about.
> Bias: who wrote the play and why.
> Message: what the play is telling us about the period/event.

These plays offer us the opportunity to look at a historical period or event from three temporal contexts which offer students an alternative approach to the study of history: the present, the period when the play was written and the period that the play is about. Thinking about the intention, reception and impact of the play in each of these particular temporal contexts introduces students to the idea that how history is positioned, perceived and examined is relative. It is often dependent on what a state or a witness chooses to remember or to forget.

What history is studied is also, of course, often determined by a political or social agenda. The study of a play, where the playwright or creator has clearly selected, edited and structured the depiction of events to fulfill a particular artistic or political purpose, is an effective way of engaging learners with concepts regarding who chooses history and how it can be manipulated to present a particular message or point of view.

Another effective task is to give different groups or pairs the same historical event from different perspectives (can be different governments, leaders or people) and ask them to write a short scene to show that particular point of view.

Conclusion

Drama and theatre provide teachers with strategies for active, student-centred learning that engage students with concepts, moments, characters, situations, events and periods of history. The past is brought alive and students are given access to the significance of human agency, action, consequence and impact in the study of history.

The practical nature of drama and theatre brings the past to life, providing us with the opportunity to bring history into the classroom *as if* it is happening now, before our eyes. By providing students with the possibility of looking at the world from different perspectives we build empathy and an understanding of different world views and attitudes that encourage international mindedness and genuine conceptual understandings.

Chapter 13

Whose methodology?
Chronology versus theme

Malcolm Davis

"Where shall I begin?" asked the White Rabbit. "Begin at
the beginning and go on till you come to the end: then stop"
the King said gravely.

Lewis Carroll, *Alice's Adventures in Wonderland*

What to teach and how to teach it are the two basic concerns of any teacher
with which ever subject they are involved. With respect to history the
content can be guided by any number of factors: the teacher's interests; the
student's interests; the available text book and other resources, external
examinations; and increasing government directives. The how to teach; the
style, the approach, and the structure of the course was often the domain
of the school or the individual teacher.

Certainly in most countries until the Second World War a young history
student learned facts from a text book and then was tested to check if those
facts were well embedded. Mr Gradgrind's system *par excellence*. What facts
were selected depended on one's nationality and the final examination.
Invariably the journey was chronologically through time. For the West,
often the start would be Mesopotamia and the Fertile Crescent – the cradle
of civilisation. After that content would tell the development of a nation,
varying according to country, but invariably showing progress. History was
a long and often difficult path to nationhood.

Increasingly, however, government directives began to be applied to
methodology and general delivery of lessons. In Britain what became
known as 'the great debate' about the teaching of history erupted in the
1970s, mainly as a result of questions about the role of history and how it
should be taught in the planned National Curriculum. What this prolonged
discourse across the 1970s and 1980s did was instigate a whole series of
questions about the way history should be taught that would not just create
lasting divisions of methodology but vitalise the teaching of history. Indeed
it would also affect the philosophy of the subject, the way it was taught in
the universities and, ultimately, the way historians wrote their books.

Content versus skills, national history versus world history, Marxist versus
Elton, chronology versus projects – all became cause for a lasting heated
division. This chapter will investigate the different approaches to the latter.

History cannot be disaggregated and plundered for bits and pieces
that can validly inform the present. Its value is as a big picture that
gives perspective to the present. History teachers as well as politicians
have been disaggregating and plundering history for bits and pieces

not for malign political purposes but in search of ever more intriguing and challenging enquiries to enthuse our pupils.

(Shemilt 2006)

An analysis of the advantages and disadvantages of these different approaches to the delivery of history reveal as many views as there are education systems. Therefore examples and arguments will be drawn from a cross section of education systems to show perhaps that the issues remain the same, even if the location of the education process changes. The focus will be largely on the age range of both primary (elementary) and secondary (middle and high school). Only passing reference will be made to activities at a tertiary level.

History and politics
Both content and delivery methods have tended to be fair game for politicians. In 1934 Stalin drew together historians to decide what history should be taught and concluded that it should be a run through of Russian heroes: the great men (and usually not women) of the nation's past[1]. In what order you did it seems irrelevant but there was a most definable political agenda as to who should be included and who was to be excluded, but with no mention of how to deliver the content.

Similarly, in a more democratic environment, a recent Education Minister in the UK argued in yet another revamp of the English history National Curriculum to remove Winston Churchill from a prescribed list of greats to be replaced by Rosa Parks, Neil Armstrong and L S Lowry. Perhaps here was a degree of tokenism towards a broader perspective of the English nation (a language nation including the USA) in response to previous criticisms about an over-emphasis on English history, restricted to England at the exclusion of Wales, Scotland and Ireland.

Stalin did not venture into the sequencing of delivery, but in the British example a number of government draft proposals had MUSTS clearly stated. The first 'must' was for chronology for five to 11 year-olds: 48 bullet points stressed historical events and personalities to be encountered from the Stone Age up to the Union with Scotland in 1707 and then a similar listing from 1707 to 1989 for up to 14 year olds[2]. More recent revisions lessened the 'musts' to suggestions, yet still included so-called 'great' people but with more of a desire to build in the idea of change and the interplay between national, international and local history.

How history is delivered as opposed to what can also be a reason for political interference. Much as a backward chronology began to be discussed in 2000 and was extensively presented as a methodology in 2012, it was in 2005 that Michael Baker was forbidden by the school district of Lincoln in Nebraska, USA, from using a backward chronological approach. The argument was put that by such innovation students would be disadvantaged in State-wide tests[3].

It would seem that in some cases delivery does become a political football. Within the United States district directives outline the content with a stress on both state and national heritage and are supported by the various publishing houses with text books. These texts, although often full of historical skills and methodology development, largely give a focus on a beginning to end approach. Start at the earliest times and try and get to the present day. Likewise in Australia[4] the trend to use history as a tool for nation-building is being developed but in the same start at the earliest times and see how far you get.

Chronology

Political decisions, be they at a local level like a state or district, directive in the USA or in England at a national level, all stress that the essence of what is being required in history is a coherent knowledge and understanding of Britain's (the State or USA's) past. The emphasis is coherent knowledge and understanding of the need to have a sense of development of the state or nation.

However, within the English national curriculum, the approach is also prescribed. The way to teach the content is prescribed. The first aim of the programme published in September 2013 is 'a coherent, chronological narrative from the earliest time to the present day...'[5]. Chronology is seen to be very important. Within the Welsh national curriculum structure the skill of chronological awareness is seen as different from historical knowledge and understanding and interpretation of history (at Key Stage 2, 11 year-olds and Key Stage 3 14 year-olds)[6].

Chronology, an understanding of sequence, seems to be important in both these cases. Such a delivery approach has been a basic way of presenting our past since written records came into existence. The very writers of history in early modern Europe were known as chroniclers. They recorded events in sequence, they rarely offered interpretation or comment and if comment was made then it reflected the current political climate.

Chronology implies the linking of time to events or events to time. A sequence of actions is presented and some forward direction of a backward view is provided. One thing follows after another and, although simplistic, such a perspective certainly shows one thing happened before another and could raise issues of the possibilities of cause and effect.

Chronology can also establish a relationship and then a context of one happening to another. Arguments are put forward that such sequencing aids the development of memory and actually seeing the close relationship of one event to another and therefore perhaps the connection between events. It portrays history as a line, a procession.

This type of thinking is based on a number of assumptions. First, that students (of age five through 16/18) have a developing sense of time; and secondly that events are isolated in time and place and the web of interconnectivity can be reduced to a line. The issue of a sense of time is often the case put for developing a chronology so as to reinforce this sense. Increased psychological understanding of the child's brain suggests that this sense of time understanding is not as clear as first thought. To a six year-old a Palaeolithic man making a stone axe is as near or as far as a soldier in a First World War trench or a friend's birthday party last year.

Within the early part of primary education the issue is not distance but simply relationship: what is a long time ago and a very long time ago or even a very, very long time ago (one of the basic learning outcomes of the International Primary curriculum[7]). Within the mentality of the small child a future event can often be placed in time by how many sleeps way: so in response to when do we go to the cinema the answer can be phrased and understood as three sleeps away meaning, perhaps, Saturday.

Similarly in 'earlier times' and in some non-European cultures events were described not as today or by numeric date but by reference to the passing of moons or suns[8]. In medieval times there was not a complete sequencing of time but more in the years of the reign of a ruler (in the fourth year of Henry's reign). It is only relatively recently that a number delineation of the past has taken place. This shortening of time sequences or relating time to 'natural' known and repeated events might be more in keeping with the developmental process of the human brain. It was a 100 years ago or ten years ago or a 1000 years seems pretty meaningless to a six year-old. It was simply in the past, and the past to them means not now.

The advocates of chronological presentation of history in the classroom argue that such an approach addresses and is essential to our understanding of time, and is a vital instrument in the development process. As a result of many of the events a child is told about, being so far removed from them in time, they struggle to make it relevant to their own experience.

The teacher often hears "What has that got to do with me? ... This is boring." There is an assumption that by using a chronological approach students will understand a relationship simply by its sequence and place in time. Research tends to show that because there is a changing time relationship then change has taken place, but what is not grasped perhaps, because of lack of knowledge, is that change can take many forms and that because there are two events in a time sequence, one after the other, something has changed[9]. However change, other than the passing of time, might not have actually occurred.

The Ofsted[10] evidence presented in 2007 revealed that students do not have a sense of chronology, cannot make connections nor gain overviews and deal with big questions, or have a 'big picture' because they deal with too many small events[11]. There seems to be no appreciation of the psychological research that might suggest it to be a developmental issue that hinders understanding rather than the lack of chronological teaching. It was a result of the Ofsted criticisms and the voices of a number of academic historians commenting on students' inability to grasp the overarching issues[12] that the incoming UK coalition (2010) government revisited history teaching and directed a chronological approach with the aim of establishing a central national narrative.

This claim that chronological understanding has lost it place in history teaching is nothing new. As far back as 1921 an inspector of schools claimed that the absence of dates had gone too far and 'there was little appreciation of historical time'[13]. The notion of a story of a nation or national development unfolding implies chronology but Barton in 2009 began to imply that it should not necessarily be assumed that teaching chronology is the best way to develop a child's understanding about one period and another[14]. Might there therefore be a need to integrate themes into an overall chronology so as to aid understanding?

Part of the University of East Anglia PGCSE history[15] programme has some emphasis given to the history teacher's role in developing a student's sense of time and of the past. It is not just the use of correct time words, particularly in the primary/elementary sector, but perhaps realisation that up to the age of 11 'the past before living memory is a nebulous idea'[16]. Therefore the history teacher, by using time lines, images and the sequencing of events according to time, can aid the development of a sense of time[17]. There are many simple activities that can be done at any age to develop and reinforce time sequencing. However it should be noted that 'sequencing for sequencing sake'[18] without a context or some more in-depth knowledge of what is being sequenced and why, makes the task somewhat irrelevant and possibly meaningless.

It would seem that chronology sits in the background of history teaching. The development of skill-based approaches and empathy development has in some peoples' opinions watered down the chronological approach but the pendulum swings, in the UK, back to seeing the development of an understanding of time through history as important.

The text book

Another controlling factor as to how to approach the delivery of history is the availability of text books. In some traditions a beginning-to-end approach to history in the text[19], often limited to the Western world, is the mainstay of the classroom. This is sometimes reduced to a series of 'great events' in the nation's history. This chronological presentation in the text will often simply avoid controversy and create certainty in their progress through time. The national story, and when appropriate to the message of nationhood the Western story, is expounded often without question or challenge.

In some USA states the district testing system is in place to control the teacher's activity and this testing is supported by the available texts that both the teacher and student rely on to pass the hurdle of the examination, When these tests, aided by the text book, cover the whole of time there is the race to complete everything as the school year moves towards its end. This leads to superficial coverage of what often might be most relevant to the student: that which is nearest to them. The solution in some states is to prescribe particular grade levels with the task of focusing on a narrow run through of state history or world history. These from beginning to end approaches can often result in the young student encountering the more distant time periods with no sense of the distance of time involved.

Frequently early middle school or early secondary school students study the ancient civilizations. These civilisations might be seemingly less relevant and perhaps more difficult to access and understand than near human happenings, but they are prescribed and taught because that seems to be the beginning of history and at the start of education you start at the beginning of time. Little has changed from the way the early chapter of large tomes would ask large tomes with early chapters 'What does this mean to us?', us being the world as seen from Europe[20].

Topic and theme-based texts allow the break with the conventional forms of chronology but might be arbitrary in the selection of topics included, or have topics that are focused to a particular examination system. If, as with themes, a variety of small topics is used then the issue of resource funding arises. The large 'beginning to end' book might continue to be used because of financial and economic factors rather than a commitment toward a particular delivery approach. When texts for history begin to exceed $60 a copy, choices have to be made!

Reverse chronology

Raised briefly earlier, reverse chronology is often described as teaching backwards and could be seen as a variation of the theme-based approach. Since the unfortunate treatment of Baker already mentioned, the approach has become slightly more fashionable in the USA.

The main argument put forward to justify reverse chronology is the relevance argument. Such an approach can demonstrate the remains of the past in the present day or more particularly the cause or origin of present day events and happenings. Moreover such an approach can give more credence to the argument that history helps us understand ourselves today as it can directly relate to us. The approach also addresses the issue that 'we have got to the present' chronologically, and not run out of classroom teaching time so stop in the mid-19th century. The relevance to the present is what advocates often claim as most convincing.

As early as 1971 Pfannkuche argued that conventional approaches moving towards the present never really engaged students and therefore put the case for reverse chronology. This is essentially presenting current contemporary issues as a spark to create interest in the past[21]. The cry that history 'has nothing to do with me' is countered by a backward approach because all that would be addressed is that which is relevant to the student or made to seem relevant to the student. Critics often put forward the view that such backward thinking and an increasing use of counter-factuals is not true historical enquiry as it cannot generate a natural question of why: the fundamental question of history enquiry. The challenge to this might be the viewpoint that our perception of the present is reflected in the past: historical interpretations change with the changing of the present.

Reverse chronology demands much of the teacher. In 1955 Frymier[22] saw that more knowledgeable teachers were needed to draw out what Khazzaka[23] in 1997 described as integrating the past and present and drawing out more interconnectivity with the past and present. It could be said that the good history teacher has to have a wide knowledge of the present and contemporary issues to be able to make any historical event relevant to the student. The method of reverse chronology can be seen as trying to establish connectivity to issues that are of concern to the student today.

Theme approaches

The theme approach might not be seen as a direct alternative to the chronology approach but both could be integrated together. The merits of keeping them separate will be explored first. It can be argued that a thematic approach requires more analytical thinking. The theme approach is more than just a topic study. Ideas of the history of transport or fashion might seem simplistic at first sight but can be treated in a complex way. The theme can provide the link across many topics and time periods. It can also promote reflection on current trends in the world of the student.

Many years ago I was able to see the transformation of a history programme that experienced shifts in theme focus due to a consideration of current contemporary events. In the early 1960s the programme had the theme of nationalism, and drew examples from across time and location to develop understanding. This reflected the current happenings at the time of the rise of nation states within Africa as a result of decolonization. Within eight years the programme had morphed into being guided by the theme of revolution. Again drawing examples from ancient times and from more recent times, but indicative of an upsurge of social revolutionary feeling in the latter part of the 1960s in some parts of Europe[24].

A school setting a theme for a term focusing on anarchy certainly reflected the contemporaneous social unrest of parts of the UK in the 1970s. Such a course allowed the exploration of the role of the Levellers and the True Diggers in the English Civil War, an analysis of the works of Godwin, alongside those of Lenin and Trotsky and the importance and effect of revolutionary groups in Russia and parts of South America. However the theme stirred responses as to whether it was wise, prudent or appropriate for a school to teach the history of such ideas (this programme was before national curriculum directives in England and Wales).

This raises issues as to whether state systems of education, state schools or in fact any schools should uphold and support the establishment positions of the time. History can become propaganda. Therefore the choice and justification for a theme does need careful consideration, especially if national curricula guide lines are laid down.

Themes can be drawn from many historical contexts and lend themselves to cross-cultural approaches. However they do have to be grade (age) appropriate and sensitive to the surrounding cultural mores. Themes can also have universal application. An adventurous theme of 'war is hell' could be explored in the context of a Grade 8 (Year 9) group as was developed some time ago in California[25]. The constraint or guide here would be the prescribed state/district standards. Naturally where these are laid down locally or nationally they must be considered when constructing a theme approach.

The advantages of a theme approach are numerous: primarily the chance to work in depth and move across perhaps many different aspects of the same idea and make cross-references across historic periods. The interconnectedness of events becomes more apparent and the possibility of analysing these connections makes for a more holistic historical approach. As most printed material available to students is chronological in nature or with standard themes, the innovative approach of new themes reduces the chance of borrowing material. The well-trodden essay or paper is not readily available and therefore a different quality of research, questioning and investigation could begin to develop.

Unfortunately with many teachers still hooked on dates and lists of facts, the theme can become just another condensed chronology. To prevent this, the teacher must be much more aware of the bigger picture and see things far more analytically. Understanding, analysis and evaluation become far more important than basic knowledge. These increased demands on the teacher involve extra preparation time and are often resource intensive. What must also be guarded against is the pet interests of the teacher driving the construction and delivery of themes.

Objectivity in theme setting might be achieved by identifying themes that are current as with the example earlier, of using recent political trends to focus attention. This would not necessarily produce a backward chronology as discussed earlier but create more opportunities to make cross reference to current situations. Students might then claim to see more relevance to themes when parallels can be drawn with the present.

Such an approach also gives the opportunity for the student to become more aware of the present. This can lead to more questions coming from students and could create a more discursive classroom with a raised awareness of the relevance of both past and present.

In some critical discussions about a theme approach it is often said that students find it easier to manage a chronological approach as the connections are clear, whereas a theme can be a confusing muddle. I wonder here what is the role of the teacher? It would seem that the teacher perhaps can take the lead in drawing connections and maybe even modelling analytical thinking so that students then get a 'wow' moment when they realise the links, as opposed to floundering, not quite knowing what to see. Mind mapping (or flow charts or brain storming) by students can often open the doors of realisation for them. However such an approach does require the availability of resources so that students can search and make informed contributions rather than spontaneous and outlandish ones.

One of the on-going major criticisms of a theme approach is that students have no sense of the time relationship of events (not to mention the classic cry that they do not know basic facts in the right order). Depending on the age range, a simple or complex time-line can easily address this issue. The current insight as to the significance of the Magna Carta (February, 2015) related to the 800th anniversary, gives an opportunity for an investigation of the theme of democracy.

The theme would put the 1215 event into a wider context and make links to the present and also could be cross-cultural. Much as 1215 is an English happening, it has been noted that in recent English history syllabi it has received little mention, yet USA programmes and German programmes dwell upon it as a route for the development of human rights/justice and democracy. Much as the event can be seen in isolation the use of time lines can give time and place references for themes.

In relation to the Magna Carta, those supporting the celebration of the anniversary, while working with Iranian and Chinese history teachers, have developed a complex timeline placing the Magna Carta in a broader sweep of the development of justice (again another theme that could be used) which included Cyfraith Hywel's[26] Welsh law system of the early medieval Wales alongside those of Hammurabi[27].

It is evident from this discussion that the use of timelines can also give a chronological structure to a theme. The Schools' History project[28] has developed a number of themes: 'The Development of the West' and 'Medicine' being but two. The object was very much a study of a development through time. In depth studies were integrated with broad sweeps. It was Shemilt who, with critical insight, drew attention to the sophistication of such an approach and the pressures on the teacher to manage such a study[29]. This reinforces the point made earlier that a thematic delivery could need more teacher preparation and more resources over and above a standard text book, unless the text was focused on the theme.

Contextual themes were developed in the England and Welsh curriculum initiative of 2007 with similar broad themes of GCSE and synoptic units for A level. This seemed then to be a more governmental directive to approach history on a theme bases. Even earlier, in 1997, initiatives linking themes were suggested for the 14 to 16 year age group, such as 'popular unrest' and 'poverty'. Dawson built on these ideas by proposing in the early 2000s a more thematic approach hoping that through themes students would develop a better understanding of the chronology and therefore see patterns of change and continuity[30] as well as gaining a big picture.

This notion of the big picture might be the key to the development of historical understanding and linking the present to the past[31]. Notions such as change and continuity are often key concepts that are seen as needing to be developed and can be addressed through themes and chronology or just a theme. The seeming basic advantage of a theme is that it prevents the student from being lost in a confusion of event after event without any interconnectedness other than before and after. Yet it could be questioned that such a run through does not really develop the notions of cause and effect. In contrast with the right themes, bigger pictures can emerge, a sense of relevance to the present and the interrelationship of human actions might become more apparent.

Resolution of the possible dichotomy

Some practitioners would say that such a resolution is not necessary as they are comfortable with both and might with one school year or over a number of years use both. Equally there could be no resolution as one or other approach is mandated by government regulation. There also seem to be different resolutions dependent upon the age range of the students being taught.

A review of the International Primary Curriculum (IPC)[32] and the International Middle Years Curriculum (IMYC)[33] does show how themes can be used. As one programme moves into the other, the themes that are unifying factors become more sophisticated and abstract, dependent on age. The themes of 'Travel', 'Inventions', 'Health', The Printed Word within the IPC are used in the primary situation (elementary) and would allow significant development of historical topics across both time and place.

Within other curriculum contexts more historical themes could be established, such as Rulers or, higher up the age range, Collaboration or Conflict. As students move up into the IMYC, history themes can be equally developed within overall more abstract themes such as Collaboration, Risk, Sustainability. Just taking the first one, it creates an opportunity within a particular school location for humans to work together to try and solve challenges that they face. The interconnectedness of this type of human activity could be seen by exploring, in a historical context, the Treaty of Westphalia, the Congress of Vienna (yet another anniversary at the time of writing), the League of Nations and the United Nations and the objectives of the European Union.

Another example of quite radical and creative approaches to the issue of theme has been seen in an East London (UK)[34] school creating a theme-based approach across one year for 14 year-olds. Here themes focused on Identity (how important is identity?); Voice and Representation (to what extent have people had a say?); and Progress and Technology (how far has progress improved our world?). These themes allowed the use of material from significant expanses of time and place. Just three examples that might have been explored in the second theme could be the Peasants' Revolt 1381, suffragettes and women's rights, civil rights movements in the USA in the 1960s and responses to apartheid in South Africa. A word of warning here could be not to overload the theme with too many examples. Time should be given for in-depth work and reflection.

There are possibilities to combine the two approaches and this might be the way forward. The combination could happen in a number of ways. Certainly within primary/elementary where more flexibility of use of time might exist, both approaches can run alongside one another with sessions that deal with chronology in perhaps a simplistic way of stories through time. The stories are then mapped onto a time-line so the sequencing and relationship is clearly evident.

Parallel to this can be studies focused on theme. The theme approach would then incorporate more in-depth work, development of particular historical skills and more creative and student-centred activities. It would seem that this would give the best of both worlds and maximise the use of teaching/learning time but might only be available with younger students.

Higher up the age range again, a mix of approaches in different ways might become possible if the teacher is relatively free to choose. One option could entertain a variation from year to year. An example of this across the middle school age range (Grade 6 through 8 or Years 7 through 9) is described in Chart 1.

Chart 1		
Age level year group	Approach	Topic or developmental ideas
Grade 6, English/ Wales Year 7	Theme and Chronology within the Theme *eg* People exercising power	*eg* Overthrow of the Roman Empire Peasants revolt 1381, Civil Rights in USA, Women's right in specified countries
Grade 7, English/ Wales Year 8	*eg* Development of a nation with specific time limits	*eg* Establishment of the USA from 1621 to 1914 or Medieval and Early Modern England
Grade 8, English/ Wales Year 9	Chronology with specific regions bias	Rise of Islam. Early African Civilisation, Aspect of China

169

Often the first two years of US High School or Grade 9 (Year 10) Grade 10 (Year 11) has to address clear formal State directives related to content and material. An example would be the prescription to do the History of the USA. The content is controlled but delivery might be left to an individual schools or teacher. Similarly examination syllabuses will dictate content and material and become the external control and driver of what is taught but few external drivers prescribe method and structure.

With increasingly sophisticated insight into how students learn and how humans perceive time it might have been thought that approaches to history would reflect this. Equally with the understanding that through history other skills useful beyond the pure academic pursuit of history might be developed in history teaching, that its content or delivery might have changed. However with these increasing insights other pressures have arisen. The desire or perceived need for government to step in and direct curricula in more and more detail has resulted in the freedom of the teacher diminishing. The control mechanism of the test, examination league tables and in some locations a statement of hierarchy of subjects[35] mean the opportunity to innovative in terms of delivery and methodology is not always fully realised.

The fundamental issue that must be addressed, whichever approach is taken, is the degree to which the activity of historical enquiry and an awareness of time becomes relevant to a person in later life. There is no doubt from anecdotal evidence of numbers of historical texts and buying of historical novels, the broadcasting of historical documentaries and historically-based dramas that an interest in history is established and strong in the general populous. However more important is the transfer of skills learnt through the teaching of history that might have relevance to adult life. The refinement of critical thinking and awareness of past events influencing and affecting the present and future could contribute to more reflective decision-making and might help in making good judgements.

In the end the relative merits of each approach, enhancing these lifelong attributes, rests with the quality and ability of the teacher. The quality teacher should be able to develop historical enquiry and questioning, develop narratives that are detailed yet also add to the 'big picture' both in chronological structure and the themed approach, so that students are involved, excited and eager to question and investigate the past. It is the teacher that can make the investigation of the past relevant to the present. In so doing students will be enriched, have a sense of identity and understand their heritage and its bearing on their futures.

End note

Perhaps the most ambitious and revolutionary approach to the teaching and understanding of history is the Big History Project set up by Bill Gates and David Christian[36].

> History has often been considered to be the few thousand year old written record of the human past. Big History places that written

record with the natural record of the entire past since the Big Bang, 13.82 billion years ago.

(Gustafson, 2014)

By covering history from the big bang through to the present in an interdisciplinary way, the humanities, science and social sciences are brought together in a single framework. Here chronology is linked to thematic material through a challenge to historians to redefine themselves. If we really want our students to regard history as a 'wow' subject then, according to Bill Gates:

> It made me wish that I could have taken big history when I was young, because it would have given me a way to think about all of the school work and reading that followed ... it put the sciences in an interesting context and explained how they apply to a lot of contemporary concerns.

(ibid)

References

Elton, G.R. The Practice of History, Fontana 1967.

Carroll, L. *Alice's Adventures in Wonderland*, Folio Society 1961.

Shemilt, D., *Teaching World History and Geography - Historical Analysis*, University of Leeds

www.studentsfriend.com, 11 April 2006 accessed 22.4.15

Gustafson, L.,The Big History Project ' ISJ Vol XXXlll, April 2014

End notes

1   Pg 1 Cannadine D, Keating J, Sheldon N The right kind of History Palgrave Macmillan 2012.

2   Michael Gove redrafts new history curriculum after outcry. The Guardian 21 June 2013 viewed at www.theguardian.com/education/2013/jun/21/michael-gove-history-curriculum

3   The incident is described in Kevin Drum's article in the Washington Monthly, May 2007 viewed At www.washingtonmonthly.com/archives/individual/2007 viewed 09 Nov. 2014.

4   Ferrari J. writing in the 'The Australian' about the new national curriculum, March 4, 2010.

5   www.gov.uk/government/publications/national-curriculum-in-england-history-programmes-of-study. Viewed December 2014.

6   History in the National Curriculum of Wales published by the Welsh National Assembly Jan 2008.

7   See end note xxxii.

8   Indigenous peoples of North America.

9   Pg 50 Kitson A Husband C Teaching and Learning History 11 – 18 OUP 2011.

10 Ofsted is the English school inspection service.

11 Ofsted Report 2007 History in Balance: History in English schools 2003-2007.

12 Eminent among the critical historians were Niall Ferguson (2010) and David Starkey 2005.

13 Pg 54 Dover Wilson J Humanism in the Continuation of School Pamphlet No 43 Board of Education report 1921.

14 Pg 111 Kitson A Husbands C Teaching and Learning History 11 – 18 OUP 2011.

15 www.uea.ac.uk/~m242/historypgce/time/framework.htm viewed Jan 2015.

16 www.uea.ac.uk/~m242/historypgce/time/research.htm viewed Jan 2015 making reference to the work of Bradley in 1947 and more recently Wood in 1995.

17 www.uea.ac.uk/~m242/historypgce/time/research.htm the work of P. Hoodless in *Time and Timelines in the Primary School*, London, Historical Association London 1996.

18 www.uea.ac.uk/~m242/historypgce/time/research.htm

19 Research by Loewen J. in 1995 (Lies my teacher told me, Simon and Schuster, New York 1995) and Chiodo J. and Byford J in 2004 (Do they really dislike social studies – Journal of Social Studies research, 28 (1)) tend to confirm this perception.

20 An example, of exceedingly large tome would be 'World history Patterns of Civilisation' by F Beers once published by Prentice Hall.

21 Davis G.H. and Lausley D.M. Tampering with the temporal order in History Teacher 593) 1972.

22 Frymier J.R A new approach to teaching history in The Social Studies no 46, 1955.

23 Khazzaka J Flashback: Comparing two approaches to teaching history in Social Education 62 (4) 1997.

24 Redland College Bristol UK History programme 1962 to 1970.

25 score.rims.k12.ca.us/standards/grades/?g=8, Curriculum and Instructional Steering Committee of the California County Superintendent's Education Services Association programme 1995.

26 cyfraith-hywel.cymru.ac.uk/en/llyfryddiaeth-gweithiaumawr-triads.php and www.llgc.org.uk/?id=lawsofhyweldda

27 www.ushistory.org/civ/4c.asp and avalon.law.yale.edu/ancient/hamframe.asp

28 A wealth of material is available on the project, their current website is www.schoolshistoryproject.org.uk/

29 Shemilt D. in 'Knowing Teaching and Learning History' ed. Stearns P, Seixas P, N. Wineberg S, New York University Press 2000.

30 Dawson I. 'Time for Chronology? Ideas for developing chronological understanding' in Teaching History 117 page 15.

31 Pg 116 Kitson A Husbands C Teaching and Learning History 11-18 OUP 2011.

32 This innovative international primary (elementary) programme can be explored more at www.greatlearning.com/ipc/

33 Similarly the programme for the middle school students roughly from 11 through 14 can be investigated at www.greatlearning.com/imyc/

34   The example being used relates to a curriculum development in 2007 in response to a government directive and is outlined in more detail on p108. Kitson A Husbands C Teaching and Learning History 11-18 OUP 2011.

35   Within Primary school education stress on literacy, numeracy, and science albeit important might have lowered the time allocation for quality and diverse history teaching.

36   Gastafson J. S., 'The Big History Project', International Schools Journal Vol XXXIII No.2, John Catt Eductional Ltd, 2014.

Chapter 14

Teaching history in a globalised world: the challenge of diversity in Finnish education and teacher education

Rauni Räsänen

Teaching history or indeed any subject in a globalised world requires a new approach to teacher training. The Intercultural Teacher Education (ITE) programme in Oulu that was initiated in 1994 illustrates an attempt to break ethnocentrism and monoacculturation in the training of teachers.

Background

Finland is a relatively sparsely populated country in the north. Its immediate neighbours are Norway, Sweden and Russia, with which it has 1269 kilometer border at the eastern edge of the European Union. Both politically and socially Finland has often been torn between ideologies and power struggles in the past and it has been under Swedish and later under Russian rule.

Finland declared independence in 1917 as a result of the First World War and the Russian revolutionary movements, but was soon driven to political controversies leading to a Civil War that killed almost 40,000 of the country's fewer than 3 million inhabitants. In spite of this traumatic past the country was able to unite its people and to create a strong front in the Winter War (1939-1940); to pay back massive war debts to Russia; and to develop the impoverished country through economic growth and policies of social responsibility (Simola 2005: 457).

In the 1970s and 1980s national consensus crystallised around the need for a welfare state and for all citizens to receive quality education. A comprehensive school reform of the 1970s became known as 'mother of all reforms' and inspired and energised a decades-long cycle of change in several sectors of society, the leading value being equity in its different forms (Räsänen 2009a: 26).

Finland has always been a border country between the 'East' and 'West', and both Russia and Sweden have significantly influenced Finnish cultural and everyday life. Particularly since Finland joined EU in 1995, it has strongly identified itself with Europe and sought to follow EU policies and regulations. However, in spite of that, Finland has been characterized as a very monocultural country, and there is some truth in that: it has very few old ethnic minorities (such as Sami and Roma people), a large majority of people are Lutheran and more than 90% speak the Finnish language as their mother tongue.

The number of immigrants is rather small due to many factors such as northern location; language that is spoken by very few people; and immigration policy being strict compared with the Nordic neighbours. At the moment, when unemployment has increased and Finland (like many other countries) has as a result of global financial changes suffered from slight recession, the political voices against migration have in some political groups become louder.

However, monoculturalism is mostly a myth, particularly if we look at diversity as a whole and do not focus only on nationality and ethnicity. Finland is a large country and ways of life are very different, for instance in the rural areas compared to the cities in the south. This myth about similarities has been perpetuated particularly during the wars and social crises when the requirements about one nation, one language and 'one mind' have been very visible in political agendas reflected in all spheres of society.

Education has been an efficient means of supporting the monolithic concept of Finnish culture, although some aspects of diversity were addressed in the big educational reform in the beginning of the 1970s when Finland transformed its educational system from a parallel to a comprehensive system where all ability groups were abolished and students since then have been taught in the same groups in basic education. As stated before, equity was the leading value in this reform and attention was paid to social classes, gender, language and diverse abilities of pupils.

However, there was no serious discussion about pluralism of perspectives and knowledge until larger numbers of immigrants entered Finland in the 1970s. International co-operation as a whole started to increase in 1990s, particularly after Finland joined the EU. That turned attention also to Finland's own minorities and questions of how Finland is perceived by others in the international community. All these changes have had some influence on Finnish education and teacher education, but the changes have been slow.

Diversity in schools

Many questions need to be raised when teaching a diverse group of students: what content to include; what methods to use; how to avoid complete ethnocentrism; and whose cultures to include in the curriculum. It has been asked whose schools and culture do the Finnish educational institutions represent and whose knowledge are they built on (Kiilakoski, Tomperi & Vuorikoski 2005). Some books have also been introduced to study Finnish history from the perspective of minorities such as the Sami and Roma people (Isaksson & Jokisalo 2005) or to introduce new perspectives to teaching various school subjects or subject areas (Jokisalo & Simola 2009; Virta 2008 and 2009; Virta & Yli-Panula 2012).

When analysing the core contents of various school subjects in Finnish curricula, it seems that they are very often still rather monocultural and follow the traditional concept of identity formation: first you study about the town/city where the school is located, then Finland, neighbouring countries and Europe, and finally countries and cultures outside Europe (Räsänen 2007: 21.). The monocultural approach is often justified by equity and equality principles and the same requirements for everyone.

It is worth remembering, however, that equity does not mean that everyone is treated in the same way; the newcomer from a totally new geographical and cultural context who possibly does not know the language of the school is not in the equal position with the pupil who speaks the language of instruction and was born and raised in the context where the school is situated. The newcomer can be very knowledgeable about the history, geography, and language of another context but the former knowledge base is not relevant in the new situation unless the teacher acknowledges it and makes it visible.

Approaches to how diversity should be addressed in education have differed and the methods have been divided into several categories (see Grant & Sleeter 1997, Banks 1999:31). In some approaches individual development and intercultural competences are the focus of education, whereas in others societal problems and structural inequities are the starting point in order to change things for the better (James 2005: 313-317). Banks (1997: 232-249) discusses the various approaches:

> Approaches where minority cultures are regarded as a deviance to be 'cured' and normalized.

> Approaches where other cultures are recognised but are included in the curriculum as separate courses or content areas, as exceptions from the 'normal' and mainstream teaching.

> Approaches where the entire curriculum is reconstructed in a way that acknowledges various perspectives and viewpoints, and thus makes students aware of the tendencies of monoacculturation and ethnocentrism in schools.

According to the first approach, particularly at the times when assimilation policies have been applied, states and schools have taken cultural difference as a handicap. The majority has been considered a norm – immigrants should catch up to through special education and other remedial arrangements. In the other two approaches the presence of other perspectives is recognised as such, but not necessarily as an integral part of school activities.

The school curriculum can still be ethnocentric and monocultural and other cultures are introduced as separate courses, books and theme weeks or through the celebration of certain festivals, heroes and significant incidents of the respective groups. A major problem in mainstream-centric education is that it provides pupils with only one way of seeing the world, a way that is usually taken for granted.

The third alternative represents more comprehensive approaches that aim to break monoacculturation and make students conscious of the possible hegemony of mainstream culture and power structures in the society. The goal is to work towards an equal and just society through care, consciousness-raising, critical thinking and democratic societal action. In these approaches, it is acknowledged that a truly intercultural education, which recognises diversity as a starting point, requires a holistic reform, which includes policy, contents, curricula, methods, school material and the entire school ethos. Higher education institutions need special attention in intercultural and global education, as it is their responsibility to develop both teaching and research in these respective areas (Räsänen 2007: 22-23).

Intercultural and global education is often, both in schools and in teacher education in Finland, realised through theme weeks and separate courses or projects. Nieto (2000, 305-320) has criticised this simplistic approach and has suggested guidelines for more thorough and pervasive attempts. She emphasises that education that acknowledges diversity is not a question of methods and projects but a philosophy, a way of looking at the world from several perspectives; and that is why it should be present throughout education and would require changes in the entire curriculum.

She also states that multi-perspective education is not for minority students or ethnically mixed groups, but it is about all people and for all people. Nieto (2000, 310) remarks that monocultural education deprives all students of recognising the value of diversity in their immediate environment and in the global context. It constructs ethnocentrism and makes perspective transformation and mental border crossing increasingly difficult.

Nora Godwin (1993), one of the developers of the idea of global citizenship, has suggested the following principles for future citizenship education:

Understanding the interdependence of different areas of the world, people, and parts of the ecosystem.

Acknowledging the relativity of perceptions, images, views and knowledge.

Understanding the interconnectedness of the past, present, and future.

Learning from conflicts and for conflict resolution.

Understanding the need for social justice.

Godwin speaks on behalf of understanding the interconnectedness of matters: cultures, states, people, the past and future, and people and the environment. She emphasises the processes and the balance in the ecosystem, and the vision for a sustainable future and development. She also points out that realising the narrowness and limits of one's own perceptions, beliefs, and knowledge is the key to understanding the relativity and diversity of worldviews.

This would also lead to a consciousness of one's ethnocentrism and tendency to create stereotypes and uphold prejudices, and would hopefully lead to transformative learning processes. The last two content areas presented by Godwin can be understood as lessons from reality; from what has been learnt about the tragedies of wars, and from the consequences of inequity and injustice. However, they are closely associated to value commitments, as well (Räsänen 2005: 29-30).

Diversity and transformative learning

Understanding the learning processes is essential for developing more relevant educational programmes and for identifying the factors that can aid students in encountering new ideas and experiences. Bennett (1993) and Taylor (1994) are among those who have concentrated on the aspect of learning in intercultural encounters. Taylor has applied Mezirow's transformative learning theory to illustrate the process of developing intercultural competence, and Bennett has developed an individual's growth model from ethnocentrism – through various stages – to a greater understanding and sensitivity of differences.

Taylor emphasizes that becoming interculturally competent requires perspective transformation, which usually occurs either through a series of changes in meaning schemes or as a result of an acute personal crisis or shock. These meaning schemes are like a 'double-edged-sword' – they give meaning to our own experiences but at the same time limit our perception of reality. These meaning perspectives are often acquired uncritically, in the course of our childhood, through socialisation, mostly through significant experiences with parents and teachers. The assumptions may constrain us, but can also be widened or transformed if new ideas are introduced and conditions are favourable for learning (Anderson 1994: 320-322).

Bennett is especially interested in the way people construe and encounter cultural difference and in the diverse experiences that accompany these different constructions. He argues that intercultural sensitivity and the ability to view things from several perspectives are not natural skills, but must grow and be developed through learning and education. Sensitivity to various perspectives grows from the realisation that my own culture is only one meaning-making context in a variety of worldviews. Learning can be expanded to an understanding and awareness of other perspectives. Instead of perspective transformation, Bennett talks about the ability to make perspective shifts and development of intercultural sensitivity, which is usually gradual and includes several stages.

The outcomes of an intercultural learning process can be recognized in cognitive, affective and behavioral aspects (Kim 1988: 94-103; Taylor 1994: 399-400; Bennett 1993:27-69). Cognitive outcomes are seen as an increase in a person's capacity for perspective taking and acknowledging the relativity of knowledges. Affective outcomes manifest themselves in a person's development of emotional co-orientation with the members of other cultures. Behaviorally the person is able to perform many of the required social roles in another context and to have constructive dialogue with representatives of various other views.

As prerequisites for change, Taylor names, referring to Mezirow (1991), critical reflection and particularly self-reflection. However, he points out that critical reflection alone will not lead to perspective transformation, but it needs to take place in conjunction with action and discourse. One should explore, experiment and experience new roles in the other culture. It also implies seeking out new skills and knowledge. Furthermore, one needs to be in dialogue with the others, to get constant feedback. It is through a learning process that includes encountering others, reflecting the experiences, seeking out new skills and knowledge, action and dialogue, that this 'stranger' interprets the meaning of his/her experiences and develops intercultural competences (Taylor 1994: 401-403).

Although Bennett's and Taylor's theories sound very comprehensive in many respects, certain questions emerge when educational contexts are considered. They base their theories mostly on situations where learners stay in contact with another culture for a longer period of time and experience the need to change in order to survive and cope with the context. Pedagogical situations, for instance in the classroom, are different, however, and raise questions of how perspective shift or transformation can take place in such an 'artificial' situation.

In classroom teaching and in most formal education, experiences, intercultural encounters, dialogue and cognitive tension have to be specifically planned and monitored. That is why such methods as role-plays, dramas, debates, visitors from other cultures, visits and exchange programmes, are important methods to apply. A diverse group in itself is a very fruitful starting point for intercultural education as it naturally provides different perspectives and possibilities for cross-cultural feedback and dialogue. However, a holistic approach is needed to address diversity, and for instance the knowledge base of teaching contents needs special attention. Noddings (2002: 190-192) also reminds of the importance of modelling and caring relations and points out the significance in teachers' models in providing various perspectives and forms of knowledge. True dialogue and presence of various perspectives requires safe and respectful atmosphere where all voices are heard.

Particularly representatives of critical pedagogy have emphasised teachers' role as social actors and 'transformative intellectuals' (Giroux 1985, Raivola 1993). The influence of critical theorists has been prominent in linking multicultural education with wider issues of socioeconomic and political inequity and ethical considerations. For instance Bennett (1995: 263) argues that acquiring multicultural literacy and appreciation of diversity is not enough to put an end to prejudice, but the emphasis should also be on clearing up myths that foster beliefs about the evils and inferiority of certain races, cultures or geographical areas. Education should include an awareness of institutional and cultural racism and economical and political power structures in the world.

Stephen May (1999, 11-45) has further discussed the conditions for critical pedagogy and has developed three key principles for its success:

> To become aware of and deconstruct the apparent neutrality of education – and particularly citizenship education – and realize that knowledge and values that often are presented as universal are neither common nor available to all.

To situate cultural differences within the wider nexus of power relations of which they form part and to interrogate the normalization and universalisation of the cultural knowledge of majority groups and put it into juxtaposition with other knowledges and practices.

To maintain a reflexive critique of specific cultural practices that avoids the vacuity of cultural relativism and allows for criticism (both internal and external), transformations, and change.

In addition to the above-mentioned principles, McLaren and Torres (1999, 71) remind that critical multicultural ethics must be performed and it must not be reduced to only reading texts about various perspectives. Multicultural ethics requires educators to be informed by ethics of compassion and social justice, ethos based on solidarity and interdependence and practical engagement in activities where these principles are practiced. They remind of the importance of taking into account students' lived experiences and engaging their minds, bodies and affections in the learning processes. They also point out the importance of practice and arranging opportunities to work in various communities and for other people in the near-by and remote environment.

Intercultural learning is a rather young study area in Finland although research in the field has increased (*eg* Jokikokko 2010; Järvelä & Jokikokko 2013; Salakka 2006). Numerous nongovernmental organisations have developed programmes and material for diverse classrooms but they have been unevenly and unsystematically integrated into the mainstream teaching (Kansinvälisyyskasvatus 2010 ohjelman arviointi 2011). A comprehensive national effort to acknowledge diversity in education was made in 2007 when a national strategy, 'Global education 2010', was published.

It analysed the need for diverse perspectives and global awareness as a lifelong and life-wide approach that permeates formal, non-formal and informal education from childhood to old age. There are some ideas about the means of teaching and learning in the strategy, but as the concrete action plan for the strategy is missing, its effects have, according to the national evaluation, been rather modest (Kansinvälisyyskasvatus 2010 ohjelman arviointi 2011).

Teachers' competences in encountering diversity
When planning and evaluating teacher education programmes that pay attention to changing environments, discussion about the permanent and new aspects of the profession is needed. The core tasks and responsibilities of the teaching profession largely remain the same, but new competence areas emerge or become more significant in new environments. That is why it is important to analyse what is essential in one's work and what are the requirements that need more attention in the changed context. Such qualifications as caring for children, creativity, innovativeness, reflection and basic teaching skills are required in all teaching posts. In addition, special criteria for working in multicultural global contexts must be added, and their development should be observed as well.

Both Bennett and Noel talk about the importance of being confronted by outside views in teacher education and of becoming aware of the relativity of knowledge and multiple perspectives (Bennett 1995: 262; Noel 1995: 270). Confronting other views and becoming aware of multiple perspectives is particularly important for representatives of mainstream cultures, because they are seldom forced to question their views or have little experience about what it is like to be different or to belong to a group with low economic or social status. However, it is important to avoid stereotypes as well. It is essential to know people's histories, know where they come from and learn about their cultures. But it is equally important to remember that people are above all individuals – they belong to several cultural groups (*eg* ethnicity, religion, language, gender, social class) and differences within cultures are big both in our own groups and in other cultures.

The second important requirement for culturally sensitive teacher education is awareness of how our community and background has affected us (Bennett 1995: 261; Noel 1995: 269-270). That is difficult unless we have encountered others who think differently and we have other cultures as a mirror for our assumptions. On the other hand, understanding one's own historically constructed biases and ethnocentrism helps to be more open to others' meaning and making efforts to look at one's own culture through the other's eyes. In addition to understanding one's personal history and its effects, collective memories and histories of nations and cultural groups are vital in consciousness-raising as well.

Bennett compares cultural consciousness-raising to cultural therapy which is a process of bringing one's own culture to the level of awareness, which makes it possible to perceive it as a potential bias in social interaction. Understanding this helps to realise that things are seldom black or white, but mostly historically and culturally developed phenomena. It is generally claimed that one's own culture forms a solid foundation for one's development and growth. That is partly true, but it can also become a mental prison if one never dares to go outside its walls or look beyond its boundaries.

The third criterion in intercultural teacher education is developing special intercultural skills and sensitivity. Bennett (1995, 263) quotes Gudykunst & Kim (1984) stating that intercultural competence includes intellectual and emotional commitment to the fundamental unity of all humans, but at the same time, acceptance and appreciation of the differences. Interculturally competent teachers are aware of the diversity of cultures, but they know that cultures are not static but dynamic, and they are conscious of the dangers of stereotyping. They know that if they do not make constant efforts to see the cultural attributes of others and to consider cultures from their perspectives, their own cultural lenses will guide them. Bennett emphasises that key elements in intercultural competences are openness to new perspectives, informed empathy and various communication skills.

The fourth requirement for the global citizen, and particularly for the teacher, is to understand that human species have a crucial role and responsibility in maintaining the balance in the ecosystem and cherish conditions where future generations can live on the globe. Both intra- and inter-generational ethics need to be observed and sustainable development includes ecological, economic, social, cultural, political and technological aspects. One aspect that must be included in all the aspects but must be specifically pointed out is ethical sustainability: how to build world order and societies which are led by human values and ethical principles that protect human dignity and human rights as well as wellbeing of human societies and ecosystems on the globe.

In addition to the above-mentioned criteria, there are special pedagogical skills that educational experts in the globalised world need. They should be aware of the various approaches to address diversity in education, and of how the approaches could be implemented in schools and educational institutions. They should be conscious of the basic values, aims, contents, methods, curricula and the requirements set by the environment. They should realise that intercultural education and education for global awareness is not a technique or a set of methods but a perspective or a philosophy that influences all aspects of education and school life including the re-evaluation of knowledge base (Nieto 2000, 313). Teachers should have practice in transforming their knowledge and philosophies about diversity and similarity as well as about sustainable development into comprehensive plans of education (Räsänen 2009b: 35-40).

Diversity and teacher education in Oulu

Developing teacher education as a collaborative action research process has long traditions in the Faculty of Education in Oulu, Finland. The process in the 1990s was particularly unique in its scope: it changed contents and structures as well as many basic assumptions about teacher education. The objectives were defined to be to develop Ethically Conscious, Skillful and Professionally Competent Teachers who:

> develop their professional skills and school communities;
> have a constructive, critical and future-oriented attitude towards their work and society;
> are aware of the cultural and societal effects of their work;
> respond to the new challenges in the field of education, such as multiculturalism, technology and environmental issues.
> (Syrjälä & Sohlo, 1996; Sohlo, 1999)

During the development process several new research areas emerged, some of them through students' initiatives such as the need to study teachers' professional ethics and other moral aspects in education. From the very beginning, diversity and multicultural aspects became central challenges in studying human encounters and co-operation. Special attention has been given to the development of pedagogy that would prevent social barriers and would increase cultural sensitivity and dialogue between individuals and groups. This pedagogy has particularly been developed within the Intercultural Teacher Education programme (ITE, previously called MEd International Programme), which is a special five-year degree programme within teacher education and which provides students with a teacher's diploma.

The ITE, which was started in 1994, is targeted at students who, in addition to education and teaching, are interested in diversity, international and multicultural aspects. The programme follows mainly the aims and structure of 'ordinary' primary teacher education programme, but pays special attention to intercultural sensitivity and transformative learning processes all through the programme in all the contents. The aim has been to utilise the experiences and results gained with this special group in all teacher education.

Since 1994 20 students have been chosen for the programme yearly. As in all teacher education, the first criterion in order to be chosen is interest in education and the skills essential in educational tasks. However, attention has also been paid to experience or interest in multicultural issues, diversity and societal questions. The selection boards have emphasised that they are looking for critical and collaborative innovators who are interested in the role of education for individual people's but also humankind's future. A minor selection criterion has been to choose groups of students which would be diverse in themselves representing various groups and geographical areas.

The home places of the Finnish students have ranged from Utsjoki in the far north to Helsinki in the south; some candidates have experience of living abroad, others have come to university straight from school. There is also a quota for international degree students, and exchange students study with this particular group. Although English is used a lot as the *lingua franca*, students are encouraged to study other cultures and languages as well.

Many courses in the programme have the same name as the 'ordinary' teacher education but are focused according to the special orientation. For instance history courses deal with the history of Finnish minorities as well as women's and children's experiences. Religion classes discuss dialogue between different denominations and music classes spend considerable amount of time on ethno-music. The national physical education curriculum needs to be reconsidered as there are student teachers who have never skied or skated, and in the handicraft classes there are students who have never knitted or do it in a totally different way to that taught in Finnish primary schools.

One third of the studies is especially planned for the ITE group. Special courses deal with intercultural education, education and cultures in different countries, comparative education and global issues and education (*eg* human rights, peace, equity, environment, globalisation and theories of knowledge and development).

At the very beginning of their studies, after the orientation stage, students take part in the simulation project called International Communication and Negotiation Skills (ICONS), where students representing governments of different countries discuss current issues in world affairs via computers and video. The simulations are preceded by thorough study of the topics and of the respective country. The students in Oulu have represented Britain, India and South Africa, which has meant familiarising themselves with these countries and it has given an idea of their role and position when negotiating with the world powers about trade, health, education, environment and human rights.

The aim of the project is to open a global perspective and to show the interrelatedness of the different parts of the world. Its purpose is also to start societal and ethical deliberations from the very beginning. Representing the government of some other country, instead of Finland, usually reveals concretely the tendencies of ethnocentrism and monoacculturation. ICONS also offers possibilities to practice intercultural communication, negotiation and diplomacy, in addition to media literacy.

Within the first two years students learn about European educational systems and cultures, educational philosophies and policies. The study units include courses on Russia and/or Baltic states, some Scandinavian and European country/countries; the representatives of the respective groups mostly give lectures about their countries and cultures. In the past when the financial situation of the teacher education department was better, the programme included several excursions to various areas outside Finland. The tutor accompanied the students for their excursions but students planned the excursions themselves with the help of the staff.

Thus students are systematically offered various possibilities for meetings and discussions with people from other cultures, particularly with their future colleagues in other countries. Erasmus-connections and North-South-South programmes offer excellent possibilities for staff and student exchange and networking. Exchange periods are compulsory for students in this programme and the large number of exchange students who study with the group provide the presence of alternative viewpoints in the discussions.

Exchanges, excursions and internships have played a special role in students' learning processes. To illustrate this, excursions to two areas are given as an example: the Balkans and Russia. Russia is an important area as a neighbour but also because of the legacies of the joint wars. Although students' parents are too young to have been involved in the fights between Finland and the Soviet Union, they have been subjected to their grandparents' narratives and they have gone through the Finnish education system and thus inherited its interpretations of the historical events.

The visits to places that previously belonged to Finland always raised a lot of emotions among students. That is why it was essential to hear other narratives told by Russian colleagues, to visit schools and to get to know ordinary people. It was also essential to visit the battlefield of Soviet-Finnish Winter War near Petrozavodsk where both sides lost thousands of young men. In the middle of this area there is a monument called Cross of Sorrow, a five-metre cross, on opposite sides of which there are figures of Finnish and Russian mothers who cry for their lost and dead sons.

Another excursion that has provoked a lot of thought has been the visit to the Balkans, to study its history and discuss with colleagues the relationship between education and society. The history of the area demonstrates how different the official interpretations about the same historical events can be among various groups, and how that is reflected in the school curricula and practices, including the language policies.

Discussions with local colleagues help create an understanding that education everywhere can be used to divide people, but it can also be used for uniting people and for peaceful co-existence. What is needed is understanding of various interpretations, political will and dialogue based on trust and acknowledgement. The visits to various places have every year expanded students' views about past events, increased understanding of diverse interpretations and raised awareness of how Finland has been part of political movements and agendas on the global scene.

Teaching practice in the programme is partly done in the practice school, which is attached to the Department of Teacher Education; it is part of the University and teachers have been especially trained for tutoring and guidance. The other half of students' internships can be planned individually according to their special interests and the aims of the programme. In addition to learning the basic skills of teaching, experience about different pedagogical cultures and contexts is considered important.

That is why students have, for instance, worked in small rural schools, urban schools, refugee centres, immigrant classes, international schools in Finland and abroad, teaching Finnish minorities, working in various organisations and development co-operation projects. In addition to guidance before and during practice, discussions after the working period are essential for individual and shared learning. Well-structured diaries have proved to be important for reflection and dialogue. The rich data of real life situations, dilemmas, narratives and encounters forms an excellent source for pedagogical and intercultural learning for the whole group.

Special attention in the programme has also been paid to tutoring, individual guidance and collaborative learning in the group. During the first three years, tutoring sessions and studies in intercultural education run parallel to all other studies. They aim to provide long-term and continuous reflection on cultural experiences and students' professional development in a secure atmosphere. The tutors follow and mentor the learning processes, develop the programme together with students and collect feedback about its meaningfulness. An important part of these sessions are visits by older professionals in the field with whom students can share knowledge and experiences.

The themes for a Master's thesis are free to be chosen in the field of education, but most of them concern diversity in some respect. Some comparative research with students from other cultures has started to emerge, which is very important for multi-perspective approach. The Master's thesis students work in close collaboration with the research group Education, Diversity, Globalisation and Ethics (EDGE), which was originally started for doctoral students in autumn 1994 (Räsänen & Sunnari 1997; Sunnari & Räsänen, 2000).

Students have indicated several conditions or prerequisites that are favourable for transformative intercultural learning. They have been described in detail in various reports, articles or theses (Jokikokko & Waris, 1999; Räsänen 2000 and 2009a; Jokikokko 2010), and are summarised below:

> Supportive and safe learning environment and study group where people dare express their own views, beliefs and opinions. Students should feel that they are listened to and respected, they are given space and voice.

Dialogue where people and cultures meet on equal terms. Representations of different cultures, expertise and life experiences have an important role in opening new perspectives.

Encountering representatives of other cultures and working in different contexts.

Knowledge and learning contents which force to evaluate and reconstruct one's own views, assumptions and culture.

Combining experiences and reflection (individual and shared), knowledge and action, in the learning circles.

Discussing the value basis and ethical aspects in intercultural education and the role of education in society and for the future.

Tutors have an important role in inspiring, challenging and supporting the learning process. The caring relationship is emphasised.

Learning units should be long and many-sided enough in the central aims and content areas. One of the main problems in teacher education is its fragmented nature, which sometimes makes it difficult for students to concentrate on the essential questions and for teachers to organise deep learning experiences.

According to students, learning is influenced by social and affective aspects and action; experiences, reflection and different forms of knowledge that help to construct and transform to one's own views. Experiences and knowledge that challenge to re-evaluate earlier views and mainstream thinking are considered essential for perspective-shifts and transformation. Students set requirements for learning environment, contents, methods and particularly human relations in their feedback. Attention is also paid to some structural factors in teacher education; the tight and inflexible schedule is particularly criticised. The central role given to relations is particularly important at the time when distant learning and virtual universities are developed even in the cases where it would be possible and sensible for the groups to meet face-to-face.

International Master's programme and epistemological pluralism

Finland introduced its national strategy for the internationalisation for higher education in Finland in 2009 (Finnish Ministry of Education 2009: 23). This strategy sets five primary aims for higher education:

A genuinely international higher education community.

Increasing the quality and attractiveness of higher education institutions.

Promoting the export of expertise.

Supporting a multicultural society.

Promoting global responsibility.

The strategy clearly states that people with immigrant backgrounds or foreign exchange and degree students as well as foreign personnel of higher education are an important and valuable resource. It also emphasises that higher education institutions must actively support the multicultural higher education community as well as civil society. International Master's programmes are mentioned as an important means to realise the aims of internationalisation.

The faculty of education in Oulu had already in 2006 started an English-medium two-year Master's programme with a yearly intake of 20 students. This programme, Education and globalisation, further challenged the previous methods and contents of teaching as well as many aspects of the learning environment as the students usually represent almost as many countries as there are students in the yearly intake. For learning purposes it is considered important that students represent 'North' and 'South' as well as 'East' and 'West'.

The orientation phase in a diverse group like this is essential in order to acquaint students with the traditions of Finnish higher education and its ideas about learning, teaching, teacher-student relationship or assessment. It is equally important that students have presentations about their backgrounds and educational systems to build a learning community for open dialogue and understanding of each others' conceptions. It is essential that the key members of the teaching team get access to these presentations, however internationally experienced they are, because they need to adjust their contents and methods according to the group or at least be aware that the knowledge bases are very different compared to most Finnish students.

Students need time to get to know the new learning environment but they also need to learn to work with each other. Student-centred methods such as group work and workshops are excellent ways to learn from each other and gain new perspectives to the subject matters. However, the philosophy behind the used methods must be explained and techniques must be learnt before joint learning can take place.

Successful learning requires realisation that pedagogical cultures are very different in different contexts, and conceptions about the best teaching and teacher can vary; practices and valued pedagogical principles such as active participation and critical thinking are not universal. The higher education teachers are also products of their context but it helps if one is aware of the various educational traditions and backgrounds and if one uses methods where these different voices are heard and listened to.

Methods of teaching and learning are a central aspect when developing methods of working with a diverse group, but so are the contents of teaching. This is certainly an area that has caused most discussions among the staff, particularly when the subject matter is education which is closely connected with culture and society. The philosophy of education course changes dramatically when, in addition to the usual western thinkers, for instance *Ubuntu, Ujamaa, Ahimsa* and Confucianism are included in the discussion. Any topic, whether it is teaching methods, inclusion, evaluation or teachers' ethics gets new, unexpected perspectives in diverse groups.

187

The learning processes are not easy because many taken-for-granted assumptions are challenged, but perspectives also widen and transform. This comparative approach does not mean that discussions would lead to total cultural relativity; on the contrary, a multiple range of options and theories are tested together, some are agreed on and new, often very creative ones, emerge as a result of discussions. One eternal topic of discussions is the relationship between culture-specific values and possible universally agreed ethical principles such as human rights.

The international groups have caused changes in the activities of the faculty as a whole. Information that previously was given in Finnish (sometimes also in Swedish), must be given also in English. As a consequence, the language requirements for the staff also change. The new situation requires further training for the staff, particularly for those who are involved in the learning processes of the students, but also for those who work in the offices, libraries, cafeterias, student health care and counselling services. For teachers of multicultural groups it is not enough to be trained in languages; the fairly common misconception is that teaching international groups means teaching the same contents as before but now in English or in some other *lingua franca*. If diversity is really taken into account, it means a much more profound discussion about the methods, teaching material and relevant contents.

Libraries need special attention as well as they tend to represent western knowledge and theories. Working with international groups has revealed how ethnocentric the academic knowledge base can be. Fortunately, internationalisation inevitably expands the range of theories, particularly in social sciences, when the amount of non-western literature increases and this knowledge is added to the discussion about various social phenomena.

Globalisation is a phenomenon that has changed lives and world views of human beings, and due to technology and mobility the scope of knowing about other cultures, ways of thinking and knowledge has become more and more visible. This challenges education systems, which were traditionally, at least in a country like Finland, based on a rather monolithic idea of cultural contents to be mediated to the next generations both in compulsory education and in teacher training.

There are various paths out of this dilemma: either to force mainstream knowledge on everyone or to develop new pedagogy, which is increasingly based on dialogue, various perspectives and joint knowledge construction. The former, monocultural approach has been applied both nationally and internationally, and in the latter case it has sometimes led to new types of colonialism in the form of one-sided knowledge transmission, for example through e-learning programmes which are not culturally sensitive. The latter approach, which I have called comparative pedagogy, promises thinking of the diversity of knowledge and is thus potential for new ideas and perspectives.

Researchers in intercultural and global education have made pioneering work in researching culturally diverse groups. However, much more development work is needed in order to address the most fundamental issues such as epistemological questions of teaching. This seems to be an area that has been much neglected, particularly in higher education. Because of that, much potential for transformative and creative learning is wasted, for instance in the international Master's programmes, which could be real sources of innovation for individuals and societies. On the other hand, diversity of perspectives and acknowledging multiple forms of knowledge does not apply only to international groups but, to certain extent, concerns teaching of any group.

References

Anderson, L. (1994). A new look at an old construct: Cross-cultural adaptation. *International Journal of Intercultural Relations*, 18(3), 293-328.

Banks, J. (1997) Approaches to multicultural curriculum reform. In J. Banks & C. McGee-Banks (Eds.) Multicultural education. Issues and perspectives. Boston: Allen and Bacon, 229 – 250.

Banks, J. (1999). An introduction to multicultural education. Boston: Allyn & Bacon.

Bennett, C. (1995). Preparing teachers for cultural diversity and national standards of academic excellence. *Journal of teacher education*, 46(4), 259-266.

Bennett, M.J. (1993). Towards ethnorelativism: A developmental model of intercultural sensitivity. In R. M. Paige (Ed.) Educating for the intercultural experience. Yarmouth: Intercultural Press, 27 – 69.

Global education 2010 Programme. Publications of the Ministry of Education 2007: 12.

Godwin, N. (1993). Miten kasvaa maailmankansalaiseksi? YK-tiedote 3, 5-7.

Giroux, H. A. (1985) Introduction to the politics of education by Paulo Freire. New York: Bergin & Garvey.

Grant, C., & Sleeter, C. (1997). Race, class, gender, exceptionality, and disability in the classroom. In J. Banks & C. McGee-Banks (Eds.), Multicultural education. Issues and perspectives. Boston: Allyn & Bacon, 61 – 84.

Gudykunst, W.B., & Kim, Y.Y. (1984). Communicationg with strangers: An approach to intercultural education. Reading: Addison-Wesley.

Isaksson, P. & Jokisalo, J. (2005) Historian lisälehtiä. Suvaitsevaisuuden ongelma ja vähemmistöt kansallisessa historiassa. Keuruu: Like.

James, K. 2005. International education: The concept, and its relationship to intercultural education. *Journal of Research in International Education* 4 (3), 313–332.

Jokikokko, K., & Waris, S. (1999). Intercultural growth. A case study of the M.Ed. students and their tutor. Master's thesis. Oulu department of teacher education.

Jokikokko, K. (2010) Teachers' intercultural learning and competence. Acta Universitatis Ouluensis E 114.

Jokisalo, J. & Simola, R. (2009) Monikulttuurisuus luokanopettajakoulutuksessa – monialaisten opintojen läpäisevä juonne. Kasvatustieteiden tiedekunnan selosteita n:o 7.

Jokikokko, K. Järvelä, M-L. (2013) Opettajan interkulttuurinen kompetenssi - Produkti vai prosessi? *Kasvatus* 3, 245-257.

Kansainvälisyyskasvatus 2010 –ohjelman arviointi. Opetus- ja kulttuuriministeriön työryhmämuistioita ja selvityksiä 2011: 13.

Kiilakoski, T. Tomperi, T. & Vuorikoski, M. (2005) Kenen kasvatus? Kriittinen pedagogiikka ja toisinkasvatuksen mahdollisuus. Tampere: Vastapaino.

Kim Y.Y. (1988). Communication and cross-cultural adaptation: An integrative theory. Philadelphia: Multilingual matters.

May, S. (1999). Critical multiculturalism and cultural difference: Avoiding essentialism. In S. May (Ed.) Critical multiculturalism. Rethinking multicultural and antiracist education. London: Falmer Press, 11-45.

Mc Laren, P. & Torres, R. (1999). Racism and multicultural education: Rethinking 'race' and 'whiteness' in late capitalism. In S. May (Ed.) Critical multiculturalism. London: Falmer Press, 46-76.

Mezirow, J. (1991). Transformative dimensions of adult learning. San Francisco: Jossey-Bass.

Nieto, S. (1996). Affirming diversity. White Plains: Longman.

Nieto, S. (2000). Affirming diversity: The sociopolitical context of multicultural education (3rd ed.). New York: Longman.

Noddings, N. (2002). Educating moral people. New York: Teachers' College Press.

Noel, J. (1995). Multicultural teacher education: From awareness through emotions to action. *Journal of teacher education*, 46(4), 267-274.

Raivola, R. (1993). Onko opettaja säilyttävän tehtävänsä vanki? In O. Luukkainen (Ed.) Hyväksi opettajaksi. Juva: WSOY, 9-30.

Räsänen, R., & Sunnari, V. (Eds.) (1997). Challenges for growth within boundaries. Oulun yliopiston kasvatustieteiden tiedekunnan tutkimuksia 98.

Räsänen, R. (2000). The global village as a challenge for teacher education. In V. Sunnari & R. Räsänen (Eds.) Ethical challenges for teacher education and teaching. Acta Universitatis Ouluensis E 45, 115-130.

Räsänen, R. 2005. Intercultural co-operation as an ethical issue. In R. Räsänen & J. San (Eds.) Conditions for intercultural learning and co-operation. Turku: Finnish Educational Research Association, 15-34.

Räsänen, R. (2007) Intercultural education as education for global responsibility. In T. Kaivola & M. Melen-Paaso (Eds.) Education for global responsibility – Finnish perspectives. Publications of the Ministry of Education 2007:31, 17-32.

Räsänen, R. (2009a) Transformative global education and learning in teacher education in Finland. *International journal of development education and global learning* 1(2), 25-40.

Räsänen, R. (2009b). Teachers' intercultural competence and education for global responsibility. In M. Talib, J. Loima, H. Paavola & S. Patrikainen (Eds.) Dialogs on diversity and global learning. Frankfurt am Main: Peter Lang, 29-50.

Salakka, M. (2006) Suomeen palaavien lähetystyöntekijöiden paluuta koskevat puhetavat: paluushokki ja identiteetin monikulttuuriset jännitteet E:81.

Simola, H. (2005) The Finnish miracle of PISA: historical and sociological remarks on teaching and teacher education. *Comparative education* 41(4), 455-470.

Sohlo, S. (Ed.) (1999). On the road again. Views on the development of teacher education in Oulu during the 1990's. Oulun yliopiston kasvatustieteellisen tiedekunnan opetusmonisteita ja selosteita 79.

Strategy for the internationalisation of higher education in Finland 2009-2015. Ministry of education 2009: 23.

Sunnari, V., & Räsänen, R. (Eds.) (2000). Ethical challenges for teacher education and teaching. Acta Universitatis Ouluensis E 45.

Syrjälä, L., & Sohlo, S. (1996). Co-operatively towards new teacher education in Oulu. In Tella, S. (Ed.) Teacher education in Finland. Present and future trends and challenges. University of Helsinki: Department of Teacher Education, 123-132.

Taylor, E. (1994). A learning model for becoming interculturally competent. International Journal of Intercultural Relations, 18(3), 389-408.

Virta, A. (2008) Kenen historiaa monikulttuurisessa koulussa. Suomen kasvatustieteellisen seuran Kasvatusalan tutkimuksia 39.

Virta, A. (2009) Learning to teach culturally diverse classrooms. *Intercultural education* 20 (4), 285-297.

Virta, A. & Yli-Panula, E. 2012) History, social science and geography education in Finnish schools and teacher education. In H. Niemi, A. Toom & A. Kallioniemi (Eds.) Miracle of education, principles and practices of teaching and learning in Finnish schools. AW Rotterdam: Sense publishers, 189-207.

Chapter 15

Whose history? Is the past such a foreign country?

Rediscovering history as a way to understanding the micro-politics of the present. International schools and the importance of historical context

Richard Caffyn

Introduction

Investigations into organisations often overlook the critical lens of history. Many studies ignore what has gone before, the historical context, preferring to understand the organisation as only situated in the present. This chapter looks at extending the discussion as to why an organisation's history is so important in constructing a complete understanding of its existence, purpose, stakeholders and behaviour.

Schools are powerful case studies into history as these organisations demonstrate the myriad array of human development and dynamics, both synergistic and conflicting. In particular, international schools offer a fascinating and kaleidoscopic angle into the complexities of organisational history, school culture and micro-political interplay.

All schools have histories as much as they have distinct locations, people, cultures and curricula. History shapes organisations such as schools and these are also multiple histories; those of the groups and individuals within the organisation as well as the collective historical memory of the school itself. History in organisations is about collective and selective memory; what you wish to demonstrate of the events that make up the fabric of the organisation. Such a view is inherently political as it strengthens power or established views through selective knowledge or controlling interpretation. This is critical in understanding any organisational history, especially that of a school with its social and emotional focus of the community.

To understand the present one must consider the past even though, as L P Hartley suggests, it is a different place. The use of history as a lens is critical in having a sophisticated and in-depth knowledge of organisations such as schools. Politics is interwoven with organisational history; the traumas, events, systems and people which make up the very fabric of the building. Politics is often part of the dynamics of interpersonal relationships, power, conflict and synergy that are what any organisation, particularly a school, is about (Caffyn, 2013).

> Micro-politics can be said to consist of the strategies by which
> individuals and groups in organisational contexts seek to use their
> resources of authority and influence to further their interests
>
> (Hoyle, 1986: 126).

Both from within the school and outside there are powerful forces at
work to control, normalise, coerce and empower. Schools are organic,
changing, shifting and determined by a complex array of variables such as
context, history, culture and location. The school's location can also have
a powerful impact as can the quest for identity and meaning amongst staff
and stakeholders (Evans, 1998).

An institution is not static; it has developed and changed over the years
since its foundation. Its history makes it unique, shapes its cultures and has
been affected by the people associated with it. Politics are interwoven with
the institution's history and have been formed by it. Organisations have
history, traditions and environments (Handy & Aitken, 1986). The effects
of incidents and individuals within institutional history have long-term
significance (O'Farrell, 1999; Lave, 2003; Morris, 2000). It is important
to look at schools as social structures and as places of emotional energy
(James, 2006).

Micro-politics in schools
A number of foci can be useful in understanding the impact of history
on the micro-politics of international schools. International schools have
added factors that are important to understand and discuss as unique
examples of the complexities of schools as human organisations.

Manifestations of power
No two schools are ever totally alike and, although one can try to apply
theory to explain micro-politics, it is important to investigate each school
as a product of its structure, people, history and environment (Howes &
Kaplan, 2004; Busher, 2006). As Rizvi (1989) points out, 'Each situation
has to be examined in the content of its own unique historical and social
features' (227). International schools have their own balance of issues
occurring from environment, interest groups, players and curriculum.
It is critical to consider the history of any school or individual, because
that dimension has affected and will affect any picture of the school at any
one time. A school needs to be looked at as part of an ongoing dialogue
between the present and the past, because the past changes in significance
and power depending on the nature of the present.

Management and leadership
The Head's leadership style and goals can develop diverse reactions in staff
and the school community. Morris (2000) discusses charismatic leadership
and the effects it had on the rest of a case study school. He criticises the
personality cult associated with a dominant leadership style and concludes
that this led to a leadership crisis. It is not only the style of leadership,
but also the after-effects of such leadership, bound into the history of the
institution, that are vital to acknowledge.

Institutions and their characteristics are also influenced by their
particular location, surroundings and, perhaps most significantly,
their history.

(Morris, 2000: 405)

Culture and history are not just about leadership as power, but also about
power within and without the school. Who else has power as influence,
authority or access (Caffyn, 2013)? Reactions and attitudes to leadership
can also be significant in a school. Existing staff and parental cultures
impact on leaders, and imbedded practice, views and power bases add to
these complexities. Leadership may be crucial but it is not the only aspect
in the historical culture of a school that determines its present or future
(Ball, 1987).

However, though leadership is central to school culture (Stoll, 1999) it is,
paradoxically, particularly vulnerable to school culture and the vagaries that
individuals, groups and clientele bring. 'School culture is one of the most
complex and important concepts in education' (Stoll, 1998: 9). Humans are
not predictable and culture is not controlled; both change, evolve and react,
often with complexity and capriciousness.

Problems of authority
History and the impact of significant events are important to understand
when looking at power and micro-politics in schools (Foucault, 1984;
Clegg, 1998; Goodson and Downbiggin, 1990). Foucault sees the history of
normalisation and control affecting organisations, although he does regard
it through the binary lenses of dominance and subjugation (Hoy, 1986).
Obedience and absolute power in managers is contrary to the flexible
collaborative initiatives of recent times (Wright, 2001).

This relates to Hargreaves' paradoxes of post-modernity (1997), where
the principal's role is the manipulation of the school culture and staff,
either to conform to a corporate vision or achieve specific goals. Power in
leadership, especially managerial power, can be and is often invariably at
odds with a professional organisational structure, and it is the contemporary
educational pressures of accountability and economics that impact heavily
on leadership and its use of power. Heads and managers can be caught
between two different conceptual views of schools and education. Power in
other groups such as staff, parents, boards and external agencies challenge
and compete to pull the school in different directions.

Departmental conflict
Department structures are places of power where competition and
dominance can be extensive (Hargreaves, 1994; Milliken, 2001; Sullivan,
2000). Schools change, develop and have their own histories, as do
departments and the staff within them. Ball (1987) sees conflict through
micro-politics as the natural state of most departments. In his discussion of
baronial politics, he argues that the underlying political nature of schools
means that departments act in a political manner to secure advantage. This
becomes part of their fabric, their genesis.

> Once established in the culture and history of the institution,
> collective assumptions of this kind are difficult to break down.
>
> (Ball, 1987: 232)

The culture of a school can also work against the culture of a department and give rise to conflict and friction where loyalties are compromised. This aspect of institutional life is problematic when, especially in a large school, departments have a lot of power and autonomy and thus can operate quite independently and sometimes at odds to the rest of the organisation. Groups and subcultures are demarcated by power, ideology and structure, creating independence and distance (Achinstein, 2002). Such balkanised departments (Hargreaves, 1994; 1995) often feature eventful histories and powerful personalities, suggesting high levels of autonomy and resistance to outside interference (Retallick and Butt, 2004). Departments and subcultures have their own histories, sometimes synergistic to the whole school history, sometimes diverse or at odds.

Diversity

Different biographical details of staff members can suggest different levels of satisfaction and that no one management style will satisfy all (Evans, 1998). This is especially true of international schools with the diversity in experience, views and national-cultural backgrounds. What may work in one school as a management system or style could be the worst in another due to the history, staff profile and power, and the needs of the school at a given point in time.

This is part of the problem of transient and individualised management styles. Morris (2000) gives a useful illustration of this in investigating the historical context of leadership in a catholic school. He concludes that dominant charismatic leadership and management created power vacuums when individual leaders left and that the staff had differing views on the Heads and their management styles. Morris argues that the mythology of the school sustained polarised views, typically staff views on the leadership of a particularly dominant Head.

Parents too can have differing views on the management of the school, usually due to experience, background and personal goals (Naybour, 1989). All schools have differing levels of diversity in tenure, age, gender, nationality and position. In addition, diversity is intrinsically about what the school means to the individual or group.

In looking in-depth at two international schools I concluded that each meant different things to every individual in the staff and leadership (Caffyn, 2009). Even though there is always some overlap and convergences in organisations, schools are ultimately dynamic places with swaths of emotion, autonomy and ideological friction.

International school histories

There is a limit of critical discussion of the significance of understanding history within the literature on international schools. One of the most interesting and relevant articles into the impact of history on expatriate

195

groups in international settings is Lave (2003). Addressing expatriate groups in Porto, Lave argues that long-term residents struggle with transient groups for the control, especially over the local international school. Lave suggests this is due to fears and vulnerability over identity (*idem*: 501), linking politics with the psycho-dynamics of individuals and groups in organisations (Watson 2002; James *et al*, 2006). The school is caught up and becomes an arena for these local historical struggles (Lave, 2003: 509). School cultures are part of and shaped by their history (Stoll, 1999), as is the identity of those within (Busher, 2006).

Trauma and events

History is marked by events, significant or otherwise that impact and shape the cultures and systems integral in a school. Viewing schools as social organisations means that historical events take on a greater significance; these influence people, systems and goals. Trauma is a more powerful event, one that impacts deeply within the history of a place or organisation. This could be an economic downturn, a death, curriculum change or other. It must be something that causes disturbance either throughout the whole organisation or in a section.

Trauma effects can be felt years later and affect how individuals or sections react. Such trauma can mean powerful counter reactions to subsequent events or change. History is about patterns: patterns of events, patterns of political issues and patterns of reaction. In investigating two international schools as case studies (Caffyn, 2009), I found instances of repeated reaction to events by staff based on a past trauma and personal vendettas. The present was, in part, an active living past.

Discussing history - different histories

In understanding any institution, it is important to consider history, not just of the whole organisation but also of the different fragmented groups within it. Collective history and fragmented history reveal the reasons why a school exists in the present (Clegg, 1998). History can be seen on the following levels:

> School – collective memory.
>
> Locality – history of the school in the local environment.
>
> Division – the history of each separate school division such as primary and secondary.
>
> Department – histories of each year group and department.
>
> Subculture – histories of subcultural groups such as enclaves and cliques (both within and outside the school).
>
> Individual – the personal history, experience and background that shape the person in the present; and their relationships, both working and social.

Rites, rituals, traditions, trauma and events have significance in the historical lens and shape the individual, group and institution. As Day and Leitch (2001) argue, emotional power and individual history impact on the workplace, stressing the critical importance of considering the socio-political context in any educational institution.

It is therefore valuable to develop Foucault's view of history as subjugation and discipline, arguing that diversity, resistance and location afford a clearer understanding of organisations (Crossley & Watson, 2003; O'Neill, 1997; Donnelly, 2000). Knowledge of history and events can also give power to individuals and groups in how to lead an organisation, how to gain influence, and how to achieve goals. Hitler's failed Beer Hall Putsch in 1923 gave architecture to the rise of the Nazis through propaganda and knowledge of how to access platforms of power (Evans, 2003).

Different locations
Schools are powerfully determined by their location; immediate and nationally. In understanding the location of international schools, theoretical ideas from this discourse can be transposed to wider educational settings. Location plays a critical factor in an international school through the impact of identity, rules, ways of practice, culture and idiosyncratic local conditions (Caffyn, 2010).

Knowledge of how the location has impacted on the school, the changing relationship between the school and its locality, and the dynamics of politics, identity and control, demonstrate a complex and at times unpredictable discourse. In an international school, the local influence has to be understood even though most schools straddle uneasy and contentious borderlands between the national and international (Caffyn, 2013).

The significant impact of events and traumas
Certain events are significant in the history of a school and within departments and subcultures. Traumas, such as the non-renewal of staff, power coups or autocratic leadership, demonstrate that powerful events affect the political and sociological structure of the school. These are often very difficult to follow as the effects are hidden and can take a long time to surface.

However, trauma affects inter-relationships at a personal level and resulting micro-political conflict can have repercussions for staff and management at a departmental level. Trauma can have significant historical impact, acting as ripples in a pond (Figure 1, page 90). The effects of this can be seen immediately, and with time, in individuals, structure and practice.

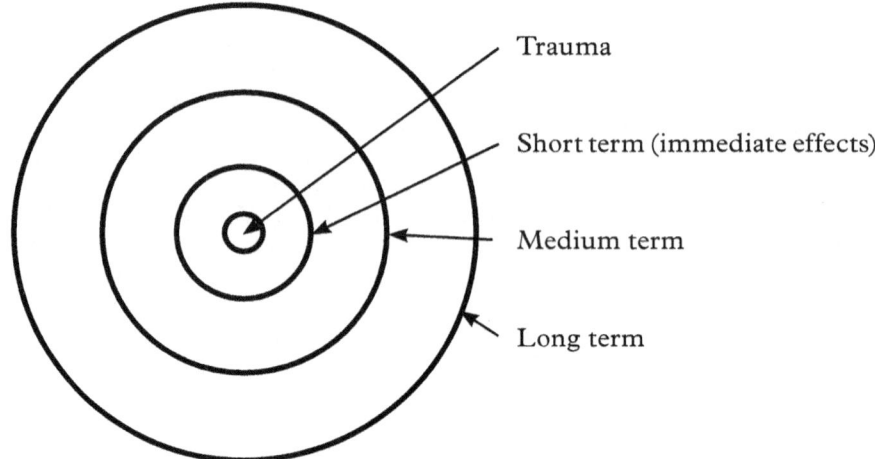

Figure 1. Ripple effect of traumas on organisations.

Individuals

Rather like events, individuals have history and cultural baggage that they bring with them. Individuals such as managers, pupils, teachers and parents can also affect institutional history. Actions and incidents caused by individuals, especially in powerful positions (both through authority and influence), will in turn impact on a school. Management can often be placed in a difficult situation, having to deal with problems of vulnerability, fear and isolation in a school setting (Evans, 1998). This vulnerability to events both inside the school, outside in its locality and within individuals' and groups' own external settings (*ie* the home or local community), can cause huge repercussions and ramifications when played out in the school (Lave, 2003).

Groups and enclaves

Departments and subcultures have history and, to understand their present dynamics, it is important to look at events, individuals and structures within the past. For example, groups made up of nationals from the same country or culture, or those with families or divorced women, are the products of the history of individuals and socio-political interrelationships. Trauma, personal rifts, events, changes and external issues will all affect these groups.

The location of an international school and the different perceptions and relationships within it can also create enclaves based on permanence (Lave, 2003) and transience (Dustmann, 1999; Gold, 2001). More established enclaves often have structure, rituals and stability, whereas transient enclaves can be more fluid and often based on social convergence such as interest groups, social focal points and clubs (Caffyn, 2009).

Likewise, groups made of parents can become very powerful, often protecting their position of advantage and privilege, the school being part of this political world. These clientele groups form enclaves marked by nationality and friendship. They also exist in isolated and closed realities where the school's *status quo* represents, for many, protection, the furtherance of intergenerational advantage and the acquisition of social and cultural capital (Ball, 2003). To extend this, case studies into individual schools, their locations and cultures would be very useful. The work of Lave (2003) into permanent and transient transnational enclave structures, and the work of James *et al* (2006) on the psychodynamics of national UK schools is important in understanding the psychological impact of identity, fear and diverse goals in communities on the school.

Historical icons and myths

Myths and icons supposedly have institutional memory and are part of school culture. Examples of these would be portraits of past directors or common stories about a school's past. Portraits can suggest founding myths or hierarchical ideology. The danger of myth creation, its sustenance and acceptance, can mask fragmentation and micro-political control by using nostalgia and history to recreate the present. Cultures of blame and attributing blame on various groups or issues create myths, and both sustain and develop prejudice. Such cultures can also mask and deflect from real issues such as political manoeuvring, personal agendas, vendettas and power plays.

Structures

Any organisational structure or system within the schools, such as rules, regulations, policies, procedures, educational programmes and established ways of operating, have a historical context. School statutes and policies can create political conflict between staff and the board regarding pay and conditions as well as the non-renewal of contracts. Structures and systems can indirectly and directly affect the micro-political conflict within a school causing imbalances of power and opportunities for creating conflict or resistance.

Conclusion

Historical events and problems can cause micro-political issues and provide an answer as to why conflict occurs. Trauma causes 'ripples' and affects individuals and structures in both overt and hidden ways (Figure 1). For example, the effects of autocratic and dictatorial management can have huge ramifications and this may directly affect the behaviour of those with this experience or knowledge. Similarly, reactive parental or staff groups to change or economic constraint, in turn, can seriously affect leadership. Structures and systems also have histories and can reveal the reasons to who has power and how politics occur. The structure of the school can create the conditions for fragmented groups and conflict later on.

The diverse histories of a school can be viewed through a typology to disengage the various lenses that can be found in the organisation. Importantly, this includes the critical focus of politics as a lens on the psychodynamic interplay between individuals and groups.

The diverse histories of a school can be viewed through a typology to disengage the various lenses that can be found in the organisation. In expanding the original typology (2008), I look to include the critical focus of politics as a lens on the psychodynamic interplay between individuals and groups.

Focus	Detail
Events	Incidents and events, especially traumatic
Individuals	Repercussions and effects of people's actions
Groups	Rites, rituals and events of departments and subcultural groups
Structures	Rules, regulations, signs and symbols, procedures and policies
Politics	Power, conflict, identity and goals

Figure 2. History as an investigative typology.

As with location, history can be used to analyse institutions, investigating how the past has influenced the present. This lens suggests schools are historically produced through political, social, personal and cultural interactions. These histories can be revealed by looking at distinct modalities (Figure 2), and, like location, create an investigative lens to enquire into international schools and how micro-politics are caused. The history of any school, its groups and events, can go a long way to explaining its present micro-political state, even though history is often continuously re-imagined, changed and redefined depending on what one wishes for the present.

School micro-politics are made up of both psychodynamics and power (Caffyn, 2013). History is of the rich interplay, synergistic and conflictual, between individuals and groups; it is always present. Likewise, in understanding the historical lens on schools as human organisations, it is knowledge of what has gone before that is needed to realise why one is in the present, and furthermore and possibly most critically, what will be the future.

'The past is never dead. It's not even past'
Requiem for a Nun, Thomas Faulkner

References

Achinstein, B. (2002) Conflict Amid Community: The Micropolitics of Teacher Collaboration, *Teachers College Record*, 104 (3): 421-455.

Ball, S.J. (1987) *The Micropolitics of the School*, London, Routledge.

Ball, S, J. (2003) *Class Strategies and the Education Market: The middle classes and social advantage*, London, RoutledgeFalmer.

Caffyn, R. (2007) Fragmentation in international schools: a micropolitical discourse of management, culture and postmodern society, in Hayden, M.C., Thompson, J. J., and Levy, J. (eds) *The SAGE Handbook of Research in International Education*, London, Sage, pp 339-350.

Caffyn, R. (2008) Understanding the Historical Context: History as an Investigative Lens in Studying the Micropolitics of International Schools, *International Schools Journal*, XXVII (2): 29-36. Woodbridge, John Catt Educational.

Caffyn, R. (2009) *Micropolitics of International Schools*, Saarbrucken, VDM.

Caffyn, R. (2010) 'We are in Transylvania, and Transylvania is not England': Location as a Significant Factor in International School Micropolitics', *Educational Management, Administration and Leadership, 38 (3): 320-340* .

Caffyn, R. (2011) International schools and micropolitics: fear, vulnerability and identity in fragmented space, in Bates, R. (ed) *Schooling Internationally: Globalisation, Internationalisation and the future for International Schools*, Routledge, Abingdon, pp 59-82.

Caffyn, R. (2013) Boundaries and Boundary Management in International School: Psychodynamics and Organisational Politics, in Pearce, R. (ed) *International Education and Schools*, Bloomsbury, London, pp 205-221.

Clegg, S. (1998) Foucault, Power and Organisations, in McKinlay, A. and Starkey, K. (eds) *Foucault, Management and Organisational Theory*, London, Sage, pp 29-48.

Crossley, M. and Watson, K. (2003) *Comparative and International Research in Education*, London, RoutledgeFalmer.

Day, C. and Leitch, R. (2001) Teachers' and teacher educators' lives: the role of emotion, Teaching and Teacher Education, 17: 403-415.

Donnelly, C. (2000) In Pursuit of School Ethos, British Journal of Educational Studies, 48 (2): 134-154.

Dustmann, C. (1999) Temporary Migration, Human Capital, and Language Fluency of Migrants, *Scandinavian Journal of Economics*, 101 (2): 297-314.

Evans, L. (1998) *Teacher Morale, Job Satisfaction and Motivation*, London, PCP.

Evans, R. J. (2003) *The Coming of the Third Reich*, London, Penguin.

Foucault, M. (1984) Des Espaces Autres, Architecture, *Mouvement et Continuité*, October: 1-10.

Gold, S. J. (2001) Gender, Class and Network: Social structure and migration patterns among transnational Israelis, *Global Networks*, 1 (1): 57-78.

Handy, C. and Aitken, R. (1986) *Understanding Schools of Organisations*, London, Penguin.

Hargreaves, A. (1994) *Changing Times, Changing Teachers*, Toronto, OISE Press.

Hargreaves, A. (1995) Renewal in the Age of Paradox, *Educational Leadership*, 52 (7): 1-5, www.ascd.org/readingroom/edlead/9504/hargreaves.html.

Hargreaves, A. (1997) Reconstructing Restructuring: Postmodernity and the Prospects for Educational Change, in Halsey, A.H., Lauder, H., Brown, P. and Stuart Wells, A. (eds) *Education: Culture, Economy and Society*, Oxford, Oxford University Press, pp 338-353.

Howes, A. and Kaplan, I. (2004) A school responding to its cultural setting, *Improving Schools*, 7 (1): 35-48.

Hoy, D. C. (1986) Power, Repression, Progress: Foucault, Lukes, and the Frankfurt School, in Hoy, D. C. (ed) *Foucault: A Critical Reader*, Oxford, Blackwell, pp 1-27.

201

Hoyle, E. (1986) *The Politics of School Management*, London, Hodder and Stoughton.

James, C. R., Connolly, M., Dunning, G. and Elliott, T. (2006) *How Very Effective Primary Schools Work*, London, PCP.

Lave, J. (2003) Producing the Future: Getting To Be British, *Antipode*, 492-511.

Milliken, J. (2001) 'Surfacing' the Micropolitics as a Potential Management Change Frame in Higher Education, *Journal of Higher Education Policy and Management*, 23 (1): 75-84.

Morris, A. (2000) Charismatic Leadership and its After-effects in a Catholic School, *Educational Management Administration and Leadership*, 24 (4): 405-418.

Naybour, S. (1989) Parents: Partners or Customers? in Sayer, J. and Williams, V. (eds) *Schools and External Relations: Managing the New Partnership*, London, Cassell, pp 108-115.

O'Farrell, C. (1999) Postmodernism for the Uninitiated, in Meamore, D., Burnett, B. and O'Brien, P. (eds) *Understanding Education: Contexts and Agendas for the New Millennium*, Sydney, Prentice Hall, pp 11-17.

O' Neill, J. (1997) Managing Through Teams, in Bush, T. and Middlewood, D. (eds) *Managing People in Education*, PCP, London, pp 76-90.

Retallick, J. and Butt, R. (2004) Professional well-being and learning: a study of teacher-peer workplace relationships, *Journal of Educational Enquiry*, 5 (1): 85-99.

Rizvi, F. (1989) In Defense of Organisational Democracy, in Smyth, J. (ed) *Critical Perspectives on Educational Leadership*, London, Falmer Press, pp 205-234.

Stoll, L. (1998) School Culture, *School Improvement Network Bulletin*, No.9, pp 9-14.

Stoll, L. (1999) School Culture: Black Hole or Fertile Garden for School Improvement, in Prosser, J, (ed) *School Culture*, London, PCP, pp 30-47.

Sullivan, K. P. H. (2000) Identity, Conflict and Reputation in the University Setting: an illustrative case study, *Journal of Higher Education Policy and Management*, 22 (2): 177-185.

Watson, T. J. (2002) *Organising and Managing Work: Organisational, managerial and strategic behaviour in theory and practice*, Harlow, Pearson.

Wright, N. (2001) Leadership, 'Bastard Leadership' and Managerialism: Confronting Twin Paradoxes in the Blair Education Project, *Educational Management Administration and Leadership*, 29 (3): 275-290.

Epilogue

The teacher's role

The poorest day that passes over us is the conflux of two eternities.
It is made up of currents that issue from the remotest past and flow
onwards into the remotest future. We were wise indeed, could we
discern truly the signs of our own time and by knowledge of its wants
and advantages wisely adjust to our own position in it. Let us instead
of gazing idly into the obscure distance; look calmly around for a
little, on the perplexed scene where we stand.

Signs of the Times, Thomas Carlyle

Carlyle wrote these words in 1829 as part of an essay where, in words
that were hardly 'calm', he decried the way in which 'mechanisation' had
overwhelmed so many aspects of society. The machine had even encroached
on education. As teachers of all subjects are now forced to acknowledge, the
importance of 'machines' in their teaching the scene is still 'perplexed' and
no more so than in the practice of the teaching of history.

For more than a century after Carlyle decried the growing mechanisation
'of head and heart', most students learning history in schools followed a
similar track. They acquired from a textbook a version of their own country's
history in order to pass an examination that was based on these facts. Only
at university level was it considered important to research the origins and
authenticity of those facts and study sources. In addition universities avoided
any consideration of current history, 'calm' or otherwise, as their courses
stopped well before anything that could be considered 'contemporary'.
Thus until comparatively recently history teachers had a straightforward
task, to follow curriculum guidelines so as to enthuse the student to learn
for an examination. For some this produced a lifelong interest, but for many
history was 'boring' and 'deadly dull' (Ellwood, 2014).

The post Second World War period produced a number of developments,
particularly in Europe, that brought new attitudes to the curriculum and
specifically to teaching history (Lynch, 1983; Goodson, 1993). What
became important were not the facts, nor what you were studying, but
the skills you required to do so. Indeed, if the aim is to produce students
who can evaluate evidence, describe and explain historical change and
understand different interpretations of history (DES, 1991) then the study
of any theme or era could provide the foundation.

Study of sources, selection and interpretation moved out of the university
enclave and the world of the professional historian into the wide open
ranges of schools. Encouragement of exploration and judgement revealed
that, unlike the information from the old style textbooks, history can be
interpreted differently, historians disagree, and a great deal of modern

history teaching forces students themselves to take sides and defend decisions over evidence. Gradgrind's facts are of course still important but it is the cause that produced an event and the effect that resulted that fires the engine of history. The history teacher's role had in many ways become more exciting and indeed challenging, although when the end result remains assessment there is a conflict.

Alan Bennett illustrates this problem in *The History Boys*. Using a class of boys taking the British A level he illustrates how teaching of history is fraught with difficulties. Intellectual exploration needs the imaginative approach of a Hector, but practically the pragmatic Irwin's analysis of examination technique is what will get a place at Oxford. Bennett's play is set in the 1980s; roll forward 35 years and the history teacher has not only to consider a discrepancy between methodology and assessment but has to adjust to a new 'mechanised' world.

The world of the internet has changed the process of the study of history dramatically. Instead of a text book, the student now has the equivalent of the Bodleian Library in a box on his desk. The web opens up a world of evidence and opinion: access to documents; books on line; essays; examination of artefacts in museums; pictures in galleries; details of architecture; TED talks; news reels of actual events in time. Constantly updating, the internet provides pathways of communication that the students know and use constantly and the teacher has to learn in order to not just keep up but use as an almost unbelievably rich source of information and opportunity.

Nor is the past the only place open to enquiry. Current events, through immediate access to news flashes, bring a working knowledge of political, economic and social change and an awareness of the dangers of war and terrorism.

This digital world is the future and in that not too distant future the 'dinosaurs' will have died off and everyone will have joined the i-generation. As examination gurus discover the efficacy of i-marking and R M Assessor (190 million scripts marked from 150 countries), there are legitimate forebodings about measurement of creativity and the need for a human judgement beyond the machine.

There is a dichotomy between an open methodology of exploration and the factual 'test'. Assessment is not going away, but testing can take more innovative forms as the creative possibilities of the web are explored. Systems are still at early stages and no doubt will be refined. In the meantime, for the working history teacher the new technologies present an exciting opportunity. The availability of resources enables immediate links across nations, between subjects and through time. As movement of peoples increases and classrooms become ever more inter-cultural, instant ability to make comparisons, reveal similarities, hear music, check other nations' histories, means that history need no longer be confined to one nation's outlook.

The teacher becomes the facilitator and the guide; the students, by joining in the search and making their own decisions, become 'historians'. Whose history, what point of view, is up to them for as long as there is the evidence to interpret, defend or promote. Nor is 'history' confined to the classroom.

The availability of excellent and popular TV series, factual and fiction, means that the thousands of students who never enter a history lesson after 16 will still over time have the opportunity to enjoy the subject. The digital age will still, for many of the young, be a 140-character Tweet, and this second great mechanical revolution, like any great paradigm change, will need in Carlyle's terms 'a great adjustment'.

However, if history teachers join the i-generation and use resources well to inculcate a critical faculty that recognises that all history is selection and requires interpretation, then the adult classes of the future will not remember history lessons as 'utter boredom' but as the start of an insight into 'the perplexed scene where we stand'.

References

Bennett, A. *The History Boys*, Faber and Faber, 2004.

Carlyle, T. 'Signs of the Times' from volume three of *The Collected Works of Thomas Carlyle*, London Chapman and Hall, 1858.

DES. 'History in the National Curriculum' 1991, HMSO.

Ellwood, C. Survey of WEA Students attitudes to school history lessons, 2014.

Goodson, I., 'School Subjects and Curriculum Change', Croom Helm, 1993.

Lynch, J., *Multicultural Education Principles and Practice*, Batsford Academic, 1983

RM Assessor, *ib-marking.**assessor.rm**.com* accessed 22 1. 2016.

Lightning Source UK Ltd.
Milton Keynes UK
UKOW06f2158111016

285034UK00001B/52/P